The Four Gospels Arranged As A Single Narrative

by Chester Wilkins

WILKINS PUBLICATIONS
P. O. 3232
Bartlesville, Oklahoma 74003

© Chester Wilkins, 1974

Selected portions of this arrangement of the Four Gospels may be used by writers, and commentators as long as the source is acknowledged.

Printed By
DANIELS PUBLISHERS, INC.
1209 29th Street
Orlando, Florida 32805

ACKNOWLEDGMENT

Although I have not referred to other sources for guidance in this arrangement of the Gospels, a presentation of the Gospels in this form would have been impossible for me without the aid of competent typists. These were to be found in the persons of Miss Judy Paris, my niece, and Miss Beulah Hooker, one of my former students, who readily saw the purpose and plan of the task before us, and they worked untiringly at the tedious and painstaking task of typing the manuscript in this form. Their suggestions concerning both form and subject matter have been most helpful.

INTRODUCTION

I have examined this remarkable new book of Chester Wilkins'. I am very happy to recommend it to every Bible reader.

It is a fresh, well developed and organized new approach to deep Bible study as well as everyday Bible reading. One will enjoy the total life of Christ as presented in this entirely new and different approach to His life much more than in any other attempt to portray Christ's life which I have seen over the years.

The life and works of Christ come through better and clearer in this collated narrative. Also, every outstanding event, record, and teaching in the four Gospels has been brought together in such a way as to give it the full strength of its original presentation as it must have been spoken or done by Christ or others appearing in the four Gospels.

Copious footnotes all through the work also provide a brief commentary that will become very useful. There are many nuggets of truths in this work which one does not find in any other late version or translation of the Gospels. Also, the many references holding truths together by a remarkable system of connected Scripture passages make this work extra valuable.

This volume will be very helpful for college and seminary students in their studies of the four Gospels. Ministers, Sunday school teachers, and other Christian workers will also find this a ready reference to any passage in the four Gospels, which one needs to examine again in short order. Laymen wishing to relate the many stories of Christ and his teachings to each other will find here a gold mine of wealth for such undertakings.

Chester Wilkins is certainly amply qualified for the production of this book. Educated at God's Bible School where he received his Ministerial Diploma, at Marion College where he received the Bachelor of Arts Degree, and at Butler University from which he received his M. A., he has served Christian colleges for a period of fourteen years as professor and as Chairman of the Department of Biblical Literature, as well as other administrative responsibilities. He has done exceedingly much research in producing this remarkable volume, which shows not only a well-trained mind, but also ripe scholarship and a devout, humble spirit.

This work should become a very popular reference work and serve to help multitudes of both Christian workers and laymen for many years to come.

—William S. Deal, M. A., Th. D.

PREFACE

As I have read again and again the gospels through the years, each time they seemed to open up new truths which I had not seen before. This was especially true when I began to compare the gospels. Two things which the comparison of the gospels revealed was that **they are amazingly alike and at the same time they are amazingly different**. Different, not in that they each had a different message, but in that they presented the same message with much that was not even mentioned by the other writers. Even then there can be no question about their referring to the same incident, each one presents it in his own way as he was inspired by the Holy Spirit. Some giving a very detailed account of the event and others a very brief account. Often in the brief account most of the material was not even mentioned by the other writers. These comparisons gave me a desire to see all the gospels compiled as a single narrative whereby one could read the whole account and get a fuller picture as to what took place in the life of our Lord.

The undertaking of a work of this nature has been challenging and approached with fear, excitement, and I trust with some measure of humility. In fear, lest the rearrangement might be distorting the inspired Word. Fear because I might leave out something which had great doctrinal value or might rearrange it in such a way as to give it an improper emphasis, and fear that I might add to or take away from the inspired record. None of which I wanted to be guilty of under any condition. But the burning desire to see such a work in print drove me on, and it is now presented to the reading public.

This work was approached with excitement in the anticipation of new truths which would be discovered in the painstaking experience in trying to give every incident the total emphasis which is given to it in all the gospel yet combining it to read as a single narrative.

Challenging in that I knew that it would be impossible to arrange the events in correct chronological order. While at the same time I recognized that there would be key words which would add much enlightenment as to just what took place and where it took place. Much of the ministry of our Lord would of necessity have to be left out of the sacred record. Therefore the writers of the Gospels had to make a choice, aided by the Holy Spirit as to just what they should include. Often the terms, "And it came to pass", "now . . .", "and . . .", all such leaving an uncertainty as to just when the event took place. However when the writer says, "While he yet spake" certain things took place, or "on the same day" or "the following day" or "about eight days after" these are to be accepted as correct and inspired as to the time of the event. Therefore after much had been done to come up with what might be considered a possible chronological order, one of these terms would come to my attention and this would require a complete reanalysis of the context. Facing these facts I can only say that an attempt has been made in placing the events in chronological order. Possibly many will disagree with the arrangement. With them I shall have no quarrel. One thing this study has convinced me of more than before, is that God is more interested in the truth of the events than the order in which they are given. With this conviction, I am not too disturbed if I have failed in my effort as to the chronological arrangement, if I have not distorted the truth in the arrangement.

In presenting this work, no inspiration is admitted. Although I have prayed much for guidance, I make no claims as to being led of our Lord. I accept all responsibility for any errors which may be found. If this work proves to be a blessing to anyone, my God shall have all the praise.

REFERENCES

When I began this task, I was under the impression that I would find much help in the many volumes which had been written on the harmony of the Gospels and in the many outlines of events which are to be found in many Bibles and textbooks on the study of the Bible. But I soon found these were so conflicting and contradictory that I laid them all aside and pursued the task without reference to any work. While at the same time I had not forgotten the scores of pages and many works which I reviewed in preparation for class instruction. Although the source was forgotten the truths or lack of logic of some presentations have had some bearing upon my choices of arrangements.

FOOTNOTES

The footnotes have been kept brief, but I trust complete enough to give the information which is necessary to explain my reasons for any choice which I have made in the arrangement, or to point out some truth that might be of interest to, although unnoticed by, a casual reader.

DOCTRINAL EMPHASIS

Few times have I felt that it might be enlightening to add a doctrinal emphasis in the footnotes—none of which I felt would be offensive to anyone, thereby leaving it as acceptable as possible to all who may desire to read the Gospels arranged in this order, The Gospels will speak for themselves on this matter.

CONTRADICTIONS

The different accounts of the narratives, read separately, seem at times to have some contradiction. These have given me the greatest of all challenges. I believe the record is inspired and therefore without contradictions. I believe that they have a logical explanation, which I have used in the footnotes. These, I believe, will be generally acceptable to the majority of the readers.

PECULIARITIES OF THE GOSPELS

Matthew seems to place much more emphasis on the fulfillment of prophecy than the other writers. This is generally accounted for because it is believed that he was writing to the Jews, since they were looking for the Messiah as prophesied in the Old Testament and would thus be convinced that Jesus was the Messiah. He also seems to place more emphasis on the events than on the order in which they took place. He places more emphasis on the parables than the other writers. Mark and Luke are quite consistent in the order of events which they record, much being left out of each gospel that is included by the other. Mark gives more emphasis to the dramatic and as a general rule, goes much more into explanation of the miracles than the others. Luke gives much detail to the physical aspects of the life of Christ and his dealings with men. John gives us some of the greatest truths that can be found in sacred writ. At times condensing the "expanse of an eternity" into a few words as in his opening remarks of his gospel, and at other times he goes to great lengths to explain the events of a few hours, such as the experience of the woman at the well. All of chapters thirteen through eighteen take place within a few hours. Chapters twelve through twenty are entirely on the last week of our Lord's earthly ministry, which covers approximately half of his gospel.

REPETITION

It will be noted that Jesus often repeated certain truths. This is characteristic of a good teacher. Also, in every audience there was the possibility of newcomers who would need the same truth which had been taught before. There have been some problems at times trying to decide whether the writers were referring to the same event or if it was on a different occasion. When I have been in doubt, I have left in the text what seemed to be repetitious. Some subjects have been repeated in the same gospel on different occasions. The following are examples:

The sign of Jonah, Matt. 12:39-41 and Matt. 16:4

Divorce and Remarriage, Matt. 5:27 and Matt. 19:9-18

Faith to remove mountains, Matt. 17:20 and Matt. 21:21

Losing and finding life, Matt. 10:39 and 16:25

Watch for coming of Christ, Luke 12:35-40 and Luke 21:34-36 Matt. 24:42, Matt. 25:13, and Matt. 26:41 Mark 13:35 and Mark 14:38

Loosing an ass or ox on Sabbath, Luke 13:15 and Luke 14:5

Before adversaries, Luke 12:11-12 and Luke 21:12-19

There will be some repetition in the footnotes. This is to eliminate searching for some needed information on the topic at hand. The subject matter of a given text, as is often found in some Bibles, has been used to outline this arrangement so as to make it easy to refer to any given subject with the least difficulty. However, no one form has been followed. The subject matter of some texts makes it impossible to use any other subject heading and still be consistent with the text. Therefore the same headings will appear here as in many other sources. The Table of Contents includes both the subject matter and the scripture reference.

GUIDE TO THE ARRANGEMENT

To arrange the gospels as a single narrative without their scripture reference to the former arrangement would not have been difficult. But to arrange the material in such a way as to make it easy for a check on the original source from which it is quoted and yet easy to follow has not been without its problems. However, I trust the chosen form will be an aid to those who wish to refer occasionally to the original source. This should be especially helpful to those who desire to use this arrangement as a text for the study of the Gospels.

REFERENCES, SYMBOLS, ETC.

When the reference to the Gospel text is in large capitals (MATT., MARK, LUKE, JOHN) following a subject division it usually refers to the Gospel from which the major portion of the material has been taken or when a verse has been quoted in its entirety. The "1", "2", etc., above the italicized portion refers to that hich has been inserted from the other gospel or gospels to make the narrative complete. The Gospel references (¹Mark 10:6) are on the left margin. When the references are in large capitals after the first verse is given in the subject division it means that the major portion of that verse is used and it may have inserts from any of the other gospels in . These would be italicized and identified with a number 1, 2, 3, etc. above the beginning of the italicized insert. However, this verse with n inserted verse may be followed with the beginning reference in rge capitals. This means that the former text has been taken up gain. When there is no marginal reference to the verse it will refer back to the last reference given in capitals. The numerals are also used to direct one to the margin where the reference is given and the different word from one of the other gospels would be used to explain the same thing ("Son of man" another gospel might use the term "Son of od"). A word in brackets ([and], etc.) indicates that it has been added to make the reading connected and smooth.

An asterisk (*) refers one to a footnote; * is for the first footnote, * is for the second and so on.

The Four Gospels Arranged As A Single Narrative

MARK 1 :1 *The beginning of the gospel of Jesus Christ, the Son of God.

THE INCARNATION OF THE WORD

JOHN 1 :1 In the beginning was the Word, and the Word was with God, and the Word was God.

2 The same was in the beginning with God.

3 **All things were made by him; and without him was not any thing made that was made.

4 ***In him was life; and the life was the light of men.

5 And the light shineth in darkness; and the darkness comprehended it not.

JOHN 1 :9 That was the true Light, which lighteth every man that cometh into the world.

10 He was in the world, and the world was made by him, and the world knew him not.

11 He came unto his own, and his own received him not.

12 But as many as received him, to them gave he power to become the sons of God, even to them that believe on his name:

13 Which were born, not of blood, nor of the will of the flesh, nor of the will of man, but of God.

14 And the Word was made flesh, and dwelt among us (and we beheld his glory, the glory as of the only begotten of the Father), full of grace and truth.

THE GENEALOGY OF JESUS CHRIST BEGINNING WITH ABRAHAM

MATT. 1 :1 The book of the generation of Jesus Christ, the son of David, the son of Abraham.

2 Abraham begat Isaac; and Isaac begat Jacob and Jacob begat Judah and his brethren;

---

*The beginning of the gospel was before the Incarnation. Col. 1:17 Eph. 1:4 I Peter 1:20.

*The creator becomes incarnate so that he can be our redeemer, Col. 1:16 Hebrews 1:2.

**Col. 1:19-22, Phil. 2:5-11, Acts 17:28.

MATT. 1

3 And Judah begat Pharez and Zerah of Tamar; and Pharez begat Hezron: and Hezron begat Ram;

4 And Ram begat Ammin'adab; and Ammin'adab begat Nahshon; and Nahshon begat Salmon;

5 And Salmon begat Boaz of Rachab; and Boaz begat Obed of Ruth; and Obed begat Jesse;

6 And Jesse begat David the king. And David the king begat Solomon of her that had been the wife of Uri'ah;

7 And Solomon begat Rehobo'am; and Rehobo'am begat Abi'jah; and Abi'jah begat Asa;

8 And Asa begat Jehosh'aphat; and Jehosh'aphat begat Jeho'ram; and Jeho'ram begat Uzzi'ah;

9 And Uzzi'ah begat Jotham; and Jotham begat Ahaz; and Ahaz begat Hezeki'ah;

10 And Hezeki'ah begat Manas'seh; and Manas'seh begat Amon; and Amon begat Josi'ah;

11 And Josi'ah begat Jeconi'ah and his brethren, about the time they were carried away to Babylon.

12 And after they were brought to Babylon, Jeconi'ah begat She-al'ti-el; and She-al'ti-el begat Zerub'babel;

13 And Zerub'babel begat Abi'ud; and Abi'ud begat Eli'akim; and Eli'akim begat Azor;

14 And Azor begat Zadok; and Zadok begat Achim; and Achim begat Eli'ud;

15 And Eli'ud begat Ele-a'zar; and Ele-a'zar begat Matthan; and Matthan begat Jacob;

16 And Jacob begat Joseph the husband of Mary, of whom was born Jesus, who is called Christ.

17 So all the generations from Abraham to David are fourteen generations; and from David until the carrying away into Babylon are fourteen generations; and from the carrying away into Babylon unto Christ are fourteen generations.

THE BIRTH OF JOHN THE BAPTIST, THE FORERUNNER OF JESUS CHRIST, FORETOLD

LUKE 1

:5 There was in the days of Herod, the king of Judea, a certain priest named Zechari'ah, of the course of Abi'jah: and his wife was of the daughters of Aaron, and her name was Elisabeth.

LUKE 1

6 And they were both righteous before God, walking in all the commandments and ordinances of the Lord blameless.

7 And they had no child, because that Elisabeth was barren; and they both were now well stricken in years.

8 And it came to pass, that, while he executed the priest's office before God in the order of his course,

9 According to the custom of the priest's office, his lot was to burn incense when he went into the temple of the Lord.

10 And the whole multitude of the people were praying without at the time of incense.

11 And there appeared unto him an *angel of the Lord standing on the right side of the altar of incense.

12 And when Zechari'ah saw him, he was troubled, and fear fell upon him.

13 But the angel said unto him, Fear not, Zechari'ah: for thy prayer is heard; and thy wife Elisabeth shall bear thee a son, and thou shalt call his name John.

14 And thou shalt have joy and gladness; and many shall rejoice at his birth.

15 For he shall be great in the sight of the Lord, and shall drink neither wine nor strong drink; and he shall be filled with the Holy Ghost, even from his mother's womb.

16 And many of the children of Israel shall he turn to the Lord their God.

17 And he shall go before him in the spirit and power of Eli'jah, to turn the hearts of the fathers to the children, and the disobedient to the wisdom of the just; to make ready a people prepared for the Lord.

18 And Zechari'ah said unto the angel, Whereby shall I know this? for I am an old man, and my wife well stricken in years.

19 And the angel answering said unto him, I am

---

*This angel of the Lord is not to be confused with the angel of the Lord that appeared to Abraham and others. The latter was Christ pre-incarnate appearing in the form of man.

LUKE 1

Gabriel, that stand in the presence of God; and am sent to speak unto thee, and to show thee these glad tidings.

20 And, behold, thou shalt be dumb, and not able to speak, until the day that these things shall be performed, because thou believest not my words, which shall be fulfilled in their season.

21 And the people waited for Zechari'ah, and marveled that he tarried so long in the temple.

22 And when he came out, he could not speak unto them: and they perceived that he had seen a vision in the temple; for he beckoned unto them, and remained speechless.

23 And it came to pass, that, as soon as the days of his ministration were accomplished, he departed to his own house.

24 And after those days his wife Elisabeth conceived, and hid herself five months, saying,

25 Thus hath the Lord dealt with me in the days wherein he looked on me, to take away my reproach among men.

GABRIEL APPEARS UNTO MARY AND FORETELLS JESUS' BIRTH

LUKE 1

:26 And in the sixth month the angel Gabriel was sent from God unto a city of Galilee, named Nazareth,

27 To a virgin espoused to a man whose name was Joseph, of the house of David; and the virgin's name was Mary.

28 And the angel came in unto her, and said, Hail, thou art highly favored, the Lord is with thee: blessed art thou among women.

29 And when she saw him, she was troubled at his saying, and cast in her mind what manner of salutation this should be.

30 And the angel said unto her, Fear not, Mary: for thou hast found favor with God.

31 And, behold, thou shalt conceive in thy womb, and bring forth a son, and shalt call his name JESUS.

32 He shall be great, and shall be called the Son of

LUKE 1

the Highest; and the Lord God shall give unto him the throne of his father David:

33 And he shall reign over the house of Jacob for ever; and of his kingdom there shall be no end.

34 Then said Mary unto the angel, How shall this be, seeing I know not a man?

35 And the angel answered and said unto her, The Holy Ghost shall come upon thee, and the power of the Highest shall overshadow thee: therefore also that holy thing which shall be born of thee shall be called the Son of God.

36 And, behold, thy cousin Elisabeth, she hath also conceived a son in her old age; and this is the sixth month with her, who was called barren.

37 For with God nothing shall be impossible.

38 And Mary said, Behold the handmaid of the Lord; be it unto me according to thy word. And the angel departed from her.

MARY GOES TO JUDAH TO VISIT ELISABETH

LUKE 1

:39 And Mary arose in those days, and went into the hill country with haste, into a city of Judah;

40 And entered into the house of Zechari'ah, and saluted Elisabeth.

41 And it came to pass, that, when Elisabeth heard the salutation of Mary, the babe leaped in her womb; and *Elisabeth was filled with the Holy Ghost.

42 And she spake out with a loud voice, and said, Blessed art thou among women, and blessed is the fruit of thy womb.

43 And whence is this to me, that the mother of my Lord should come to me?

44 For, lo, as soon as the voice of thy salutation sounded in mine ears, the babe leaped in my womb for joy.

45 And blessed is she that believed: for there shall

---

*The Holy Spirit has always been present as the administrator of the Divine Trinity. He was, is, and always will be omnipresent. Luke 1:35, Luke 1:65, Luke 2:25, Matthew 1:18.

be a performance of those things which were told her from the Lord.

LUKE 1

46 And Mary said, My soul doth magnify the Lord,

47 And my spirit hath rejoiced in God my Saviour.

48 For he hath regarded the low estate of his handmaiden: for, behold, from henceforth all generations shall call me blessed.

49 For he that is mighty hath done to me great things; and holy is his name.

50 And his mercy is on them that fear him from generation to generation.

51 He hath showed strength with his arm; he hath scattered the proud in the imagination of their hearts.

52 He hath put down the mighty from their seats, and exalted them of low degree.

53 He hath filled the hungry with good things; and the rich he hath sent empty away.

54 He hath holpen his servant Israel, in remembrance of his mercy;

55 As he spake to our fathers, to Abraham, and to his seed for ever.

56 And Mary abode with her about three months, and returned to her own house.

THE BIRTH OF JOHN
THE BAPTIST

LUKE 1

:57 Now Elisabeth's full time came that she should be delivered; and she brought forth a son.

58 And her neighbors and her cousins heard how the Lord had showed great mercy upon her; and they rejoiced with her.

59 And it came to pass, that on the eighth day they came to circumcise the child; and they called him Zechari'ah, after the name of his father.

60 And his mother answered and said, Not so; but he shall be called John.

61 And they said unto her, There is none of thy kindred that is called by this name.

LUKE 1   62 And they *made signs to his father, how he would have him called.

63 And he asked for a writing table, and wrote, saying, His name is John. And they marveled all.

64 And his mouth was opened immediately, and his tongue loosed, and he spake, and praised God.

65 And fear came on all that dwelt round about them: and all these sayings were noised abroad throughout all the hill country of Judea.

66 And all they that heard them laid them up in their hearts, saying, What manner of child shall this be? And the hand of the Lord was with him.

ZECHARIAH IS FILLED WITH THE HOLY SPIRIT AND PROPHESIES

LUKE 1   :67 And his father Zechari'ah was filled with the Holy Ghost, and prophesied, saying,

68 Blessed be the Lord God of Israel; for he hath visited and redeemed his people,

69 And hath raised up a horn of salvation for us in the house of his servant David;

70 As he spake by the mouth of his holy prophets, which have been since the world began:

71 That we should be saved from our enemies, and from the hand of all that hate us;

72 To perform the mercy promised to our fathers, and to remember his holy covenant;

73 The oath which he sware to our father Abraham,

74 That he would grant unto us, that we, being delivered out of the hand of our enemies, might serve him without fear,

75 In holiness and righteousness before him, all the days of our life.

76 And thou, child, shalt be called the prophet of the Highest: for thou shalt go before the face of the Lord to prepare his ways;

77 To give knowledge of salvation unto his people by the remission of their sins,

78 Through the tender mercy of our God; whereby the dayspring from on high hath visited us,

---

*He must have been deaf as well as dumb.

LUKE 1

79 To give light to them that sit in darkness and in the shadow of death, to guide our feet into the way of peace.

80 And the child grew, and waxed strong in spirit, and was in the deserts till the day of his showing unto Israel.

THE WORD BECOMES FLESH IN THE BIRTH OF JESUS THE CHRIST*

MATT. 1

:18 Now the birth of Jesus Christ was on this wise: When as his mother Mary was espoused to Joseph, before they came together, she was found with child of the Holy Ghost.

19 Then Joseph her husband, being a just man, and not willing to make her a public example, was minded to put her away privily.

20 But while he thought on these things, behold, the angel of the Lord appeared unto him in a dream, saying, Joseph, thou son of David, fear not to take unto thee Mary thy wife: for that which is conceived in her is of the Holy Ghost.

21 And she shall bring forth a son, and thou shalt call his name JESUS: for he shall save his people from their sins.

22 Now all this was done, that it might be fulfilled which was spoken of the Lord by the prophet, saying,

23 Behold, a virgin shall be with child, and shall bring forth a son, and they shall call his name Imman'u-el, which being interpreted is, God with us.

24 Then Joseph being raised from sleep did as the angel of the Lord had bidden him, and took unto him his wife:

25 And knew her not till she had brought forth her firstborn son:

---

*Mary returns from the home of Elisabeth. Luke 1:39 implies that Mary departed from Nazareth immediately after the annunciation to visit Elisabeth, and Luke 1:57 implies that she left the home of Elisabeth just before the birth of John the Baptist, a period of about three months. Evidently she did not tell Joseph of the annunciation by Gabriel. Upon return, she possibly opened her heart and it is likely that Joseph disbelieved her. A pregnancy of only three months might not have been noticable enough for Joseph to be suspicious.

Arranged As a Single Narrative

LUKE 2 :1 And it came to pass in those days that there went out a decree from Caesar Augustus, that all the world should be taxed.

:2 (And this taxing was first made when Cyre'nius was governor of Syria.)

3 And all went to be taxed, every one into his own city.

4 And Joseph also went up from Galilee, out of the city of Nazareth, into Judea, unto the city of David, which is called Bethlehem, (because he was of the house and lineage of David:)

5 To be taxed with Mary his espoused wife, being great with child.

6 And so it was, that *while they were there, the days were accomplished that she should be delivered.

7 And she brought forth her firstborn son, and wrapped him in swaddling clothes, and laid him in a manger; because there was no room for them in the inn. ¹*And he [Joseph] called his name Jesus.*

¹Matt. 1:25

THE SHEPHERDS VISITED
BY THE ANGELS

LUKE 2 :8 And there were in the same country shepherds abiding in the field, keeping watch over their flock by night.

9 And, lo, the angel of the Lord came upon them, and the glory of the Lord shone round about them; and they were sore afraid.

10 And the angel said unto them, Fear not: for, behold, I bring you good tidings of great joy, which shall be to all people.

11 For unto you is born this day in the city of David a Saviour, which is Christ the Lord.

12 And this shall be a sign unto you: Ye shall find the babe wrapped in swaddling clothes, lying in a manger.

13 And suddenly there was with the angel a multitude of the heavenly host praising God, and saying,

---
*There is no scriptural reason to believe Jesus was born on the first night Mary and Joseph were in Bethlehem. They may have been in Bethlehem several days before the Christ Child was born.

LUKE 2

14 Glory to God in the highest, and on earth peace, good will toward men.

15 And it came to pass, as the angels were gone away from them into heaven, the shepherds said one to another, Let us now go even unto Bethlehem, and see this thing which is come to pass, which the Lord hath made known unto us.

16 And they came with haste, and *found Mary and Joseph, and the babe lying in a manger.

17 **And when they had seen it, they made known abroad the saying which was told them concerning this child.

18 And all they that heard it wondered at those things which were told them by the shepherds.

19 But Mary kept all these things, and pondered them in her heart.

20 And the shepherds returned, glorifying and praising God for all the things that they had heard and seen, as it was told unto them.

MARY AND JOSEPH TAKE JESUS TO THE TEMPLE TO PRESENT HIM TO THE LORD

LUKE 2

:21 And when eight days were accomplished for the circumcising of the child, his name was called JESUS, which was so named of the angel before he was conceived in the womb.

22 And when the days of her purification according to the law of Moses were accomplished, they brought him to Jerusalem, to present him to the Lord;

23 ***(As it is written in the law of the Lord,

---

*By the time the shepherds arrived, Mary and Joseph had probably retired for the remainder of the night just as in any other home. The visit and report of the shepherds was an unexpected visit.

**This was not a secret event. The news was spread far and wide. There is no question about the fact of this event being common knowledge among many. The Pharisees once said to Jesus, "We be not born of fornication". They would have to have had some knowledge of the nature of his birth to have made such a remark.

***This is still Old Testament time. This continued through the Gospels up until the crucifixion. This presentation was necessary because he was man as well as God. As a man he walked before God as all men should walk, without sin. When Jesus cried, "It is finished!", the Old Testament ceremonial law was all fulfilled; the moral law was never changed.

LUKE 2

Every male that openeth the womb shall be called holy to the Lord;)

24 And to offer a sacrifice according to that which is said in the law of the Lord, A pair of turtledoves, or two young pigeons.

25 And, behold, there was a man in Jerusalem, whose name was Simeon; and the same man was just and devout, waiting for the consolation of Israel: and the Holy Ghost was upon him.

26 And it was revealed unto him by the Holy Ghost, that he should not see death, before he had seen the Lord's Christ.

27 And he came by the Spirit into the temple: and when the parents brought in the child Jesus, to do for him after the custom of the law,

28 Then took he him up in his arms, and blessed God, and said,

29 Lord, now lettest thou thy servant depart in peace, according to thy word:

30 For mine eyes have seen thy salvation,

31 Which thou hast prepared before the face of all people;

32 A light to lighten the Gentiles, and the glory of thy people Israel.

33 And Joseph and his mother marveled at those things which were spoken of him.

34 And Simeon blessed them, and said unto Mary his mother, Behold, this child is set for the fall and rising again of many in Israel; and for a sign which shall be spoken against;

35 (Yea, a sword shall pierce through thy own soul also;) that the *thoughts of many hearts may be revealed.

36 And there was one Anna, a prophetess, the daughter of Phanu-el, of the tribe of Asher: she was of a great age, and had lived with a husband seven years from her virginity;

37 And she was a widow of about fourscore and four years, which departed not from the temple, but served God with fastings and prayers night and day.

38 And she coming in that instant gave thanks

---

*The rejection of Christ and His crucifixion revealed the sinfulness of man.

likewise unto the Lord, and spake of him to all them that looked for redemption in Jerusalem.

*THEY RETURN TO NAZARETH

LUKE 2

:39 And when they had performed all things according to the law of the Lord, they returned into Galilee, to their own city Nazareth.

40 And the child grew, and waxed strong in the spirit, filled with wisdom; and the grace of God was upon him.

THE VISIT OF THE WISE MEN

MATT. 2

:1 Now when Jesus was born in Bethlehem of Judea in the days of Herod the king, behold, there came wise men from the east to Jerusalem,

2 Saying, Where is he that is born King of the Jews? for we have seen his **star in the east, and are come to worship him.

3 When Herod the king had heard these things, he was troubled, and all Jerusalem with him.

4 And when he had gathered all the chief priests and scribes of the people together, he demanded of them where Christ should be born.

5 And they said unto him, In Bethlehem of Judea: for thus it is written by the prophet,

6 And thou Bethlehem, in the land of Judah, art not the least among the princes of Judah; for out of thee shall come a Governor, that shall rule my people Israel.

7 Then Herod, when he had privily called the wise men, inquired of them diligently ***what time the star appeared.

8 And he sent them to Bethlehem, ****and said,

---

*There is no reason to believe that they remained in Bethlehem until the wise men arrived. (See notes of Matt. 2:2, below)

**The star appeared in the east at the time of Jesus' birth. It reappeared again after the wise men left Jerusalem for Bethlehem. (See v. 9) If they had been following the star all the way, they would not have gone to Jerusalem and made inquiry.

***His knowledge as to the time the star first appeared was evidently the reason why he had the children slain up to two years old.

****Evidently Joseph and Mary had gone back to Nazareth and returned again. (See Luke 2:41) Jesus is now a young child, not a baby or infant. At this time he was in a house not a stable or manger. (See v.11)

ARRANGED AS A SINGLE NARRATIVE

Go and search diligently for the young child; and when ye have found him, bring me word again, that I may come and worship him also.

MATT. 2

9 When they had heard the king, they departed; and, lo, the *star, which they saw in the east, went before them, till it came and stood over where the young child was.

10 **When they saw the star, they rejoiced with exceeding great joy.

11 And when they were come into the house, they saw the young child with Mary his mother, and fell down, and worshipped him: and when they had opened their treasures, they presented unto him gifts; gold, and frankincense, and myrrh.

12 And being warned of God in a dream that they should not return to Herod, they departed into their own country another way.

HEROD HAS ALL THE INFANTS SLAIN UP TO TWO YEARS OLD

MATT. 2

:13 And when they were departed, behold, the angel of the Lord appeareth to Joseph in a dream, saying, Arise, and take the young child and his mother, and flee into Egypt, and be thou there until I bring thee word: for Herod will seek the young child to destroy him.

14 When he arose, he took the young child and his mother by night, and departed into Egypt:

15 And was there until the death of Herod: that it might be fulfilled which was spoken of the Lord by the prophet, saying, ***Out of Egypt have I called my son.

16 Then Herod, when he saw that he was mocked of the wise men, was exceeding wroth, and sent forth, and slew all the children that were in Bethlehem, and in all the coasts thereof, from two

---

*The same star which appeared in the east re-appears. This could not have been a planet or planets as some astrologers suggest.
**They had not seen it for some time.
***This prophecy is given a double meaning—first the exodus from Egypt; second as stated here.

MATT. 2

years old and under, according to the *time which he had diligently inquired of the wise men.

17 Then was fulfilled that which was spoken by Jeremiah the prophet, saying,

18 In Ramah was there a voice heard, lamentation, and weeping, and great mourning, Rachel weeping for her children, and would not be comforted, because they are not.

19 But when Herod was dead, behold, an angel of the Lord appeareth in a dream to Joseph in Egypt,

20 Saying, Arise, and take the young child and his mother, and go into the land of Israel: for they are dead which sought the child's life.

21 And he arose, and took the young child and his mother, and came into the land of Israel.

22 But when he heard that Archela'us did reign in Judea in the room of his father Herod, he was afraid to go thither: notwithstanding, being warned of God in a dream, he turned aside into the parts of Galilee:

23 And he came and dwelt in a city called Nazareth: that it might be fulfilled which was spoken by the prophets, He shall be called a Nazarene.

JESUS IN THE TEMPLE—
AGE TWELVE

LUKE 2

:41 Now his parents **went to Jerusalem every year at the feast of the passover.

42 And when he was twelve years old, they went up to Jerusalem after the custom of the feast.

43 And when they had fulfilled the days, as they returned, the child Jesus tarried behind in Jerusalem; and Joseph and his mother knew not of it.

44 But they, supposing him to have been in the company, went a day's journey; and they sought him among their kinsfolk and acquaintance.

45 And when they found him not, they turned back again to Jerusalem, seeking him.

46 And it came to pass, that after three days they

---

*See notes on Matthew 2:7, page 12.
**This would explain the reason for them being back in Judea when Jesus was about two years old when the wise men arrived.

LUKE 2

found him in the temple, sitting in the midst of the doctors, both hearing them, and asking them questions.

47 And all that heard him were astonished at his understanding and answers.

48 And when they saw him, they were amazed: and his mother said unto him, Son, why hast thou thus dealt with us? behold, thy father and I have sought thee sorrowing.

49 And he said unto them, How is it that ye sought me? wist ye not that I must be about my Father's business?

50 And they understood not the saying which he spake unto them.

51 And he went down with them, and came to Nazareth, and was subject unto them: but his mother kept all these sayings in her heart.

52 And Jesus *increased in wisdom and stature, and in favor with God and man.

JOHN THE BAPTIST BEGINS HIS MINISTRY

LUKE 3

:1 Now in the fifteenth year of the reign of Tibe'ri-us Caesar, Pontius Pilate being governor of Judea, and Herod being tetrarch of Galilee, and his brother Philip tetrarch of Iturae'a and of the region of Trachoni'tis, and Lysa'ni-as the tetrarch of Abile'ne,

2 Annas and Cai'aphas being the high priests, the word of God came unto John the son of Zechari'ah in the wilderness.

JOHN 1

:6 There was a man sent from God, whose name was John.

MARK 1

:2 As it is written in the prophets, Behold, I send my messenger before thy face, which shall prepare thy way before thee.

LUKE 3

:5 Every valley shall be filled, and every mountain and hill shall be brought low; and the crooked shall be made straight, and the rough ways shall be made smooth;

6 And all flesh shall see the salvation of God.

---

*This is the way it appeared to men. Otherwise, this was impossible, for he was God as well as man. He possessed all wisdom, knowledge and understanding.

JOHN 1 :7 The same came for a witness, to bear witness of the Light, that all men through him might believe.

8 He was not that Light, but was sent to bear witness of that Light.

THE PREACHING OF REPENTANCE FOR THE REMISSION OF SINS

MATT. 3 :1 In those days came John the Baptist, preaching in the wilderness of Judea,

LUKE 3 :3 And he came into all the country about Jordan, preaching the baptism of repentance for the remission of sins;

MATT. 3 :2 And saying, Repent ye: for the kingdom of heaven is at hand.

3 For this is he that was spoken of by the prophet Esaias, saying, The voice of one crying in the wilderness, Prepare ye the way of the Lord, make his paths straight.

4 And the same John had his raiment of camel's hair, and a leathern girdle about his loins; and his meat was locusts and wild honey.

5 Then went out to him Jerusalem, and all Judea, and all the region round about Jordan,

6 And were baptized of him in Jordan, confessing their sins.

JOHN REPROVES THE PHARISEES AND SADDUCEES

MATT. 3 :7 But when he saw [1]many of the Pharisees and Sadducees come to his baptism, he said unto them,
[1]Luke 3:7 the multitude O generation of vipers, who hath warned you to flee from the wrath to come?

LUKE 3 :8 Bring forth therefore fruits [2]worthy of repentance, and begin not to say within yourselves, We have Abraham to our father: for I say unto you,
[2]Matt. 3:8 meet* That God is able of these stones to raise up children unto Abraham.

9 And now also the axe is laid unto the root of the trees: every tree therefore which bringeth not forth good fruit is hewn down, and cast into the fire.

---
*Answerable to amendment of life.

CONVERSION LEADS TO ETHICAL CONDUCT AND DEMANDS

LUKE 3 :10 And the people asked him, saying, What shall we do then?

11 He answered and saith unto them, He that hath two coats, let him impart to him that hath none; and he that hath meat, let him do likewise.

12 Then came also publicans to be baptized, and said unto him, Master, what shall we do?

13 And he said unto them, Exact no more than that which is appointed you.

14 And the soldiers likewise demanded of him, saying, And what shall we do? And he said unto them, Do violence to no man, neither accuse any falsely; and be content with your wages.

15 And as the people were in expectation, and all men mused in their hearts of John, whether he were the Christ, or not;

CHRIST SHALL BAPTIZE WITH THE HOLY GHOST AND FIRE

LUKE 3
[1]**Matt. 3:11** unto repentance
[2]**Matt. 3:11**
[3]bear

:16 John answered, saying unto them all, I indeed baptize you with [1]water; but one mightier than I cometh [2]*after me,* the latchet of whose shoes I am not worthy to [3]unloose: he shall baptize you with the Holy Ghost and with fire:

17 Whose fan is in his hand, and he will thoroughly purge his floor, and will gather the wheat into his garner; but the chaff he will burn with fire unquenchable.

18 And many other things in his exhortation preached he unto the people.

LUKE 3 :21 Now it came to pass when all the people were baptized,

THE BAPTISM OF JESUS

MATT. 3
[1]**Mark 1:9**

:13 Then cometh Jesus from [1]*Nazareth of* Galilee to Jordan unto John, to be baptized of him [1]*in Jordan.*

14 But John forbade him, saying, I have need to be baptized of thee, and comest thou to me?

15 And Jesus answering said unto him, Suffer it

to be so now; for thus it becometh us to fulfill all righteousness. Then he suffered him.

16 And Jesus, ²when he was baptized, went up straightway out of the water: and, lo, the heavens were opened unto him, and he saw the Spirit of God descending like a dove, and lighting upon him:

17 And lo a voice from heaven, saying, This ⁴is my beloved Son, in whom I am well pleased.

²Luke 3:21 being baptized, and praying
MATT. 3
⁴Mark 1:11
Luke 3:22
Thou art

LUKE 3

THE GENEALOGY OF JESUS GOING BACK TO ADAM*

:23 And Jesus himself began to be about thirty years of age, being (as was supposed) the son of Joseph, which was the son of Heli,

24 Which was the son of Matthat, which was the son of Levi, which was the son of Melchi, which was the son of Janna, which was the son of Joseph,

25 Which was the son of Mattathi'as, which was the son of Amos, which was the son of Nahum, which was the son of Esli, which was the son of Nag'gai,

26 Which was the son of Ma'ath, which was the son of Mattathi'as, which was the son of Sem'e-i, which was the son of Joseph, which was the son of Judah,

27 Which was the son of Joanna, which was the son of Rhesa, which was the son of Zerub'-babel, which was the son of She-al'tiel, which was the son of Neri,

28 Which was the son of Melchi, which was the son of Addi, which was the son of Cosam, which was the son of Elmo'dam, which was the son of Er,

29 Which was the son of Jose, which was the son

---

*Much controversy has arisen over the recorded genealogy of Jesus. There are major differences between Luke's account and those of Matthew. How the genealogy was established has been lost. Many conjectures have been made by scholars concerning it. Whatever might be said to throw light upon the subject is to our benefit. But, there is one fact that stands out, no one, friend or enemy of Christ, during the first centuries, left any records of what might be considered discrepancies. If there had been any contrary to the accepted form, one can stand assured that Christ's enemies would not have hesitated to bring it to light in order to discredit the Gospels.

LUKE 3

of Eli-e'zer, which was the son of Jorim, which was the son of Matthat, which was the son of Levi,

30 Which was the son of Simeon, which was the son of Judah, which was the son of Joseph, which was the son of Jonan, which was the son of Eli'akim,

31 Which was the son of Me'le-a, which was the son of Menan, which was the son of Mat'tatha, which was the son of Nathan, which was the son of David,

32 Which was the son of Jesse, which was the son of Obed, which was the son of Boaz, which was the son of Salmon, which was the son of Nahshon,

33 Which was the son of Ammin'adab, which was the son of Ram, which was the son of Hezron, which was the son of Pharez, which was the son of Judah,

34 Which was the son of Jacob, which was the son of Isaac, which was the son of Abraham, which was the son of Terah, which was the son of Nahor,

35 Which was the son of Serug, which was the son of Re'u, which was the son of Peleg, which was the son of Eber, which was the son of Salah,

36 Which was the son of Ca-i'nan, which was the son of Arphax'ad, which was the son of Shem, which was the son of Noah, which was the son of Lamech,

37 Which was the son of Methu'selah, which was the son of Enoch, which was the son of Jared, which was the son of Mahal'-aleel, which was the son of Cai-i'nan,

38 Which was the son of Enos, which was the son of Seth, which was the son of Adam, which was the son of God.

THE TEMPTATION OF JESUS

LUKE 4

:1 And Jesus being full of the Holy Ghost returned from Jordan,

MARK 1
¹Luke 4:1 led
²Luke 4:2 devil

:12 And immediately the Spirit ¹driveth him into the wilderness.

13 And he was there in the wilderness forty days tempted of ²Satan; and was with the wild beasts; and the angels ministered unto him.

LUKE 4
[3]Matt. 4:2
  fasted
[4]Matt. 4:3
  Tempter
[5]Matt. 4:3
  stones
MATT. 4

LUKE 4
[6]Matt. 4:8
  exceeding
[7]Matt. 4:8

MATT. 4
[8]Luke 4:7
LUKE 4

:2 ... And in those days he [3]did eat nothing: and when they were ended, he afterward hungered.

3 And the [4]devil said unto him, If thou be the Son of God, command this [5]stone that it be made bread.

:4 But he answered and said, It is written, Man shall not live by bread alone, but by every word that proceedeth out of the mouth of God.

:5 And the devil, taking him up into a [6]high mountain, showed unto him all the kingdoms of the world in a moment of time, [7]*and the glory of them,*

6 And the devil said unto him, All this power will I give thee, and the glory of them: for that is delivered unto me; and to whomsoever I will, I give it.

:9 ... All these things will I give thee, if thou wilt fall down and worship me [8]*all shall be thine.*

:8 And Jesus answered and said unto him, Get thee behind me, Satan: for it is written, Thou shalt worship the Lord thy God, and him only shalt thou serve.

9 And he brought him to Jerusalem, and set him on a pinnacle of the temple, and said unto him, If thou be the Son of God, cast thyself down from hence:

10 For it is written, He shall give his angels charge over thee, to keep thee:

11 And in their hands they shall bear thee up; lest at any time thou dash thy foot against a stone.

12 And Jesus answering said unto him, It is said, Thou shalt not tempt the Lord thy God.

13 And when the devil had ended all the temptation, he departed from him for a season.

MATT. 4

:11 ...and, behold, angels came and ministered unto him.

THE TESTIMONY OF JOHN THE BAPTIST

JOHN 1

:15 And John bare witness of him, and cried, saying, This was he of whom I spake, He that

JOHN 1

cometh after me is preferred before me, *for he was before me.

16 And of his fulness have all we received, and grace for grace.

17 For the law was given by Moses, **but grace and truth came by Jesus Christ.

18 No man hath seen God at any time; the only begotten Son, which is in the bosom of the Father, he hath declared him.

19 And this is the record of John, when the Jews sent priests and Levites from Jerusalem to ask him, Who art thou?

20 And he confessed, and denied not; but confessed, I am not the Christ.

21 And they asked him, What then? Art thou Eli'jah? And he saith, I am not. Art thou that Prophet? And he answered, No.

22 Then said they unto him, Who art thou? that we may give an answer to them that sent us. What sayest thou of thyself?

23 He said, I am the voice of one crying in the wilderness, Make straight the way of the Lord, as said the prophet Isaiah.

24 And they which were sent were of the Pharisees.

25 And they asked him, and said unto him, Why baptizest thou then, if thou be not that Christ, nor Eli'jah, neither that Prophet?

26 John answered them, saying, I baptize with water: but there standeth one among you, whom ye know not;

27 He it is, who coming after me is preferred before me, whose shoe-latchet I am not worthy to unloose.

---

*Christ was the angel of the Lord in the Old Testament that appeared in bodily form to Abraham, (Gen. 12:7; Gen. 17:1; Gen. 18:33), to Hagar, (Gen 16:7-13), to Manoah, (Judges 13:3, Judges 13:21-22). He was the "I Am" that spoke to Moses, (Ex. 3:13-15). Christ is contemporary with eternity past, in the Old Testament and the Gospels, and today, "Jesus Christ the same yesterday, and today, and forever", (Heb. 3:8).

**Grace and truth have always been available to all men, (Noah, Gen. 6:8, Gen. 7:1; Enoch, Gen. 5:24), because Christ always was co-existent, co-eternal, and co-equal with the Father. He was the Eternal Word that became incarnate.

JOHN 1

28 These things were done in Bethab'ara beyond Jordan, where John was baptizing.

JESUS IS THE LAMB OF GOD

JOHN 1

:29 The next day John seeth Jesus coming unto him, and saith, *Behold the Lamb of God, which taketh away the sin of the world!

30 This is he of whom I said, After me cometh a man which is preferred before me: for he was before me.

31 And I knew him not: but that he should be made manifest to Israel, therefore am I come baptizing with water.

32 And John bare record, saying, I saw the Spirit descending from heaven like a dove, and it abode upon him.

33 And I knew him not: but he that sent me to baptize with water, the same said unto me, Upon whom thou shalt see the Spirit descending, and remaining on him, the same is he which baptizeth with the Holy Ghost.

34 And I saw, and bare record that this is the Son of God.

THE DISCIPLES OF JOHN
SEEK JESUS

JOHN 1

:35 Again the next day after, John stood, and two of his disciples;

36 And looking upon Jesus as he walked, he saith, Behold the Lamb of God!

37 And the two disciples heard him speak, and they followed Jesus.

38 Then Jesus turned, and saw them following, and saith unto them, What seek ye? They say unto him, Rabbi, (which is to say, being interpreted, Master,) where dwellest thou?

39 He saith unto them, Come and see. They came and saw where he dwelt, and abode with him that day: for it was about the tenth hour.

---

*The lamb was a symbolic sacrifice in the Old Testament of Christ's perfect sacrifice for sin.

JOHN 1

40 One of the two which heard John speak, and followed him, was Andrew, Simon Peter's brother.

41 He first findeth his own brother Simon, and saith unto him, We have found the Messiah, which is, being interpreted, the Christ.

42 And he brought him to Jesus. And when Jesus beheld him, he said, Thou art Simon the son of Jona: thou shalt be called Cephas, which is by interpretation, A stone.

THE CALL OF PHILIP AND NATHANAEL

JOHN 1

:43 *The day following Jesus would go forth into Galilee, and findeth Philip, and saith unto him, Follow me.

44 Now Philip was of Bethsai'-da, the city of Andrew and Peter.

45 Philip findeth Nathan'a-el, and saith unto him, We have found him, of whom Moses in the law, and the prophets, did write, Jesus of Nazareth, the son of Joseph.

46 And Nathan'a-el said unto him, Can there any good thing come out of Nazareth? Philip saith unto him, Come and see.

47 Jesus saw Nathan'a-el coming to him, and saith of him, Behold an Israelite indeed, in whom is no guile!

48 Nathan'a-el saith unto him, Whence knowest thou me? Jesus answered and said unto him, **Before that Philip called thee, when thou wast under the fig tree, I saw thee.

49 Nathan'a-el answered and saith unto him, Rabbi, thou art the Son of God; thou art the King of Israel.

50 Jesus answered and said unto him, Because I said unto thee, I saw thee under the fig tree, believest thou? thou shalt see greater things than these.

51 And he saith unto him, Verily, verily, I say unto you, Hereafter ye shall see heaven open, and

---

*This would be Christ's first return to Galilee after his baptism.
**Jesus, being divine was omnipresent. (See John 2:24-25.)

the angels of God ascending and descending upon the Son of man.

BEGINNING OF MIRACLES AT THE WEDDING IN CANA OF GALILEE

JOHN 2

:1 And the third day there was a marriage in Cana of Galilee; and the mother of Jesus was there:

2 And both Jesus was called, and his disciples, to the marriage.

3 And when they wanted wine, the mother of Jesus saith unto him, They have no wine.

4 Jesus saith unto her, Woman, what have I to do with thee? mine hour is not yet come.

5 His mother saith unto the servants, Whatsoever he saith unto you, do it.

6 And there were set there six waterpots of stone, after the manner of the purifying of the Jews, containing two or three firkins apiece.

7 Jesus saith unto them, Fill the waterpots with water. And they filled them up to the brim.

8 And he saith unto them, Draw out now, and bear unto the governor of the feast. And they bare it.

9 When the ruler of the feast had tasted the water that was made into wine, and knew not whence it was, (but the servants which drew the water knew,) the governor of the feast called the bridegroom,

10 And saith unto him, Every man at the beginning doth set forth good wine; and when men have well drunk, then that which is worse: but thou hast kept the good wine until now.

11 This beginning of miracles did Jesus in Cana of Galilee, and manifested forth his glory; and his disciples believed on him.

12 After this he went down to Caper'na-um, he, and his mother, and his brethren, and his disciples; and they continued there not many days.

THE FIRST CLEANSING OF THE TEMPLE

JOHN 2 :13 And the Jews' *passover was at hand, and Jesus went up to Jerusalem,

14 And found in the temple those that sold oxen and sheep and doves, and the changers of money sitting:

15 And when he had made a scourge of small cords, he drove them all out of the temple, and the sheep, and the oxen; and poured out the changers' money, and overthrew the tables;

16 And said unto them that sold doves, Take these things hence; make not my Father's house a house of merchandise.

17 And his disciples remembered that it was written, The zeal of thine house hath eaten me up.

18 Then answered the Jews and said unto him, What sign showest thou unto us, seeing that thou does these things?

19 Jesus answered and said unto them, Destroy this temple, and in three days I will raise it up.

20 Then said the Jews, Forty and six years was this temple in building, and wilt thou rear it up in three days?

21 But he spake of the temple of his body.

22 When therefore he was risen from the dead, his disciples remembered that he had said this unto them; and they believed the Scripture, and the word which Jesus had said.

JESUS BEING DIVINE, KNOWS THE CHARACTER OF ALL MEN

JOHN 2 :23 Now when he was in Jerusalem at the passover, in the feast day, many believed in his name, when they saw the miracles which he did.

24 But Jesus did not commit himself unto them, because he knew all men,

25 And needed not that any should testify of man; for he knew what was in man.

---

*First recorded trip to Jerusalem after Jesus begins his ministry. Luke 3:23 implies that Jesus was about 30 years of age at the time of his baptism. The events from this baptism until this event were within a few days or a very few weeks. This would date the Birth of Christ near this time of the year, March or April.

JOHN 3

NICODEMUS VISITS JESUS

:1 There was a man of the Pharisees, named Nicodemus, a ruler of the Jews:

2 The same came to Jesus by night, and said unto him, Rabbi, we know that thou art a teacher come from God: for no man can do these miracles that thou doest, except God be with him.

3 Jesus answered and said unto him, Verily, verily, I say unto thee, Except a man be born again, he cannot see the kingdom of God.

4 Nicodemus saith unto him, How can a man be born when he is old? can he enter the second time into his mother's womb, and be born?

5 Jesus answered, Verily, verily, I say unto thee, Except a man be born of water and of the Spirit, he cannot enter into the kingdom of God.

6 That which is born of the flesh is flesh; and that which is born of the Spirit is spirit.

7 Marvel not that I said unto thee, Ye must be born again.

8 The wind bloweth where it listeth, and thou hearest the sound thereof, but canst not tell whence it cometh, and whither it goeth: so is every one that is born of the Spirit.

9 Nicodemus answered and said unto him, How can these things be?

10 Jesus answered and said unto him, Art thou a master of Israel, and knowest not these things?

11 Verily, verily, I say unto thee, We speak that we do know, and testify that we have seen; and ye receive not our witness.

12 If I have told you earthly things, and ye believe not, how shall ye believe, if I tell you of heavenly things?

13 And no man hath ascended up to heaven, but he that came down from heaven, even the Son of man which is in heaven.

14 And as Moses lifted up the serpent in the wilderness, even so must the Son of man be lifted up:

15 That whosoever believeth in him should not perish, but have eternal life.

GOD'S LOVE FOR THE WORLD

JOHN 3

:16 For God so loved the world, that he gave his only begotten Son, that whosoever believeth in him should not perish, but have everlasting life.

17 For God sent not his Son into the world to condemn the world; but that the world through him might be saved.

18 He that believeth on him is not condemned: but he that believeth not is condemned already, because he hath not believed in the name of the only begotten Son of God.

19 And this is the condemnation, that light is come into the world, and men loved darkness rather than light because their deeds were evil.

20 For every one that doeth evil hateth the light, neither cometh to the light, lest his deeds should be reproved.

21 But he that doeth truth cometh to the light, that his deeds may be made manifest, that they are wrought in God.

DISCIPLES OF JOHN AND JESUS BAPTIZE BELIEVERS

JOHN 3

:22 After these things came Jesus and his disciples into the land of Judea; and there he tarried with them, and baptized.

23 And John also was baptizing in Ae'non near to Salim because there was much water there: and they came, and were baptized.

24 For John was not yet cast into prison.

25 Then there arose a question between some of John's disciples and the Jews about purifying.

26 And they came unto John, and said unto him, Rabbi, he that was with thee beyond Jordan, to whom thou barest witness, behold, the same baptizeth, and all men come to him.

27 John answered and said, A man can receive nothing, except it be given him from heaven.

JOHN AGAIN BEARS WITNESS OF CHRIST

JOHN 3

:28 Ye yourselves bear me witness, that I said, I am not the Christ, but that I am sent before him.

JOHN 3

29 He that hath the bride is the bridegroom: but the friend of the bridegroom, which standeth and heareth him, rejoiceth greatly because of the bridegroom's voice: this my joy therefore is fulfilled.

30 He must increase, but I must decrease.

31 He that cometh from above is above all: he that is of the earth is earthly, and speaketh of the earth: he that cometh from heaven is above all.

32 And what he hath seen and heard, that he testifieth; and no man receiveth his testimony.

33 He that hath received his testimony hath set to his seal that God is true.

34 For he whom God hath sent speaketh the words of God: for God giveth not the Spirit by measure unto him.

35 The Father loveth the Son, and hath given all things unto his hand.

36 He that believeth on the Son hath everlasting life: and he that believeth not the Son shall not see life; but the wrath of God abideth on him.

JOHN THE BAPTIST IMPRISONED

LUKE 3

:19 But Herod the tetrarch, being reproved by him for Hero′di-as his brother Philip's wife, and for all the evils which Herod had done,

20 Added yet this above all, that he shut up John in prison.

JESUS' MINISTRY IN SAMARIA

JOHN 4

:1 When therefore the Lord knew how the Pharisees had heard that Jesus made and baptized more disciples than John,

[1]Matt. 4:12

2 (Though Jesus himself baptized not, but his disciples,) [and] [1]*heard that John was cast into prison,*

3 He left Judea, and departed *again into Galilee.

4 And he must needs go through Samaria.

5 Then cometh he to a city of Samaria, which is called Sychar, near to the parcel of ground that Jacob gave to his son Joseph.

6 Now Jacob's well was there. Jesus therefore,

---

*Second trip into Galilee.

JOHN 4

being wearied with his journey, sat thus on the well: and it was about the sixth hour.

7 There cometh a woman of Samaria to draw water: Jesus saith unto her, Give me to drink.

8 (For his disciples were gone away unto the city to buy meat.)

9 Then saith the woman of Samaria unto him, How is it that thou, being a Jew, askest drink of me, which am a woman of Samaria: for the Jews have no dealings with the Samaritans.

10 Jesus answered and said unto her, If thou knewest the gift of God, and who it is that saith to thee, Give me to drink; thou wouldest have asked of him, and he would have given thee living water.

11 The woman saith unto him, Sir, thou hast nothing to draw with, and the well is deep: from whence then hast thou that living water?

12 Art thou greater than our father Jacob, which gave us the well, and drank thereof himself, and his children, and his cattle?

13 Jesus answered and said unto her, Whosoever drinketh of this water shall thirst again:

14 But whosoever drinketh of the water that I shall give him shall never thirst; but the water that I shall give him shall be in him a well of water springing up into everlasting life.

15 The woman saith unto him, Sir, give me this water, that I thirst not, neither come hither to draw.

16 Jesus saith unto her, Go, call thy husband, and come hither.

17 The woman answered and said, I have no husband. Jesus said unto her, Thou hast well said, I have no husband:

18 For thou has had five husbands; and he whom thou now hast is not thy husband: in that saidst thou truly.

19 The woman saith unto him, Sir, I perceive that thou art a prophet.

20 Our fathers worshipped in this mountain; and ye say, that in Jerusalem is the place where men ought to worship.

21 Jesus saith unto her, Woman, believe me, the

hour cometh, when ye shall neither in this mountain, nor yet at Jerusalem, worship the Father.

22 Ye worship ye know not what: we know what we worship; for salvation is of the Jews.

23 But the hour cometh, and now is, when the true worshippers shall worship the Father in spirit and in truth: for the Father seeketh such to worship him.

24 God is a Spirit: and they that worship him must worship him in spirit and in truth.

25 The woman saith unto him, I know that Messiah cometh, which is called Christ: when he is come, he will tell us all things.

26 Jesus saith unto her, I that speak unto thee am he.

27 And upon this came his disciples, and marveled that he talked with the woman: yet no man said, What seekest thou? or, Why talkest thou with her?

28 The woman then left her waterpot, and went her way into the city, and saith to the men,

29 Come, see a man, which told me all things that ever I did: is not this the Christ?

30 Then they went out of the city, and came unto him.

31 In the mean while his disciples prayed him, saying, Master, eat.

32 But he said unto them, I have meat to eat that ye know not of.

33 Therefore said the disciples one to another, Hath any man brought him aught to eat?

34 Jesus saith unto them, My meat is to do the will of him that sent me, and to finish his work.

35 Say not ye, there are yet four months, and then cometh harvest? behold, I say unto you, Lift up your eyes, and look on the fields; for they are white already to harvest.

36 And he that reapeth receiveth wages, and gathereth fruit unto life eternal: that both he that soweth and he that reapeth may rejoice together.

37 And herein is that saying true, One soweth, and another reapeth.

JOHN 4	38 I sent you to reap that whereupon ye bestowed no labor: other men labored, and ye are entered into their labors.
39 And many of the Samaritans of that city believed on him for the saying of the woman, which testified, He told me all that ever I did.
40 So when the Samaritans were come unto him, they besought him that he would tarry with them: and he abode there two days.
41 And many more believed because of his own word;
42 And said unto the woman, Now we believe, not because of thy saying: for we have heard him ourselves, and know that this is indeed the Christ, the Saviour of the world.
¹Luke 4:14	43 Now after two days ¹*Jesus returned in the power of the Spirit into Galilee: and there went out a fame of him through all the region round about.*
LUKE 4	:15 And he taught in their synagogues, being glorified of all.

JESUS MINISTERS AT NAZARETH
AND IS REJECTED

LUKE 4	:16 And he came to Nazareth, where he had been brought up: and, as his custom was, he went into the synagogue on the sabbath day, and stood up for to read.
17 And there was delivered unto him the book of the prophet Isaiah. And when he had opened the book, he found the place where it was written,
18 The Spirit of the Lord is upon me, because he hath anointed me to preach the gospel to the poor; he hath sent me to heal the brokenhearted, to preach deliverance to the captives, and recovering of sight to the blind, to set at liberty them that are bruised,
19 To preach the acceptable year of the Lord.
20 And he closed the book, and he gave it again to the minister, and sat down. And the eyes of all them that were in the synagogue were fastened on him.
21 And he began to say unto them, This day is this scripture fulfilled in your ears.
22 And all bare him witness, and wondered at the

gracious words which proceeded out of his mouth. And they said, Is not this Joseph's son?

LUKE 4

23 And he said unto them, Ye will surely say unto me this proverb, Physician, heal thyself: whatsoever we have heard done in Caper'na-um, do also here in thy country.

24 And he said, Verily I say unto you, *No prophet is accepted in his own country.

25 But I tell you of a truth, many widows were in Israel in the days of Eli'jah, when the heaven was shut up three years and six months, when great famine was throughout all the land;

26 But unto none of them was Eli'jah sent, save unto Zar'ephath, a city of Sidon, unto a woman that was a widow.

27 And many lepers were in Israel in the time of Eli'sha the prophet; and none of them was cleansed, saving Na'aman the Syrian.

28 And all they in the synagogue, when they heard these things, were filled with wrath,

29 And rose up, and thrust him out of the city, and led him unto the brow of the hill whereon their city was built, that they might cast him down headlong.

30 But he, passing through the midst of them, went his way,

JOHN 4

:44 For Jesus himself testified, that a **prophet hath no honor in his own country.

45 Then when he was come into Galilee, the Galileans, received him, having seen all the things that he did at Jerusalem at the feast: for they also went unto the feast.

---

*The context of Luke, Matt. 13:57, and Mark 6:4 would lead one to believe this same truth was repeated at different times under similar circumstances except in John 4:44.

**This is all John has to say about Jesus' rejection in Nazareth and appears to be parallel with Luke 4:24.

NOBLEMAN'S SON HEALED

JOHN 4

46 So Jesus came again into *Cana of Galilee, where he made the water wine. And there was a certain nobleman, whose son was sick at Caper'na-um.

47 When he heard that Jesus was come out of Judea into Galilee, he went unto him, and besought him that he would come down, and heal his son: for he was at the point of death.

48 Then said Jesus unto him, Except ye see signs and wonders, ye will not believe.

49 The nobleman saith unto him, Sir, come down ere my child die.

50 Jesus saith unto him, Go thy way; thy son liveth. And the man believed the word that Jesus had spoken unto him, and he went his way.

51 And as he was now going down, his servants met him, and told him, saying, Thy son liveth.

52 Then inquired he of them the hour when he began to amend. And they said unto him, Yesterday at the seventh hour the fever left him.

53 So the father knew that it was at the same hour, in the which Jesus said unto him, Thy son liveth: and himself believed, and his whole house.

54 This is again the **second miracle that Jesus did, when he was come out of Judea into Galilee.

MATT. 4

:13 And leaving Nazareth, he came and dwelt in Caper'na-um, which is upon the seacoast, in the borders of Zeb'ulun and Naphtali:

14 That it might be fulfilled which was spoken by Isaiah the prophet, saying,

15 The land of Zeb'ulun, and the land of Naph'tali, by the way of the sea, beyond Jordan, Galilee of Gentiles;

16 The people which sat in darkness saw great

---

*Cana of Galilee is between Nazareth and Tiberius. Therefore it seems that this narrative of the nobleman would best fit in the chronological order of the Gospels at this place. Also this is said to be his second miracle after coming from Judea into Cana of Galilee (v. 54). Other miracles had been performed in Capernaum (Luke 4:23) which were possibly performed on His previous tour. This is the first healing in absentia.

**Matthew does not mention the above miracle.

light; and to them which sat in the region and shadow of death light is sprung up.

MATT. 4
[1] Mark 1:15

17 From that time Jesus began to preach, and to say, [1]*The time is fulfilled,* Repent [1]*ye, and believe the gospel,* for the kingdom of heaven is at hand.

JESUS CALLS FOUR FISHERMEN*

MATT. 4

:18 And Jesus, walking by the sea of Galilee, saw two brethren, Simon called Peter, and Andrew his brother, casting a net into the sea: for they were fishers.

19 And he saith unto them, Follow me, and I will make you fishers of men.

20 And they straightway left their nets, and followed him.

21 And going on from thence, he saw other two brethren, James the son of Zeb'edee, and John his brother, in a ship with Zeb'edee their father, mending their nets; and he called them.

22 And they immediately left the ship and their father, and followed him.

JESUS' FAME REACHES INTO SYRIA

MATT. 4

:23 And Jesus went about all Galilee, teaching in their synagogues, and preaching the gospel of the kingdom, and healing all manner of sickness and all manner of disease among the people.

24 And his fame went throughout all Syria: and they brought unto him all sick people that were taken with divers diseases and torments, and those which were possessed with devils, and those which were lunatic, and those that had the palsy; and he healed them.

25 And there followed him great multitudes of people from Galilee, and from Decap'olis, and from Jerusalem, and from Judea, and from beyond Jordan.

---

*This first call of these four men is not to be confused with the second call in Luke 5:1-11 (Page 49-50). The circumstances are similar, yet there is a distinct difference. Here, Peter and Andrew were casting their net, and James and John were in their ship mending their nets. In Luke, the ships were standing by the lake and the fishermen were gone out of them and washing their nets.

JESUS' SECOND TRIP TO JERUSALEM DURING HIS MINISTRY
THE HEALING AT THE POOL

JOHN 5

:1 After this there was a feast of the Jews; and Jesus went up to Jerusalem.

2 Now there is at Jerusalem by the sheep market a pool, which is called in the Hebrew tongue Bethes'da, having five porches.

3 In these lay a great multitude of impotent folk, of blind, halt, withered, waiting for the moving of the water.

4 For an angel went down at a certain season into the pool, and troubled the water: whosoever then first after the troubling of the water stepped in was made whole of whatsoever disease he had.

5 And a certain man was there, which had an infirmity thirty and eight years.

6 When Jesus saw him lie, and knew that he had been now a long time in that case, he saith unto him, Wilt thou be made whole?

7 The impotent man answered him, Sir, I have no man, when the water is troubled, to put me into the pool: but while I am coming, another steppeth down before me.

8 Jesus saith unto him, Rise, take up thy bed, and walk.

9 And immediately the man was made whole, and took up his bed, and walked: and on the same day was the sabbath.

10 The Jews therefore said unto him that was cured, It is the sabbath day: it is not lawful for thee to carry thy bed.

11 He answered them, He that made me whole, the same said unto me, Take up thy bed, and walk.

12 Then asked they him, What man is that which said unto thee, Take up thy bed, and walk?

13 And he that was healed wist not who it was: for Jesus had conveyed himself away, a multitude being in that place.

14 Afterward Jesus findeth him in the temple, and said unto him, Behold, thou art made whole: sin no more, lest a worse thing come unto thee.

JOHN 5

15 The man departed, and told the Jews that it was Jesus, which had made him whole.

16 And therefore did the Jews persecute Jesus, and sought to slay him, because he had done these things on the sabbath day.

THE WORK OF THE FATHER AND SON ARE ONE

JOHN 5

:17 But Jesus answered them, My Father worketh hitherto, and I work.

18 Therefore the Jews sought the more to kill him, because he not only had broken the sabbath, but said also that God was his Father, making himself equal with God.

19 Then answered Jesus and said unto them, Verily, verily, I say unto you, The Son can do nothing of himself, but what he seeth the Father do: for what things soever he doeth, these also doeth the Son likewise.

20 For the Father loveth the Son, and showeth him all things that himself doeth: and he will show him greater works than these, that ye may marvel.

21 For as the Father raiseth up the dead, and quickeneth them; even so the Son quickeneth whom he will.

22 For the Father judgeth no man, but hath committed all judgment unto the Son:

23 That all men should honor the Son, even as they honor the Father. He that honoreth not the Son honoreth not the Father which hath sent him.

24 Verily, verily, I say unto you, He that heareth my word, and believeth on him that sent me, hath everlasting life, and shall not come into condemnation; but is passed from death unto life.

25 Verily, verily, I say unto you, The hour is coming, and now is, when the dead shall hear the voice of the Son of God: and they that hear shall live.

26 For as the Father hath life in himself; so hath he given to the Son to have life in himself;

27 And hath given him authority to execute judgment also, because he is the Son of man.

28 Marvel not at this: for the hour is coming, in

the which all that are in the graves shall hear his voice,

JOHN 5

29 And shall come forth; they that have done good, unto the resurrection of life; and they that have done evil, unto the resurrection of damnation.

30 I can of mine own self do nothing: as I hear, I judge: and my judgment is just; because I seek not mine own will, but the will of the Father which hath sent me.

31 If I bear witness of myself, my witness is not true.

32 There is another that beareth witness of me; and I know that the witness which he witnesseth of me is true.

33 Ye sent unto John, and he bare witness unto the truth.

34 But I receive not testimony from man: but these things I say, that ye might be saved.

35 He was a burning and a shining light: and ye were willing for a season to rejoice in his light.

JESUS HAS A GREATER WITNESS THAN JOHN

JOHN 5

:36 But I have greater witness than that of John: for the works which the Father hath given me to finish, the same works that I do, bear witness of me, that the Father hath sent me.

37 And the Father himself, which hath sent me, hath borne witness of me. Ye have neither heard his voice at any time, nor seen his shape.

38 And ye have not his word abiding in you: for whom he hath sent, him ye believe not.

39 Search the Scriptures; for in them ye think ye have eternal life: and they are they which testify of me.

40 And ye will not come to me, that ye might have life.

41 I receive not honor from men.

42 But I know you, that ye have not the love of God in you.

43 I am come in my Father's name, and ye receive

THE FOUR GOSPELS

me not: if another shall come in his own name, him ye will receive.

JOHN 5

44 How can ye believe, which receive honor one of another, and seek not the honor that cometh from God only?

45 Do not think that I will accuse you to the Father: there is one that accuseth you, even Moses, in whom ye trust.

46 For had ye believed Moses, ye would have believed me: for he wrote of me.

47 But if ye believe not his writings, how shall ye believe my words?

JOHN 6

:1 After these things Jesus went over the Sea of Galilee, which is the sea of Ti-be′ri-as.

2 And a great multitude followed him, because they saw his miracles which he did on them that were diseased.

[1]Matt. 5:1

3 And Jesus [1]*seeing the multitude* went up into a mountain, and [1]*when he was set,* his disciples [1]*came unto him,*

THE SERMON ON THE MOUNT*

MATT. 5

:2 And he opened his mouth, and taught them saying,

3 Blessed are the poor in spirit: for theirs is the kingdom of heaven.

4 Blessed are they that mourn: for they shall be comforted.

5 Blessed are the meek: for they shall inherit the earth.

6 Blessed are they which do hunger and thirst after righteousness: for they shall be filled.

7 Blessed are the merciful: for they shall obtain mercy.

8 Blessed are the pure in heart: for they shall see God.

---

*Matt 5:1 "And seeing the multitude, he went into a mountain: And when he was set, his disciples came unto him." This possibly included a great number. The Sermon on the Mount is not to be confused with Luke 6:17-49, which was given to the multitude in the Plain. Jesus, like all ministers found it necessary to repeat the same truth, at least in part when he had a different congregation. The message on the Mount had deeper truths for more established Christians.

MATT. 5

9 Blessed are the peacemakers: for they shall be called the children of God.

10 Blessed are they which are persecuted for righteousness' sake: for theirs is the kingdom of heaven.

11 Blessed are ye, when men shall revile you, and persecute you, and shall say all manner of evil against you falsely, for my sake.

12 Rejoice, and be exceeding glad: for great is your reward in heaven: for so persecuted they the prophets which were before you.

13 Ye are the salt of earth: but if the salt have lost his savor, wherewith shall it be salted: it is thenceforth good for nothing, but to be cast out, and to be trodden under foot of men.

THE LIGHT OF THE WORLD

MATT. 5

:14 Ye are the light of the world. A city that is set on a hill cannot be hid.

15 Neither do men light a candle, and put it under a bushel, but on a candlestick; and it giveth light unto all that are in the house.

16 Let your light so shine before men, that they may see your good works, and glorify your Father which is in heaven.

JESUS DECLARES THAT THE MORAL LAW IS STILL IN FORCE

MATT. 5

:17 Think not that I am come to destroy the law, or the prophets: I am not come to destroy, but to fulfil.

18 For verily I say unto you, Till heaven and earth pass, one jot or one tittle shall in no wise pass from the law, till all be fulfilled.

19 Whosoever therefore shall break one of these least commandments, and shall teach men so, he shall be called the least in the kingdom of heaven: but whosoever shall do and teach them, the same shall be called great in the kingdom of heaven.

20 For I say unto you, That except your righteousness shall exceed the righteousness of the

scribes and Pharisees, ye shall in no case enter into the kingdom of heaven.

JESUS REPROVES THEM FOR THEIR DISTORTION OF THE LAW

MATT. 5 :21 Ye have *heard that it was said by them of old time, Thou shalt not kill; and whosoever shall kill shall be in danger of the judgment:

22 But I say unto you, That whosoever is angry with his brother without a cause shall be in danger of the judgment: and whosoever shall say to his brother, Raca, shall be in danger of the council: but whosoever shall say, Thou fool, shall be in danger of hell fire.

23 Therefore if thou bring thy gift to the altar and there rememberest that thy brother hath aught against thee;

24 Leave there thy gift before the altar, and go thy way; first be reconciled to thy brother, and then come and offer thy gift.

25 Agree with thine adversary quickly, whiles thou art in the way with him; lest at any time the adversary deliver thee to the judge, and the judge deliver thee to the officer, and thou be cast into prison.

26 Verily I say unto thee, Thou shalt by no means come out thence, till thou hast paid the uttermost farthing.

LOOKING AND LUSTING

MATT. 5 :27 Ye have heard that it was said by them of old time, Thou shalt not commit adultery:

28 But I say unto you, That whosoever looketh on a woman to lust after her hath committed adultery with her already in his heart.

29 And if thy right eye offend thee, pluck it out, and cast it from thee: for it is profitable for thee that one of thy members should perish, and not that thy whole body should be cast into hell.

---

*What they had heard was one thing; what was written was another. The Pharisees had distorted the Law through their traditions. Christ is directing them back to the truth. He did not add to, or change the Law. He only corrected them in their error.

MATT. 5

30 And if thy right hand offend thee, cut it off, and cast it from thee: for it is profitable for thee that one of thy members should perish, and not that thy whole body should be cast into hell.

31 It hath been said, Whosoever shall put away his wife, let him give her a writing of divorcement:

32 But I say unto you, That whosoever shall put away his wife, saving for the cause of fornication, causeth her to commit adultery: and whosoever shall marry her that is *divorced committeth adultery.

OATHS

MATT. 5

:33 Again, ye have heard that it hath been said by them of old time, Thou shalt not forswear thyself, but shalt perform unto the Lord thine oaths:

34 But I say unto you, Swear not at all; neither by heaven; for it is God's throne:

35 Nor by the earth; for it is his footstool: neither by Jerusalem for it is the city of the great King.

36 Neither shalt thou swear by thy head, because thou canst not make one hair white or black.

37 But let your communication be, Yea, yea; Nay, nay: for whatsoever is more than these cometh of evil.

38 Ye have heard that it hath been said, An **eye for an eye, and a tooth for a tooth:

39 But I say unto you, That ye resist not evil: but whosoever shall smite thee on thy right cheek, turn to him the other also.

40 And if any man will sue thee at the law, and take away thy coat, let him have thy cloak also.

41 And whosoever shall compel thee to go a mile, go with him twain.

42 Give to him that asketh thee, and from him that would borrow of thee turn not thou away.

---

*Jesus gives a fuller discourse on this subject in Matthew 19:3-12 than is recorded here.

**The Old Testament gave no place for carnal retaliation. Should an injury occur, the offended was not permitted to decide the penalty. The offended was to take the offender before a court of judges who would consider the deed with the motive and pass sentence accordingly. Eye for eye was the maximum penalty. See Deut. 19:1-21.

LOVE YOUR ENEMIES

MATT. 5

:43 Ye have heard that it hath been said, Thou shalt love thy neighbor, and hate thine enemy.

44 But I say unto you, Love your enemies, bless them that curse you, do good to them that hate you, and pray for them which despitefully use you, and persecute you;

45 That ye may be the children of your Father which is in heaven: for he maketh his sun to rise on the evil and on the good, and sendeth rain on the just and on the unjust.

46 For if ye love them which love you, what reward have ye? do not even the publicans the same?

47 And if ye salute your brethren only, what do ye more than others? do not even the publicans so?

48 Be ye therefore perfect, even as your Father which is in heaven is perfect.

GIVING

MATT. 6

:1 Take heed that ye do not your alms before men, to be seen of them: otherwise ye have no reward of your Father which is in heaven.

2 Therefore when thou doest thine alms, do not sound a trumpet before thee, as the hypocrites do in the synagogues and in the streets, that they may have glory of men. Verily I say unto you, They have their reward.

3 But when thou doest alms, let not thy left hand know what thy right hand doeth:

4 That thine alms may be in secret: and thy Father which seeth in secret himself shall reward thee openly.

PRAYER

MATT. 6

:5 And when thou prayest, thou shalt not be as the hypocrites are: for they love to pray standing in the synagogues and in the corners of the streets, that they may be seen of men. Verily I say unto you, They have their reward.

6 But thou, when thou prayest, enter into thy closet, and when thou hast shut thy door, pray to

ARRANGED AS A SINGLE NARRATIVE

thy Father which is in secret; and thy Father which seeth in secret shall reward thee openly.

MATT. 6

7 But when ye pray, use not vain repetitions, as the heathen do: for they think that they shall be heard for their much speaking.

8 Be not ye therefore like unto them: for your Father knoweth what things ye have need of, before ye ask him.

9 After this manner therefore pray ye: Our Father which art in heaven, Hallowed be thy name.

10 Thy kingdom come. Thy will be done in earth, as it is in heaven.

11 Give us this day our daily bread.

12 And forgive us our debts, as we forgive our debtors.

13 And lead us not into temptation, but deliver us from evil: For thine is the kingdom, and the power, and the glory, for ever. Amen.

14 For if ye forgive men their trespasses, your heavenly Father will also forgive you:

15 But if ye forgive not men their trespasses, neither will your Father forgive your trespasses.

FASTING

MATT. 6

:16 Moreover when ye fast, be not, as the hypocrites, of a sad countenance: for they disfigure their faces, that they may appear unto men to fast. Verily I say unto you, They have their reward.

17 But thou, when thou fastest, anoint thine head, and wash thy face;

18 That thou appear not unto men to fast, but unto thy Father which is in secret: and thy Father which seeth in secret shall reward thee openly.

TREASURES CAN BE SECURE

MATT. 6

:19 Lay not up for yourselves treasures upon earth, where moth and rust doth corrupt, and where thieves break through and steal:

20 But lay up for yourselves treasures in heaven, where neither moth nor rust doth corrupt, and where thieves do not break through nor steal:

21 For where your treasure is, there will your heart be also.

THE EYE: THE LIGHT OF THE BODY

MATT. 6 :22 The light of the body is the eye: if therefore thine eye be single, thy whole body shall be full of light.

23 But if thine eye be evil, thy whole body shall be full of darkness. If therefore the light that is in thee be darkness, how great is that darkness!

GOD AND MAMMON

MATT. 6 :24 No man can serve two masters: for either he will hate the one, and love the other; or else he will hold to the one, and despise the other. Ye cannot serve God and mammon.

GOD ACCEPTS RESPONSIBILITY TO CARE FOR US

MATT. 6 :25 Therefore I say unto you, Take no thought for your life, what ye shall eat, or what ye shall drink; nor yet for your body, what ye shall put on. Is not the life more than meat, and the body than raiment?

26 Behold the fowls of the air: for they sow not, neither do they reap, nor gather into barns; yet your heavenly Father feedeth them. Are ye not much better than they?

27 Which of you by taking thought can add one cubit unto his stature?

28 And why take ye thought for raiment? Consider the lilies of the field, how they grow; they toil not, neither do they spin:

29 And yet I say unto you, That even Solomon in all his glory was not arrayed like one of these.

30 Wherefore, if God so clothe the grass of the field, which today is, and tomorrow is cast into the oven, shall he not much more clothe you, O ye of little faith?

31 Therefore take no thought, saying, What shall we eat? or, What shall we drink? or, Wherewithal shall we be clothed?

32 (For after all these things do the Gentiles seek:) for your heavenly Father knoweth that ye have need of all these things.

MATT. 6

33 But seek ye first the kingdom of God, and his righteousness; and all these things shall be added unto you.

34 Take therefore no thought for the morrow: for the morrow shall take thought for the things of itself. Sufficient unto the day is the evil thereof.

JUDGING OTHERS

MATT. 7

:1 Judge not, that ye be not judged.

2 For with what judgment ye judge, ye shall be judged: and with what measure ye mete, it shall be measured to you again.

3 And why beholdest thou the mote that is in thy brother's eye, but considerest not the beam that is in thine own eye?

4 Or how wilt thou say to thy brother, Let me pull out the mote out of thine eye: and, behold, a beam is in thine own eye?

5 Thou hypocrite, first cast out the beam out of thine own eye: and then shalt thou see clearly to cast out the mote out of thy brother's eye.

6 Give not that which is holy unto the dogs, neither cast ye your pearls before swine, lest they trample them under their feet, and turn again and rend you.

THE PRAYER OF FAITH

MATT. 7

:7 Ask, and it shall be given you; seek, and ye shall find; knock, and it shall be opened unto you:

8 For every one that asketh receiveth; and he that seeketh findeth; and to him that knocketh it shall be opened.

9 Or what man is there of you, whom if his son ask bread, will he give him a stone?

10 Or if he ask a fish, will he give him a serpent?

11 If ye then, being evil, know how to give good gifts unto your children, how much more shall your Father which is in heaven give good things to them that ask him?

12 Therefore all things whatsoever ye would that men should do to you, do ye even so to them: for this is the law and the prophets.

TWO WAYS

MATT. 7 :13 Enter ye in at the strait gate: for wide is the gate, and broad is the way, that leadeth to destruction, and many there be which go in thereat:

14 Because strait is the gate, and narrow is the way, which leadeth unto life, and few there be that find it.

FRUIT IDENTIFIES THE TREE

MATT. 7 :15 Beware of false prophets, which come to you in sheep's clothing, but inwardly they are ravening wolves.

16 Ye shall know them by their fruits. Do men gather grapes of thorns, or figs of thistles?

17 Even so every good tree bringeth forth good fruit; but a corrupt tree bringeth forth evil fruit.

18 A good tree cannot bring forth evil fruit, neither can a corrupt tree bring forth good fruit.

19 Every tree that bringeth not forth good fruit is hewn down, and cast into the fire.

20 Wherefore by their fruits ye shall know them.

21 Not every man that saith unto me, Lord, Lord, shall enter into the kingdom of heaven; but he that doeth the will of my Father which is in heaven.

22 Many will say unto me in that day, Lord, Lord, have we not prophesied in thy name? and in thy name have cast out devils? and in thy name done many wonderful works?

23 And then will I profess unto them, I never knew you: depart from me, ye that work iniquity.

BUILDING ON ROCK OR SAND

MATT. 7 :24 Therefore whosoever heareth these sayings of mine, and doeth them, I will liken him unto a wise man, which built his house upon a rock:

25 And the rain descended, and the floods came, and the winds blew, and beat upon that house; and it fell not: for it was founded upon a rock.

26 And every one that heareth these sayings of mine, and doeth them not, shall be likened unto a foolish man, which built his house upon the sand:

27 And the rain descended, and the floods came,

MATT. 7

and the winds blew, and beat upon that house; and it fell: and great was the fall of it.

28 And it came to pass, when Jesus had ended these sayings, the people were astonished at his doctrine:

29 For he taught them as one having authority, and not as the scribes.*

JESUS CLEANSES A LEPER**

MATT. 8

:1 When he was come down from the mountain, great multitudes followed him.

2 And, behold, there came a leper and worshipped him, saying, Lord if thou wilt, thou canst make me clean.

3 And Jesus put forth his hand, and touched him, saying, I will; be thou clean. And immediately his leprosy was cleansed.

4 And Jesus saith unto him, See thou tell no man; but go thy way, show thyself to the priest, and offer the gift that Moses commanded, for a testimony unto thee.

A CENTURION'S SERVANT HEALED***

MATT. 8
[1]Luke 4:31-32

:5 And when Jesus was entered into Caper'na-um, [1]*a city of Galilee, he taught them on the Sabbath days* [and] there came unto him a centurion, beseeching him,

6 And saying, Lord, my servant lieth at home sick of the palsy, grievously tormented.

7 And Jesus saith unto him, I will come and heal him.

8 The centurion answered and said, Lord, I am not worthy that thou shouldest come under my roof: but speak the word only, and my servant shall be healed.

---

*End of Sermon on the Mount.

**This may have been a different leper than the one recorded in Luke and Mark. Luke 5:12 speaks of the leper in a certain city. Mark 1:40-45 gives no account as to where it took place. It seems that Mark and Luke have recorded the same miracle. It would be reasonable to believe there were many such cases of healing.

***Second healing in absentia. This is not to be confused with Luke 7:1-10. Here the centurion talks with Jesus. In Luke, he sent elders to make the request.

MATT. 8

9 For I am a man under authority, having soldiers under me: and I say to this man, Go, and he goeth; and to another, Come, and he cometh; and to my servant, Do this, and he doeth it.

10 When Jesus heard it, he marveled, and said to them that followed, Verily I say unto you, I have not found so great faith, no, not in Israel.

11 And I say unto you, That many shall come from the east and west, and shall sit down with Abraham, and Isaac, and Jacob, in the kingdom of heaven:

12 But the children of the kingdom shall be cast out into outer darkness: there shall be weeping and gnashing of teeth.

13 And Jesus said unto the centurion, Go thy way; and as thou hast believed, so be it done unto thee. And his servant was healed the selfsame hour.

A MAN WITH AN UNCLEAN SPIRIT

LUKE 4

:33 And in the synagogue there was a man, which had a spirit of an unclean devil, and cried out with a loud voice,

34 Saying, Let us alone; what have we to do with thee, thou Jesus of Nazareth: art thou come to destroy us? I know thee who thou art; the Holy One of God.

35 And Jesus rebuked him, saying, Hold thy peace, and come out of him. And when the devil had

¹Mark 1:26 torn

¹thrown him in the midst, he came out of him, and hurt him not.

²Mark 1:27 What new doctrine is this?
³They do obey him
⁴Mark 1:28

36 And they were all amazed, and spake among themselves, saying, ²what a word is this! for with authority and power he commandeth the unclean spirits, ³and they came out.

37 And ⁴*immediately* the fame of him went out into every place of the country round about ⁴*Galilee*.

JESUS HEALS SIMON'S MOTHER-IN-LAW

MARK 1

¹Luke 4:38

:29 And forthwith, when they were come out of the synagogue, they entered into the house of Simon and Andrew, with James and John. ¹*And Simon's*

Arranged As a Single Narrative

²Mark 1:30   *wife's mother was taken with a great fever; and they*
tell him of her ²*besought him for her.*

LUKE 4   :39 And he stood over her, ³*And he touched her*
³Matt. 8:15   *hand* and rebuked the fever; and it left her: and immediately she arose and ministered unto them.

JESUS HEALS MANY AT EVENING

LUKE 4   :40 Now when the ¹*sun was setting* ²*and all the*
¹Matt. 8:16   *city was gathered together at the door,* all they that
even was come   had any sick with divers diseases and ³*possessed*
²Mark 1:33   *with devils* brought them unto him; and he laid his
³Matt. 8:16   hands on every one of them and healed them.

MATT. 8   :17 That it might be fulfilled which was spoken by Isaiah the prophet, saying, Himself took our infirmities, and bare our sicknesses.

LUKE 4   :41 And devils also came out of many, crying out, and saying, Thou art Christ the Son of God. And he rebuking them suffered them not to speak: for they knew that he was Christ.

JESUS DEPARTS ON A PREACHING TOUR

MARK 1   :35 And in the morning, rising up a great while
¹Luke 4:42   before day, he went out, and departed into a ¹solitary
desert   place, and there prayed.

                 36 And Si'-mon and they that were with him followed after him.

                 37 And when they had found him, they said unto
²Luke 4:42   him, All men seek for thee, ²*and the people sought him and . . . stayed him, that he should not depart from them.*

                 38 And he said unto them, Let us go into the next
³Luke 4:43   towns, that I may preach ³*the Kingdom of God* there also: for therefore came I forth.

                 39 And he preached in their synagogues throughout all Gal'i-lee, and cast out devils.

THE GREAT CATCH OF FISH

LUKE 5   :1 ¹And it came to pass, that as the people pressed
¹See note   upon him to hear the word of God, he stood by the
Matt. 4:18-22   lake of Gennes'-aret,
(Page 34)

LUKE 5

2 And saw two ships standing by the lake: But the fishermen were gone out of them, and were washing their nets.

3 And he entered into one of the ships, which was Simon's, and prayed him that *he would thrust out a little from the land. And he sat down, and taught the people out of the ship.

4 Now when he had left speaking, he said unto Simon, Launch out into the deep, and let down your nets for a draught.

5 And Simon answering said unto him, Master, we have toiled all the night, and have taken nothing: nevertheless at thy word I will let down the net.

6 And when they had this done, they inclosed a great multitude of fishes: and their net brake.

7 And they beckoned unto their partners which were **in the other ship, that they should come and help them. And they came, and filled both the ships, so that they began to sink.

8 When Simon Peter saw it, he fell down at Jesus' knees, saying, Depart from me; for I am a sinful man, O Lord.

9 For he was astonished, and all that were with him, at the draught of the fishes which they had taken:

10 And so was also James, and John, the sons of Zeb'edee, which were partners with Simon. And Jesus said unto Simon, Fear not; from henceforth thou shalt catch men.

11 And when they had brought their ships to land, they forsook all, and followed him.***

---

*Simon evidently got into the ship and then pushed it out from the shore.

**When Christ arrived they were gone out of their ship. Some time during the discourse they returned to their ship.

***Just when the disciples gave full time to the ministry is not clear. This was the second call of these men. The twelve apostles were not chosen for some months after Christ began his ministry. In Luke 8:1 it says, "as he went throughout every city and village preaching . . . and the twelve were with him," which seems to imply that they were not always with him. This might be one reason why each writer has much to say about some things which are not mentioned by the others.

ARRANGED AS A SINGLE NARRATIVE

JESUS CLEANSES A LEPER

MARK 1
¹Luke 5:12

:40 ¹*And it came to pass, when he was in a certain city,* there came a leper to him, ¹*full of leprosy,* beseeching him, and kneeling down to him, and saying unto him, ¹*Lord,* If thou wilt, thou canst make me clean.

41 And Jesus, moved with compassion, put forth his hand, and touched him, and saith unto him, I will; be thou clean.

42 And as soon as he had spoken, immediately the leprosy departed from him, and he was cleansed.

43 And he straitly charged him, and forthwith sent him away:

44 And saith unto him, See thou say nothing to any man: but go thy way, show thyself to the priest, and offer for thy cleansing those things which Moses commanded, for a testimony unto them.

45 But he went out, and began to publish it much, and to blaze abroad the matter, insomuch that Jesus could no more openly enter into the city, but was without in desert places: and ²*great multitudes came together to hear* him from every quarter, ²*and to be healed by Him of their infirmities.*

²Luke 5:15

LUKE 5

:16 And he withdrew himself into the wilderness and prayed.

JESUS HEALS A PALSIED MAN

MARK 2
¹Matt. 9:1
²Luke 5:17

:1 ¹*And he entered into a ship, and passed over, and came into his own city,* Caperna-um after some days; and it was noised that he was ²*teaching* in the house. And ²*there were Pharisees and doctors of the law sitting by, which were come out of every town of Galilee, and Judea, and Jerusalem: and the power of the Lord was present to heal them.*

MARK 2

:2 And straightway many were gathered together, insomuch that there was no room to receive them, no, not so much as about the door: and he preached the word unto them.

³Matt. 9:2
⁴Luke 5:18

3 And they come unto him, bringing one sick of the palsy, ³*lying on a bed,* which was borne of four ⁴*and they sought means to bring him in to lay him before him.*

[5]Luke 5:19	4 [5]*And when they could not find by what way they might bring him in because of the multitude, they went upon the housetop, and* uncovered the roof where he was: and when they had broken it up, they let down, [5]*through the tiling*, the bed wherein the sick of the palsy lay [6]*into the midst before Jesus.*
[6]Luke 5:19 MARK 2	
[7]Luke 5:20 Man	5 When Jesus saw their faith, he said unto the sick of the palsy, [7]Son, [8]*be of good cheer*, thy sins be forgiven thee.
[8]Matt. 9:2	
[9]Luke 5:21	6 But there were certain of the scribes [9]*and the Pharisees* sitting there, and reasoning in their hearts [9]*saying,* 7 Why doth this man thus speak blasphemies? who can forgive sins but God only?
[10]Matt. 9:4	8 And immediately, when Jesus perceived in his spirit that they so reasoned within themselves, he said unto them, Why reason ye these [10]*evil things in your hearts?* 9 Whether is it easier to say to the sick of the palsy, Thy sins be forgiven thee; or to say, Arise, and take up thy bed, and walk? 10 But that ye may know that the Son of man hath power on earth to forgive sins, (he saith to the sick of the palsy,) 11 I say unto thee, Arise, and take up thy bed, and go thy way into thine house.
[11]Luke 5:25	12 And immediately he rose [11]*up before them and* took up the bed whereon he lay, and went forth before them all [11]*to his own house, glorifying God.*
[12]Matt. 9:8 [13]Matt. 9:8 marveled [14]Luke 4:26	[12]*When the multitudes saw it*, they were all [13]amazed, and glorified God, [14]*which had given such power unto men*, saying, We never saw it on this fashion. [14]*We have seen strange things to day.**

THE CALL OF LEVI

MARK 2 [1]Luke 5:27	:13 [1]*And after these things he went forth*, by the sea side; and all the multitude resorted unto him, and he taught them.

---

*"We have seen strange things today". It is very probable that both these and other remarks were made by the multitude. The writers make their choice from the remarks that were made.

THE FEEDING OF THE FIVE THOUSAND

⁴Luke 9:11 — *them of the kingdom of God,* **and . . . to teach them many things,** *⁴and healed them that had need of healing.*

MARK 6 — :35 And when the day was now far spent, his disciples came unto him, and said, this is a desert place, and now the time is far passed:

¹Luke 9:12 — 36 Send them away, that they may go into the country round about, and into the villages, *¹and lodge,* and buy themselves bread: for they have nothing to eat.

JOHN 6 — :4 And the passover, a feast of the Jews, was nigh.

²Matt. 14:16 — 5 . . . Jesus then . . . saith unto Philip, *²They need not depart,* *³Give ye them to eat.*

³Mark 6:37 — 6 And this he said to prove him: for he himself knew what he would do.

7 Philip answered him, Two hundred pennyworth of bread is not sufficient for them, that every one of them may take a little.

MARK 6 — :38 He saith unto them, How many loaves have ye? go and see.

JOHN 6 — :8 One of his disciples, Andrew, Simon Peter's brother, saith unto him.

9 There is a lad here, which hath five barley loaves, and two small fishes: but what are they among so many? *⁴except we should* go and buy meat for all this people.

⁴Luke 9:13

MARK 6 — :39 And he commanded them to make all sit down by companies upon the green grass.

40 And they sat down in ranks, by hundreds, and by fifties.

41 And when he had taken the five loaves and the two fishes, he looked up to heaven, and blessed, and brake the loaves, and gave them to his disciples to set before them: and the two fishes divided he among the *⁵disciples to set before the multitude.*

⁵Luke 9:16

⁶Luke 9:17 — 42 And they did all eat, and were filled: [Then] *⁶he said unto his disciples, Gather up the fragments that remain, that nothing be lost.*

JOHN 6	13 Therefore they gathered them together, and filled twelve baskets with the fragments of the five barley loaves, which remained over and above unto them that had eaten.
MATT. 14	:21 And they that had eaten were about five thousand men, beside women and children.
JOHN 6	:14 Then those men, when they had seen the miracle that Jesus did, said, This is of a truth that Prophet that should come into the world.
	15 Jesus therefore perceived that they would come and take him by force, to make him a king ...
MATT. 14	:22 And straightway Jesus constrained his disciples to get into a ship, and to go before him into
[7]John 6:17	the other side, [7]*toward Caper'na-um,* [8]*unto*
[8]Mark 6:45	*Bethsai'da,* while he sent the multitudes away.
	23 And when he had sent the multitudes away, he went up into a mountain apart to pray, and when the
[9]Mark 6:47	evening was come, he was there alone [9]*on the land.*

JESUS WALKS ON THE SEA

MATT. 14	:24 But the ship was now in the midst of the sea
[1]John 6:18 great	tossed with waves: for the wind was [1]contrary, [2]*and it was now dark, and Jesus was not come to them.*
[2]John 6:17	[3]*And he saw them toiling in rowing;*
[3]Mark 6:48	25 And in the fourth watch of the night, [4]*when*
[4]John 6:19	*they had rowed about five and twenty or thirty furlongs, they see Jesus walking on the sea, and drawing nigh unto the ship:* [3]*and would have passed by them,* they were troubled, saying, It is a spirit;
[5]Mark 6:50	and they cried out for fear, [5]*for they all saw him.*
MATT. 14	:27 But straightway Jesus spake unto them, saying, Be of good cheer: it is I; be not afraid.
	28 And Peter answered him and said, Lord, if it be thou, bid me come unto thee on the water.
	29 And he said, Come. And when Peter was come down out of the ship, he walked on the water, to go to Jesus.
	30 And when he saw the wind boisterous, he was afraid; and beginning to sink, he cried, saying, Lord, save me.
	31 And immediately Jesus stretched forth his

hand, and caught him, and said unto him, O thou of little faith, wherefore didst thou doubt?

32 And when they were come, ⁶*they willingly received him* into the ship, the wind ceased, ⁷*and they were sore amazed in themselves* and wondered, ⁸*for their heart was hardened;* and immediately the ship was at the land whither they went.

33 Then they that were in the ship came and worshipped him, saying, Of a truth thou art the Son of God.

⁶John 6:21
⁷Mark 6:51
⁸Mark 6:52

JESUS HEALS THE SICK IN GENNESARET

MARK 6

:53 And when they had passed over, they came into the land of Gennes'aret, and drew to the shore.

54 And when they were come out of the ship, straightway they knew him,

55 And ran through that whole region round about, and began to carry about in beds ¹*and brought unto him all* those that were sick, where they heard he was.

¹Matt. 14:35

56 And whithersoever he entered, into villages, or cities, or country, they laid the sick in the streets, and besought him that they might touch if it were but the border of his garment: and as many as touched him were made whole.

THE PEOPLE SEEK JESUS

JOHN 6

:22 The day following, when the people, which stood on the other side of the sea, saw that there was none other boat there, save that one whereinto his disciples were entered, and that Jesus went not with his disciples into the boat, but that his disciples were gone away alone;

23 (Howbeit there came other boats from Tibe'rias nigh unto the place where they did eat bread, after that the Lord had given thanks:)

24 When the people therefore saw that Jesus was not there, neither his disciples, they also took shipping, and came to Caper'na-um, seeking for Jesus.

25 And when they had found him on the other side

of the sea, they said unto him, Rabbi, when camest thou hither?

26 Jesus answered them and said, Verily, verily, I say unto you, Ye seek me, not because ye saw the miracles, but because ye did eat of the loaves, and were filled.

27 Labor not for the meat which perisheth, but for that meat which endureth unto everlasting life, which the Son of man shall give unto you: for him hath God the father sealed.

28 Then said they unto him, What shall we do, that we might work the works of God?

29 Jesus answered and said unto them, This is the work of God, that ye believe on him whom he hath sent.

JESUS THE BREAD OF LIFE

:30 They said therefore unto him, What sign shewest thou then, that we may see, and believe thee? what dost thou work?

31 Our fathers did eat manna in the desert; as it is written, He gave them bread from heaven to eat.

32 Then Jesus said unto them, Verily, verily, I say unto you, Moses gave you not that bread from heaven; but my Father giveth you the true bread from heaven.

33 For the bread of God is he which cometh down from heaven, and giveth life unto the world.

34 Then said they unto him, Lord, evermore give us this bread.

35 And Jesus said unto them, I am the bread of life: he that cometh to me shall never hunger; and he that believeth on me shall never thirst.

36 But I said unto you, That ye also have seen me, and believe not.

37 All that the Father giveth me shall come to me; and him that cometh to me I will in no wise cast out.

38 For I came down from heaven, not to do mine own will, but the will of him that sent me.

39 And this is the Father's will which hath sent me, that of all which he hath given me I should lose nothing, but should raise it up again at the last day.

JOHN 6

40 And this is the will of him that sent me, that every one which seeth the Son, and believeth on him, may have everlasting life: and I will raise him up at the last day.

41 The Jews then murmured at him, because he said, I am the bread which came down from heaven.

42 And they said, Is not this Jesus, the son of Joseph, whose father and mother we know? how is it then that he saith, I came down from heaven?

43 Jesus therefore answered and said unto them, Murmur not among yourselves.

44 No man can come to me, except the Father which hath sent me draw him: and I will raise him up at the last day.

45 It is written in the prophets, And they shall be all taught of God. Every man therefore that hath heard, and hath learned of the Father, cometh unto me.

46 Not that any man hath seen the Father, save he which is of God, he hath seen the Father.

47 Verily, verily, I say unto you, He that believeth on me hath everlasting life.

48 I am the bread of life.

49 Your fathers did eat manna in the wilderness, and are dead.

50 This is the bread which cometh down from heaven, that a man may eat thereof, and not die.

51 I am the living bread which came down from heaven: if any man eat of this bread, he shall live for ever: and the bread that I will give is my flesh, which I will give for the life of the world.

52 The Jews therefore strove among themselves, saying, How can this man give us his flesh to eat?

53 Then Jesus said unto them, Verily, verily, I say unto you, Except ye eat the flesh of the Son of man, and drink his blood, ye have no life in you.

54 Whoso eateth my flesh, and drinketh my blood, hath eternal life; and I will raise him up at the last day.

55 For my flesh is meat indeed, and my blood is drink indeed.

56 He that eateth my flesh, and drinketh my blood, dwelleth in me, and I in him.

57 As the living Father hath sent me, and I live by the Father; so he that eateth me, even he shall live by me.

58 This is that bread which came down from heaven: not as your fathers did eat manna, and are dead: he that eateth of this bread shall live for ever.

59 These things said he in the synagogue, as he taught in Caper'na-um.

THE WORDS OF ETERNAL LIFE

:60 Many therefore of his disciples, when they had heard this, said, This is a hard saying; who can hear it?

61 When Jesus knew in himself that his disciples murmured at it, he said unto them, Doth this offend you?

62 What and if ye shall see the Son of man ascend up where he was before?

63 It is the Spirit that quickeneth; the flesh profiteth nothing: the words that I speak unto you, they are spirit, and they are life.

64 But there are some of you that believe not. For Jesus knew from the beginning who they were that believed not, and who should betray him.

65 And he said, Therefore said I unto you, that no man can come unto me, except it were given unto him of my Father.

66 From that time many of his disciples went back, and walked no more with him.

67 Then said Jesus unto the twelve, Will ye also go away?

68 Then Simon Peter answered him, Lord, to whom shall we go? thou hast the words of eternal life.

69 And we believe and are sure that thou art that Christ, the Son of the living God.

70 Jesus answered them, Have not I chosen you twelve, and one of you is a devil?

71 He spake of Judas Iscar'i-ot the son of Simon: for he it was that should betray him, being one of the twelve.

THE UNBELIEF OF JESUS' BRETHREN

JOHN 7

:1 After these things Jesus walked in Galilee: for he would not walk in Jewry, because the Jews sought to kill him.

2 Now the Jews' feast of tabernacles was at hand.

3 His brethren therefore said unto him, Depart hence, and go into Judea, that thy disciples also may see the works that thou doest.

4 For there is no man that doeth any thing in secret, and he himself seeketh to be known openly. If thou do these things, show thyself to the world.

5 For neither did his brethren believe in him.

6 Then Jesus said unto them, My time is not yet come: but your time is always ready.

7 The world cannot hate you; but me it hateth, because I testify of it, that the works thereof are evil.

8 Go ye up unto this feast: I go not up yet unto this feast; for my time is not yet full come.

9 When he had said these words unto them, he abode still in Galilee.

THINGS THAT DEFILE

MARK 7

:1 Then came together unto him the Pharisees, and certain of the scribes, which came from Jerusalem.

2 And when they saw some of his disciples eat bread with defiled, that is to say, with unwashen hands, they found fault.

3 For the Pharisees, and all the Jews, except they wash their hands oft, eat not, holding the tradition of the elders.

4 And when they come from the market except they wash, they eat not. And many other things there be, which they have received to hold, as the washing of cups, and pots, brazen vessels, and of tables.

[1]Matt. 15:2 transgress the tradition of the elders

5 Then the Pharisees and scribes asked him, Why [1]walk not thy disciples according to the tradition of the elders, but eat bread with unwashen hands?

MARK 7

²Matt. 15:3
Why do ye transgress the commandment of God by your tradition?

³Matt. 15:8
draweth nigh

⁴Matt. 15:6

MARK 7

⁵Matt. 15:10
multitude

⁶Matt. 15:12

MATT. 15

6 He answered and said unto them, ²Well hath Isaiah prophesied of you hypocrites, as it is written, This people ³honoreth me with their lips but their heart is far from me.

7 Howbeit in vain do they worship me, teaching for doctrines the commandments of men.

8 For laying aside the commandment of God, ye hold the tradition of men, as the washing of pots and cups: and many other such like things ye do.

9 And he said unto them, Full well ye reject the commandment of God, that ye may keep your own tradition.

10 For Moses said, Honor thy father and thy mother; and, whoso curseth father or mother, let him die the death:

11 But ye say, If a man shall say to his father or mother, It is Corban, that is to say, a gift, by whatsoever thou mightest be profited by me ⁴*And honor not his father or his mother, he shall be free.*

12 And ye suffer him no more to do aught for his father or his mother;

13 Making the word of God of none effect through your tradition, which ye have delivered: and many such like things do ye.

14 And when he had called all the ⁵people unto him, he said unto them, Hearken unto me every one of you, and understand:

15 There is nothing from without a man, that entering into him can defile him: but the things which come out of him, those are they that defile the man.

16 If any man have ears to hear, let him hear.

17 And when he was entered into the house from the people, ⁶*his disciples . . . said unto him, Knowest thou that the Pharisees were offended, after they heard this saying?*

:13 But he answered and said, Every plant, which my heavenly Father hath not planted, shall be rooted up.

14 Let them alone: they be blind, both shall fall into the ditch.

MATT. 15 [7]Mark 7:17 disciples MARK 7	15 Then answered [7]Peter and said unto him, Declare unto us this parable.
	:18 And he saith unto them, Are ye so without understanding also? Do ye not perceive, that whatsoever thing from without entereth it cannot defile him;
	19 Because it entereth not into his heart, and goeth out into the draught, purging all meats?
[8]Matt. 15:18	20 And he said, That which cometh out of *the mouth of the man, [8]come forth from the heart,* that defileth the man.
[9]Matt. 15:19	21 For from within, out of the heart of men, proceed evil thoughts, adulteries, fornications, murders, [9]*false witnesses.*
	22 Thefts, covetousness, wickedness, deceit, lasciviousness, an evil eye, blasphemy, pride, foolishness:
[10]Matt. 15:20	23 All these evil things come from within, and defile the man. [10]*But to eat with unwashen hands defileth not a man.*

THE SYROPHOENICIAN WOMAN'S FAITH

MARK 7	:24 And from thence he arose, and went into the borders of Tyre and Sidon, and entered into a house, and would have no man know it: but he could not be hid.
[1]Matt. 15:22	25 [1]*Behold a certain woman* [1]*of Canaan came out of the same coasts,* whose young daughter had an unclean spirit, heard of him, and came and fell at his feet: [1]*and cried unto him, saying, Have mercy on me, O Lord, thou son of David; my daughter is grievously vexed with a devil.*
	26 The woman was a Greek, a Syrophoeni'cian by nation; and she besought him that he would cast forth the devil out of her daughter.
MATT. 15	:23 But he answered her not a word. And his disciples came and besought him, saying, Send her away; for she crieth after us.
	24 But he answered and said, I am not sent but unto the lost sheep of the house of Israel.
	25 Then came she and worshipped him, saying, Lord, help me.

MARK 7

:27 But Jesus said unto her, Let the children first be filled: for it is not meet to take the children's bread, and to cast it unto the dogs.

[2]Matt. 15:27

28 And she answered and said unto him, Yes, Lord: yet the dogs under the [2]*masters'* table eat of the children's crumbs.

[3]Matt. 15:28

29 And he said unto her [3]*O Woman, great is thy faith.* For this saying go thy way; [3]*be it unto thee even as thou wilt.* And her daughter was made whole from that very hour.

30 And when she was come to her house, she found the devil gone out, and her daughter laid upon the bed.

JESUS HEALS A DEAF AND DUMB MAN

MARK 7

:31 And again, departing from the coasts of Tyre and Sidon, he came unto the sea of Galilee, through the midst of the coasts of Decap'olis, [1]*and went up into a mountain, and sat down there.*

[1]Matt. 15:29

MATT. 15

:30 And great multitudes came unto him, having with them those that were lame, blind, dumb, maimed, and many others, and cast them down at Jesus' feet; and he healed them:

MARK 7

:32 And they bring unto him one that was deaf, and had an impediment in his speech; and they beseech him to put his hand upon him.

33 And he took him aside from the multitude, and put his fingers into his ears, and he spit, and touched his tongue;

34 And looking up to heaven, he sighed, and saith unto him, Eph'phatha, that is, Be opened.

35 And straightway his ears were opened, and the string of his tongue was loosed, and he spake plain.

36 And he charged them that they should tell no man: the more he charged them, so much the more a great deal they published it;

37 And were beyond measure astonished, saying, He hath done all things well: he maketh both the deaf to hear, and the dumb to speak.

THE FEEDING OF THE FOUR THOUSAND

MARK 8 :1 In those days the multitude being very great, and having nothing to eat, Jesus called his disciples unto him, and saith unto them,

2 I have compassion on the multitude, because they have now been with me three days and have had nothing to eat:

[1]Matt. 15:32

3 And . . . I [1]*will not* send them away fasting to their own houses, they will faint by the way: for divers of them came from far.

4 And his disciples answered him, From whence

[2]Matt. 14:33 fill
[3]Multitude

can a man [2]satisfy these [3]men with bread here in the wilderness?

5 And he asked them, How many loaves have ye?

[4]Matt. 15:34

And they said, Seven [4]*and a few little fishes.*

[5]Matt. 15:35 multitude

6 And he commanded the [5]people to sit down on the ground: and he took the seven loaves, and gave thanks, and brake, and gave to his disciples to set before them; and they did set them before the people.

7 And they had a few small fishes: and he blessed, and commanded to set them also before them.

[6]Matt. 15:37

8 So they did [6]*all* eat, and were filled: and they took up of the broken meat that was left seven baskets [6]*full.*

9 And they that had eaten were about four

[7]Matt. 15:38
[8]Matt. 15:39

thousand men, [7]*beside women and children,* and he sent [8]*the multitude away.*

10 And straightway he entered into a ship with his disciples, and came into the parts of

[9]Matt. 15:39 Mag'-dala

[9]Dalmanu'tha.

THE DEMAND FOR A SIGN

MATT. 16
[1]Mark 8:11

:1 The Pharisees also with the Sadducees came [1]*forth and began to question with him,* and tempting desired him that he would show them a sign from heaven.

MARK 8

:12 And he sighed deeply in his spirit, and saith, Why doth this generation seek after a sign?

MATT. 16

:2 He answered and said unto them, When it is evening, ye say, It will be fair weather: for the sky is red.

MATT. 16

3 And in the morning, It will be foul weather today: for the sky is red and lowering. O ye hypocrites, ye can discern the face of the sky; but can ye not discern the signs of the times?

4 A wicked and adulterous generation seeketh after a sign; verily I say unto you, there shall no sign be given unto it, but the sign of the prophet Jonas.

²Mark 8:13

And he left them, ²*and entering into the ship again departed to the other side.*

THE LEAVEN OF THE PHARISEES

MARK 8
¹Matt. 16:5

:14 Now the disciples ¹*were come to the other side*, and had forgotten to take bread, neither had they in the ship with them more than one loaf.

²Matt. 16:6

15 And he, ²*Jesus*, charged them, saying, Take heed, beware of the leaven of the Pharisees, ²*and of the Sadducees*, and of the leaven of Herod.

16 And they reasoned among themselves, saying, It is because we have no bread.

³Matt. 16:8
perceived
⁴Matt. 16:8

17 And when Jesus ³knew it, he saith unto them, ⁴*O ye of little faith, why reason ye among yourselves, because ye have brought no bread?* perceive ye not yet, neither understand? have ye your heart yet hardened?

18 Having eyes, see ye not? and having ears, hear ye not? and do ye not remember?

19 When I brake the five loaves among five thousand, how many baskets full of fragments took ye up? They say unto him, Twelve.

20 And when the seven among four thousand, how many baskets full of fragments took ye up? And they said, Seven.

⁵Matt. 16:11

21 And he said unto them, How is it that ye do not understand? ⁵*I spake it not to you concerning bread, that ye should beware of the leaven of the Pharisees and of the Sadducees?*

MATT. 16

:12 Then understood they how that he bade them not beware of the leaven of bread, but of the doctrine of the Pharisees and of the Sadducees.

A BLIND MAN HEALED AT BETHSAIDA

MARK 8

:22 And he cometh to Bethsai'da; and they bring a blind man unto him, and besought him to touch him.

23 And he took the blind man by the hand, and led him out of the town; and when he had spit on his eyes, and put his hands upon him, he asked him if he saw aught.

24 And he looked up, and said, I see men as trees, walking.

25 After that he put his hands again upon his eyes, and made him look up; and he was restored, and saw every man clearly.

26 And he sent him away to his house, saying, Neither go into the town, nor tell it to any in the town.

PETER'S CONFESSION

MATT. 16
[1] Mark 8:27
[2] Mark 8:27
  towns
[3] Luke 9:18
[4] Luke 9:18
  the people
[5] Luke 9:19

:13 When Jesus [1]*went out* with his disciples, and came into the [2]coasts of Caesare'a Phil'ippi, [3]*as he was alone praying,* [1]*by the way,* [3]*his disciples were with him,* he asked his disciples, saying, Whom do [4]men say that I, the Son of man am?

14 And they said, Some say that thou art John the Baptist; some, Eli'jah; and others, Jeremiah or one of the [5]*old* prophets [5]*is risen again.*

15 He saith unto them, But whom say ye that I am?

16 And Simon Peter answered and said, Thou art the Christ, the Son of the living God.

17 And Jesus answered and said unto him, Blessed art thou, Simon Bar-jona: for flesh and blood hath not revealed it unto thee, but my Father which is in heaven.

18 And I say also unto thee, that thou art Peter, and upon this rock I will build my church; and the gates of hell shall not prevail against it.

19 And I will give unto thee the keys of the kingdom of heaven; and whatsoever thou shalt bind on earth shall be bound in heaven; and whatsoever thou shalt loose on earth shall be loosed in heaven.

MATT. 16	20 Then charged he his disciples that they should tell no man that he was Jesus the Christ.
	## JESUS FORETELLS HIS DEATH
MARK 8 ¹Matt. 16:21	:31 ¹*From that time forth began Jesus* to teach ¹*his disciples, how that he must go unto Jerusalem, and* that the Son of man must suffer many things, and be rejected of the elders, and of the chief priests,
²Luke 9:22 slain	and scribes, and be ²killed, and after three days rise up again.
	32 And he spake that saying openly. And Peter took him, and began to rebuke him, ³*saying, Be it far*
³Matt. 16:22	*from thee, Lord: this shall not be unto thee.*
	33 But when he had turned about and looked on his disciples, he rebuked Peter, saying, Get thee
⁴Matt. 16:23	behind me, Satan: ⁴*Thou art an offense unto me* for thou savorest not the things that be of God, but the things that be of men.
	34 And when he had called the people unto him with his disciples also, he said unto them,
⁵Matt. 16:24 If any man ⁶Luke 9:23	⁵Whosoever will come after me, let him deny himself, and take up his cross ⁶*daily,* and follow me.
	35 For whosoever will save his life shall lose it; but whosoever shall lose his life for my sake and the
⁷Matt. 16:25 find it	gospel's, the same shall ⁷save it.
	36 For what shall it profit a man, if he shall gain the whole world, and lose his own soul?
	37 Or what shall a man give in exchange for his soul?
	38 Whosoever therefore shall be ashamed of me and of my words, in this adulterous and sinful generation, of him also shall the Son of man be ashamed, when he cometh in the glory of his Father
⁸Matt. 16:27	with the holy angels, ⁸*and then he shall reward every man according to his works.*
MARK 9 see the Son of man coming in his kingdom	:1 And he said unto them, Verily I say unto you, That there be some of them that stand here, which shall not taste of death, till they have ⁹seen the kingdom of God come with power.

THE TRANSFIGURATION

MARK 9
¹Luke 9:28
about eight
days after
these sayings
²Luke 9:28
³Luke 9:29
⁴Luke 9:29
the fashion
of his countenance was altered
⁵Matt. 17:2
⁶Matt. 17:2
light
⁷Matt. 17:3
⁸Luke 9:31

:2 And after ¹six days Jesus taketh with him Peter, and James, and John, and leadeth them up into a high mountain apart by themselves: ²*to pray,* ³*and as he prayed,* ⁴he was transfigured before them, ⁵*and his face did shine as the sun.*

3 And his raiment became shining, exceeding white as ⁶snow; so as no fuller on earth can white them.

4 And ⁷*behold,* there appeared unto them Eli'jah with Moses; and they were talking with Jesus ⁸*who appeared in glory, and spake of his decease which he should accomplish at Jerusalem.*

LUKE 9

:32 And Peter and they that were with him were heavy with sleep: and when they were awake, they saw his glory, and the two men that stood with him.

33 And it came to pass, as they departed from him, . . .

MARK 9
⁹Matt. 17:4

:5 . . . Peter answered and said to Jesus, Master, it is good for us to be here: ⁹*if thou wilt* . . . let us make three tabernacles; one for thee, and one for Moses and one for Eli'jah.

¹⁰Luke 9:33
not knowing
what to say

6 For ¹⁰he wist not what to say; for they were sore afraid.

MATT. 17
¹¹Luke 9:34
¹²Mark 9:7

:5 While he yet spake, behold, a bright cloud overshadowed them ¹¹*and they feared as they entered into the cloud* ¹²*and a voice came out of the cloud, saying, This is my beloved Son,* in whom I am well pleased; hear ye him.

6 And when the disciples heard it, they fell on their face, and were sore afraid,

7 And Jesus came and touched them and said, Arise, and be not afraid.

MARK 9	:8 And suddenly, when ¹³*the voice was past* and they had looked round about, they saw no man any more, save Jesus only with themselves.
¹³Luke 9:36	
	9 And as they came down from the ¹⁴mountain, he charged them that they should tell no man which things they had seen, till the Son of man were risen ¹⁵*again* from the dead.
¹⁴Luke 9:37 hill	
¹⁵Matt. 17:9	
¹⁶Luke 9:36 kept it close	10 And they ¹⁶kept that saying with themselves, ¹⁷*and told no man in those days any of those things which they had seen*, questioning one with another what the rising from the dead should mean.
¹⁷Luke 9:36	
	11 And they asked him, saying, Why say the scribes that Eli'jah must first come ¹⁸*and restore all things?*
¹⁸Matt. 17:11	
	12 And he answered and told them, Eli'jah verily cometh first, and restoreth all things; and how it is written of the Son of man, that he must suffer many things, and be set at nought.
	13 But I say unto you, That Eli'jah is indeed come, and they have done unto him whatsoever they listed, as it is written of him. ¹⁹*Likewise shall also the Son of man suffer of them.*
¹⁹Matt. 17:12	
MATT. 17	:13 Then the disciples understood that he spake unto them of John the Baptist.

JESUS HEALS A BOY WITH AN UNCLEAN SPIRIT

MARK 9	:14 ¹*And it came to pass, that on the next day, when they were come down from the hill, much people met him.* And when he came to his disciples, he saw a great multitude about them, and the scribes questioning with them.
¹Luke 9:37	
	15 And straightway all the people, when they beheld him, were greatly amazed, and running to him saluted him.
	16 And he asked the scribes, What question ye with them?
²Matt. 17:14	17 And ²*there came to him a certain man,* of the multitude, ²*kneeling down to him,* and said, Master, I have brought unto thee my ³*lunatic* son ³*and he is sore vexed* ⁴*for he is mine only child.* ³*Have mercy on my son,* which hath a dumb spirit;
³Matt. 17:15	
⁴Luke 9:38	

ARRANGED AS A SINGLE NARRATIVE

MARK 9

⁵Luke 9:39
⁶Matt. 17:16
brought him
⁷Luke 9:41

⁸Luke 9:42

18 And wheresoever he taketh him, he teareth him; and he foameth, and gnasheth with his teeth and pineth away, [and] ⁵*hardly departeth from him,* and I ⁶spake to thy disciples that they should cast him out; and they could not.

19 He answereth him, and saith, O faithless ⁷*and perverse* generation, how long shall I be with you? how long shall I suffer you? bring him unto me.

20 And they brought him unto him, and when he saw him, straightway ⁸*as he was yet coming* the ⁸*devil threw him down, and tare him;* and he fell on the ground, and wallowed foaming.

21 And he asked his father, How long is it ago since this came unto him? And he said, Of a child.

22 And ofttimes it hath cast him into the fires and into the waters, to destroy him: but if thou canst do anything, have compassion on us, and help us.

23 Jesus said unto him, If thou canst believe, all things are possible to him that believeth.

24 And straightway the father of the child cried out, and said with tears, Lord, I believe; help thou mine unbelief.

⁹Luke 9:42
unclean spirit

25 When Jesus saw that the people came running together, he rebuked the foul spirit, saying unto him, ⁹Thou dumb and deaf spirit, I charge thee, come out of him, and enter no more into him.

26 And the spirit cried and rent him sore, and came out of him: and he was as one dead, insomuch that many said, He is dead.

¹⁰Luke 9:42
¹¹Matt. 17:18
LUKE 9

27 But Jesus took him by the hand, and lifted him up: ¹⁰*and delivered him again to his father,* ¹¹*and the child was cured from that very hour.*

:43 And they were all amazed at the mighty power of God.

MARK 9

¹²Matt. 17:20

:28 And when he was come into the house, his disciples asked him privately, Why could not we cast him out? ¹²*Because of your unbelief: for verily I say unto you, If ye have faith as a grain of mustard seed, ye shall say unto this mountain, Remove hence to yonder place; and it shall remove: and nothing shall be impossible unto you.*

MARK 9	:29 And he said unto them, This kind can come forth by nothing, but by prayer and fasting.

JESUS AGAIN FORETELLS HIS DEATH

MARK 9	:30 And they departed thence, and ²*passed through Galilee; and he would not that any man should know it.* ¹*But while they wondered every one at all things which Jesus did,*
¹Luke 9:43	
²Matt. 17:22 While he abode in	
	31 For he taught his disciples, and said unto them,
LUKE 9	:44 Let these sayings sink down into your ears: ³*The Son of man is* ⁴*delivered into the hands of men, and they shall kill him; and after that he is killed, he shall rise the third day.* ⁵*And they were exceeding sorry.*
³Mark 9:31	
⁴Matt. 17:22 betrayed	
⁵Matt. 17:23	
	45 But they understood not this saying, and it was hid from them, that they perceived it not: and they feared to ask him of that saying.

WHO IS THE GREATEST?

LUKE 9	:46 Then there arose a reasoning among them, which of them should be greatest.

PAYMENT OF THE TRIBUTE MONEY

MATT. 17	:24 And when they were come to Caper'na-um, they that received tribute money came to Peter, and said, Doth not your master pay tribute?
	25 He saith, Yes. And when he was come into the house, Jesus prevented him, saying; What thinkest thou, Simon? of whom do the kings of the earth take custom or tribute? of their own children, or of strangers?
	26 Peter saith unto him Of strangers. Jesus saith unto him, Then are the children free.
	27 Notwithstanding, lest we should offend them, go thou to the sea, and cast a hook, and take up the fish that first cometh up; and when thou hast opened his mouth, thou shalt find a piece of money: that take, and give unto them for me and thee.

WHICH OF THE APOSTLES SHOULD BE THE GREATEST

MARK 9
¹Luke 9:47
²Mark 9:33

:33 ¹*Jesus perceiving the thoughts of their hearts, and being in the house* [at] ²*Caper'na-um* asked them, What was it that ye disputed among yourselves by the way?

34 But they held their peace: for by the way they had disputed among themselves, who should be the greatest.

35 And he sat down, and called the twelve, and saith unto them, If any man desire to be first, the same shall be the last of all, and servant of all.

³Luke 9:47
by him

36 And he took a child, and set him ³in the midst of them: and when he had taken him in his arms, he said unto them,

⁴Luke 9:48

37 Whosoever shall receive one of such children in my name, receiveth me; and whosoever shall receive me, receiveth not me, but him that sent me, ⁴*for he that is least among you the same shall be great.*

WHO IS THE GREATEST IN THE KINGDOM OF HEAVEN?*

MATT. 18

:1 At the same time came the disciples unto Jesus, saying, Who is the greatest in the kingdom of heaven?

2 And Jesus called a little child unto him, and set him in the midst of them,

:3 And said, Verily I say unto you, Except ye be converted, and become as little children, ye shall not enter into the kingdom of heaven.

5 And whoso shall receive one such little child in my name receiveth me.

---

*The questions, though apparently about the same time and in the same place, are quite different. They first reasoned among themselves which of *them should be the greatest*. (Luke 9:46) When they arrive at Capernaum Jesus asks them what the disputation was which they had along the way. (Mark 9:34). This illustration of greatness was given to the twelve, (Mark 9:35). In Matthew 18, other disciples came and asked, Who is greatest in *the kingdom of heaven*? Here the disciples ask, Who, and in the above the twelve argue among themselves and Jesus, without their acknowledging their problem, gives them the object lesson.

HE THAT IS NOT AGAINST US IS FOR US

MARK 9

:38 And John answered him, saying, Master, we saw one casting out devils in thy name, and he followeth not us: and we forbade him, because he followeth not us.

39 But Jesus said, Forbid him not: for there is no man which shall do a miracle in my name, that can lightly speak evil of me.

40 For he that is not against us [1]is on our part.

[1]Luke 9:50
is for us

41 For whosoever shall give you a cup of water to drink in my name, because ye belong to Christ, verily I say unto you, he shall not lose his reward.

OFFENCES

MARK 9

:42 And whosoever shall offend one of these little ones that believe in me, it is better for him that a millstone were hanged about his neck, and he were [1]*drowned in the depths of the sea.*

[1]Matt. 18:6
MATT. 18

:7 Woe unto the world because of offences! for it must needs be that offences come; but woe to that man by whom the offence cometh!

MARK 9
[2]Matt. 18:8

:43 And if thy hand offend thee, cut it off: it is better for thee to enter into life [2]*halt or* maimed, [2]*rather* than having two hands to go into hell, into the [2]*everlasting* fire that never shall be quenched:

44 Where their worm dieth not, and the fire is not quenched.

45 And if thy foot offend thee, cut it off: it is better for thee to enter halt into life, than having two feet to be cast into hell, into the fire that never shall be quenched:

46 Where their worm dieth not, and the fire is not quenched.

[3]Matt. 18:9
[4]Matt. 18:9
life

47 And if thine eye offend thee, pluck it out [3]*and cast it from thee:* it is better for thee to enter into the [4]kingdom of God with one eye, than having two eyes to be cast into hell fire:

48 Where their worm dieth not, and the fire is not quenched.

49 For every one shall be salted with fire, and every sacrifice shall be salted with salt.

MARK 9   50 Salt is good: but if the salt have lost his saltness, wherewith will ye season it? Have salt in yourselves, and have peace one with another.

MATT. 18   :10 Take heed that ye despise not one of these little ones; for I say unto you, That in heaven their angels do always behold the face of my Father which is in heaven.

11 For the Son of man is come to save that which was lost.

THE LOST SHEEP

MATT. 18   :12 How think ye? if a man have a hundred sheep, and one of them be gone astray, doth he not leave the ninety and nine, and goeth into the mountains, and seeketh that which is gone astray?

13 And if so be that he find it, verily I say unto you, he rejoiceth more of that sheep, than of the ninety and nine which went not astray.

14 Even so it is not the will of your Father which is in heaven, that one of these little ones should perish.

IF A BROTHER SINS AGAINST THEE

MATT. 18
¹See Luke
17:3-4 P. 149
Many of the
same truths
are repeated
in Luke but
from Luke 17
on seems to
be at a later
date.

:15 Moreover if thy ¹brother shall trespass against thee, go and tell him his fault between thee and him alone: if he shall hear thee, thou hast gained thy brother.

16 But if he will not hear thee, then take with thee one or two more, that in the mouth of two or three witnesses every word may be established.

17 And if he shall neglect to hear them, tell it unto the church: but if he neglect to hear the church, let him be unto thee as a heathen man and a publican.

18 Verily I say unto you, Whatsoever ye shall bind on earth shall be bound in heaven; and whatsoever ye shall loose on earth shall be loosed in heaven.

19 Again I say unto you, That if two of you shall agree on earth as touching any thing that they shall ask, it shall be done for them of my Father which is in heaven.

20 For where two or three are gathered together in my name, there am I in the midst of them.

THE UNFORGIVING SERVANT

MATT. 18

:21 Then came Peter to him, and said, Lord, how oft shall my brother sin against me, and I forgive him? till seven times?

22 Jesus saith unto him, I say not unto thee, Until seven times: but, Until seventy times seven.

23 Therefore is the kingdom of heaven likened unto a certain king, which would take account of his servants.

24 And when he had begun to reckon, one was brought unto him, which owed him ten thousand talents.

25 But forasmuch as he had not to pay, his lord commanded him to be sold, and his wife, and children, and all that he had, and payment to be made.

26 The servant therefore fell down, and worshipped him, saying, Lord have patience with me, and I will pay thee all.

27 Then the lord of that servant was moved with compassion, and loosed him, and forgave him the debt.

28 But the same servant went out, and found one of his fellow servants, which owed him a hundred pence: and he laid hands on him, and took him by the throat, saying, Pay me that thou owest.

29 And his fellow servant fell down at his feet, and besought him, saying, Have patience with me, and I will pay thee all.

30 And he would not: but went and cast him into prison, till he should pay the debt.

31 So when his fellow servants saw what was done, they were very sorry, and came and told unto their lord all that was done.

32 Then his lord, after that he had called him, said unto him, O thou wicked servant, I forgave thee all that debt, because thou desiredst me:

33 Shouldest not thou also have had compassion on thy fellow servant, even as I had pity on thee?

34 And his lord was wroth, and delivered him to the tormentors till he should pay all that was due unto him.

MATT. 18 — 35 So likewise shall my heavenly Father do also unto you, if ye from your hearts forgive not every one his brother their trespasses.

JESUS REBUKES JAMES AND JOHN

LUKE 9 — :51 And it came to pass, when the time was come that he should be received up, *he steadfastly set his face to go to Jerusalem,**

52 And sent messengers before his face: and they went, and entered into a village of the Samaritans, to make ready for him.

53 And they did not receive him, because his face was as though he would go to Jerusalem.

54 And when his disciples James and John saw this, they said, Lord, wilt thou that we command fire to come down from heaven, and consume them, even as Eli'jah did?

55 But he turned, and rebuked them, and said, Ye know not what manner of spirit ye are of.

56 For the Son of man is not come to destroy men's lives, but to save them. And they went to another village.

THE COST OF DISCIPLESHIP

LUKE 9 — :57 And it came to pass, that, as they went in the way, a certain man said unto him, Lord, I will follow thee whithersoever thou goest.

58 And Jesus said unto him, Foxes have holes, and birds of the air have nests; but the Son of man hath not where to lay his head.

59 And he said unto another, Follow me. But he said, Lord, suffer me first to go and bury my father.

60 Jesus said unto him, Let the dead bury their dead: but go thou and preach the kingdom of God.

61 And another also said, Lord, I will follow thee; but let me first go bid them farewell, which are at home at my house.

62 And Jesus said unto him, No man, having put his hand to the plow, and looking back, is fit for the kingdom of God.

---

*Although this is nearing the end of His ministry, this is not his last journey to Jerusalem. See Luke 18:31-34.

JESUS' TEACHING ON DIVORCE*

MATT. 19 :1 And it came to pass, that when Jesus had finished these sayings, he departed from Galilee, and came into the coasts of Judea beyond Jordan; [1]*and the people resort unto him again; and, as he was wont, he taught them again.*

[1]Mark 10:1

2 And great multitudes followed him; and he healed them there.

3 The Pharisees also came unto him, tempting him, and saying unto him, Is it lawful for a man to put away his wife for every cause?

4 And he answered and said unto them, Have ye not read, that he which made them at the beginning made them male and female,

5 And said, For this cause shall a man leave father and mother, and shall cleave to his wife: and they twain shall be one flesh?

6 Wherefore they are no more twain, but one flesh. What therefore God hath joined together, let not man put asunder.

MARK 10 :3 And he answered and said unto them, What did Moses command you?

MATT. 19 :7 They say unto him, Why did Moses then command to give a writing of divorcement, and to put her away?

[2]Mark 10:5 wrote you this precept
[3]Mark 10:6

8 He saith unto them, Moses because of the hardness of your hearts [2]suffered you to put away your wives: but from the beginning [3]*of creation* it was not so.

MATT. 19 :9 And I say unto you, Whosoever shall put away his wife, except it be for fornication, and shall marry another, committeth adultery: and whoso marrieth her which is put away doth commit adultery.

MARK 10 :10 And in the house his disciples asked him again of the same matter.

11 And he saith unto them, Whosoever shall put away his wife, and marry another, committeth adultery against her.

12 And if a woman shall put away her husband, and be married to another, she committeth adultery.

---

*Mark 10 and Matthew 19 seem to be parallel passages. But there are other passages on this subject which were given on different occasions.

ARRANGED AS A SINGLE NARRATIVE

MATT. 19 :10 His disciples say unto him, If the case of the man be so with his wife, it is not good to marry.

11 But he said unto them, All men cannot receive this saying, save they to whom it is given.

12 For there are some eunuchs, which were so born from their mother's womb: and there are some eunuchs, which were made eunuchs of men: and there be eunuchs, which have made themselves eunuchs for the kingdom of heaven's sake. He that is able to receive it, let him receive it.

THE SEVENTY SENT FORTH*

LUKE 10** :1 After these things the Lord appointed other seventy also, and sent them two and two before his face into every city and place, whither he himself would come.

2 Therefore said he unto them, The harvest truly is great, but the laborers are few: pray ye therefore the Lord of the harvest, that he would send forth laborers into his harvest.

3 Go your ways: behold, I send you forth as lambs among wolves.

4 Carry neither purse, nor scrip, nor shoes: and salute no man by the way.

5 And into whatsoever house ye enter, first say, Peace be to this house.

6 And if the son of peace be there, your peace shall rest upon it: if not, it shall turn to you again.

---

*The directive given to the seventy is very similar to those given to the twelve apostles (Matt. 10:1-16 and Luke 9:2). The ordination address was given to the twelve, months before. The mission which the twelve made was very near the end of Christ's earthly ministry. Much of the same message is repeated after Christ's resurrection (Mark 16:18).

**It is amazing how each writes about so much which is not mentioned by the others. The recording of Luke 10:1 - 18:14 falls between the healing of the lunatic boy just after the transfiguration as recorded by all three gospels and the narrative of the rich young ruler which is preceeded each time by blessing little children: Matt. 19:16-26, 19:13-15, Mark 10:17-31 and 10:13-17, respectively. Therefore it appears that all of Luke, ch. 10:1-18:14 should be placed in this order. It is admitted that he speaks of many things which are repeated at other places by the other writers. He also repeats some of the same truths later in his gospel. Therefore it should be considered as another sermon when great truths are given needed emphasis. These were now the last few weeks of our Lord's earthly ministry. All the recorded events from all writers from the transfiguration on seem to fit into the same chronological order although not all the events are recorded by any one of the writers.

LUKE 10

7 And in the same house remain, eating and drinking such things as they give: for the laborer is worthy of his hire. Go not from house to house.

8 And into whatsoever city ye enter, and they receive you, eat such things as are set before you:

9 And heal the sick that are therein, and say unto them, The kingdom of God is come nigh unto you.

10 But into whatsoever city ye enter, and they receive you not, go your ways out into the streets of the same and say,

11 Even the very dust of your city, which cleaveth on us, we do wipe off against you: notwithstanding, be ye sure of this, that the kingdom of God is come nigh unto you.

12 But I say unto you, that it shall be more tolerable in that day for Sodom, than for that city.

13 Woe unto thee, Chora'zin! woe unto thee, Bethsai'da for if the mighty works had been done in Tyre and Sidon, which have been done in you, they had a great while ago repented, sitting in sackcloth and ashes.

14 But it shall be more tolerable for Tyre and Sidon at the judgment, than for you.

15 And thou, Caper'na-um, which are exalted to heaven, shalt be thrust down to hell.

16 He that heareth you heareth me; and he that despiseth you despiseth me; and he that despiseth me despiseth him that sent me.

THE SUCCESS OF THE SEVENTY

LUKE 10

:17 And the seventy returned again with joy, saying, Lord, even the devils are subject unto us through thy name,

18 And he said unto them, I beheld Satan as lightning fall from heaven.

19 Behold, I give unto you power to tread on serpents and scorpions, and over all the power of the enemy; and nothing shall by any means hurt you.

20 Notwithstanding, in this rejoice not, that the spirits are subject unto you; but rather rejoice, because your names are written in heaven.

JESUS REJOICES IN SPIRIT

LUKE 10 :21 In that hour Jesus rejoiced in spirit, and said, I thank thee, O Father, Lord of heaven and earth, that thou hast hid these things from the wise and prudent, and hast revealed them unto babes: even so, Father; for so it seemed good in thy sight.

22 All things are delivered to me of my father: and no man knoweth who the Son is, but the Father and who the Father is, but the Son, and he to whom the Son will reveal him.

23 And he turned him unto his disciples, and said privately, Blessed are the eyes which see the things that ye see:

24 For I tell you, that many prophets and kings have desired to see those things which ye see, and have not seen them; and to hear those things which ye hear, and have not heard them.

THE GOOD SAMARITAN

LUKE 10 :25 And, behold, a certain lawyer stood up, and tempted him, saying, Master, what shall I do to inherit eternal life?

26 He said unto him, What is written in the law? how readest thou?

27 And he answering said, Thou shalt love the Lord thy God with all thy heart, and with all thy soul, and with all thy strength, and with all thy mind; and thy neighbor as thyself.

28 And he said unto him, Thou hast answered right: this do, and thou shalt live.

29 But he, willing to justify himself, said unto Jesus, And who is my neighbor?

30 And Jesus answering said, A certain man went down from Jerusalem to Jericho, and fell among thieves, which stripped him of his raiment, and wounded him, and departed, leaving him half dead.

31 And by chance there came down a certain priest that way; and when he saw him, he passed by on the other side.

32 And likewise a Levite, when he was at the place, came and looked on him, and passed by on the other side.

LUKE 10

33 But a certain Samaritan, as he journeyed, came where he was; and when he saw him, he had compassion on him.

34 And went to him, and bound up his wounds, pouring in oil and wine, and set him on his own beast, and brought him to an inn, and took care of him.

35 And on the morrow when he departed, he took out two pence, and gave them to the host, and said unto him, Take care of him: and whatsoever thou spendest more, when I come again, I will repay thee.

36 Which now of these three, thinkest thou, was neighbor unto him that fell among the thieves?

37 And he said, He that showed mercy on him. Then said Jesus unto him, Go, and do thou likewise.

JESUS VISITS MARTHA AND MARY

LUKE 10

38 Now it came to pass, as they went, that he entered into a certain village: and a certain woman named Martha received him into her house.

39 And she had a sister called Mary, which also sat at Jesus' feet, and heard his word.

40 But Martha was cumbered about much serving, and came to him, and said, Lord, dost thou not care that my sister hath left me to serve alone? bid her therefore that she help me.

41 And Jesus answered and said unto her, Martha, Martha, thou art careful and troubled about many things:

42 But one thing is needful; and Mary hath chosen that good part, which shall not be taken away from her.

JESUS AT THE FEAST OF TABERNACLES

JOHN 7

:10 *But when his brethren were gone up, then went he also up unto the feast, not openly, but as it were in secret.

11 Then the Jews sought him at the feast, and said, Where is he?

12 And there was much murmuring among the people concerning him: for some said, He is a good man: others said, Nay; but he deceiveth the people.

---
*See footnote on next page.

JOHN 7

13 Howbeit no man spake openly of him for fear of the Jews.

14 Now about the midst of the feast Jesus went up into the temple, and taught.

15 And the Jews marveled, saying, How knoweth this man letters, having never learned?

16 Jesus answered them, and said, My doctrine is not mine, but his that sent me.

17 If any man will do his will, he shall know of the doctrine, whether it be of God, or whether I speak of myself.

18 He that speaketh of himself seeketh his own glory: but he that seeketh his glory that sent him, the same is true, and no unrighteousness is in him.

:19 Did not Moses give you the law, and yet none of you keepeth the law? Why go ye about to kill me?

20 The people answered and said, Thou hast a devil: who goeth about to kill thee?

21 Jesus answered and said unto them, I have done one work, and ye all marvel.

22 Moses therefore gave unto you circumcision; (not because it is of Moses, but of the fathers;) and ye on the sabbath day circumcise a man.

23 If a man on the sabbath day receive circumcision, that the law of Moses should not be broken; are ye angry at me, because I have made a man every whit whole on the sabbath day?

24 Judge not according to the appearance, but judge righteous judgment.

Many events have taken place between John 7:9 and 7:10. In verse 9 he is in Galilee, vs. 10 in Jerusalem. In Luke 9:51-53 we see Christ on his way to Jerusalem, Luke 10:38 he is in Bethany very near Jerusalem. In Luke 13:22 we see him journeying again toward Jerusalem. It seems quite probable that John 7:10-10:42 was given at this time when he went out from Jerusalem into beyond Jordan (10:40). Where he was praying in Luke, ch. 11 does not say, but he must have left the vicinity, because we see him again on the way to Jerusalem in Luke 13:22. In Luke 13:31-35 Christ is evidently in Herod's jurisdiction, not Jerusalem. In Luke 17:11 it says *it came to pass as he went to Jerusalem*. He had not yet arrived for we have the narrative of Christ blessing the young children followed by the narrative of the rich young ruler. The last parallel account of John is the feeding of the 5,000 and the following is that of the triumphal entry. This makes it very difficult where John 7:10-11:57 should be placed in the narrative.

IS THIS THE CHRIST?

JOHN 7

:25 Then said some of them of Jerusalem, Is not this he, whom they seek to kill?

26 But, lo, he speaketh boldly, and they say nothing unto him. Do the rulers know indeed that this is the very Christ?

27 Howbeit we know this man whence he is: but when Christ cometh, no man knoweth whence he is.

28 Then cried Jesus in the temple as he taught, saying, Ye both know me, and ye know whence I am: and I am not come of myself, but he that sent me is true, whom ye know not.

29 But I know him; for I am from him, and he hath sent me.

30 Then they sought to take him: but no man laid hands on him, because his hour was not yet come.

31 And many of the people believed on him, and said, When Christ cometh, will he do more miracles than these which this man hath done?

OFFICERS SENT TO ARREST JESUS

JOHN 7

:32 The Pharisees heard that the people murmured such things concerning him; and the Pharisees and the chief priests sent officers to take him.

33 Then said Jesus unto them, Yet a little while am I with you, and then I go unto him that sent me.

34 Ye shall seek me, and shall not find me: and where I am, thither ye cannot come.

35 Then said the Jews among themselves, Whither will he go, that we shall not find him? will he go unto the dispersed among the Gentiles, and teach the Gentiles?

36 What manner of saying is this that he said, Ye shall seek me, and shall not find me: and where I am, thither ye cannot come?

RIVERS OF LIVING WATER

JOHN 7

:37 In the last day, that great day of the feast, Jesus stood and cried, saying, If any man thirst, let him come unto me, and drink.

JOHN 7

38 He that believeth on me, as the Scripture hath said, out of his belly shall flow rivers of living water.

39 (But this spake he of the Spirit, which they that believe on him should receive: for the Holy Ghost was not yet given; because that Jesus was not yet glorified.)

DIVISION AMONG THE PEOPLE

JOHN 7

40 Many of the people therefore, when they heard this saying, said, Of a truth this is the Prophet.

41 Others said, This is the Christ. But some said, Shall Christ come out of Galilee?

42 Hath not the Scripture said, That Christ cometh of the seed of David, and out of the town of Bethlehem, where David was?

43 So there was a division among the people because of him.

44 And some of them would have taken him; but no man laid hands on him.

THE UNBELIEF OF THOSE IN AUTHORITY

JOHN 7

:45 Then came the officers to the chief priests and Pharisees; and they said unto them, Why have ye not brought him?

46 The officers answered, Never man spake like this man.

47 Then answered them the Pharisees, Are ye also deceived?

48 Have any of the rulers of the Pharisees believed on him?

49 But this people who knoweth not the law are cursed.

50 Nicode'mus saith unto them, (he that came to Jesus by night, being one of them,)

51 Doth our law judge any man, before it hear him, and know what he doeth?

52 They answered and said unto him, Art thou also of Galilee? Search, and look: for out of Galilee ariseth no prophet.

53 And every man went unto his own house.

THE WOMAN CAUGHT IN ADULTERY

JOHN 8

:1 Jesus went unto the mount of Olives.

2 And early in the morning he came again into the temple, and all the people came unto him; and he sat down, and taught them.

3 And the scribes and Pharisees brought unto him a woman taken in adultery; and when they had set her in the midst,

4 They say unto him, Master, this woman was taken in adultery, in the very act.

5 Now Moses in the law commanded us, that such should be stoned: but what sayest thou?

6 This they said, tempting him, that they might have to accuse him. But Jesus stooped down, and with his finger wrote on the ground, as though he heard them not.

7 So when they continued asking him, he lifted up himself, and said unto them, He that is without sin among you, let him first cast a stone at her.

8 And again he stooped down, and wrote on the ground.

9 And they which heard it, being convicted by their own conscience, went out one by one, beginning at the eldest, even unto the last: and Jesus was left alone, and the woman standing in the midst.

10 When Jesus had lifted up himself, and saw none but the woman, he said unto her, Woman, where are those thine accusers? hath no man condemned thee?

11 She said, No man, Lord. And Jesus said unto her, Neither do I condemn thee: go, and sin no more.

JESUS THE LIGHT OF THE WORLD

JOHN 8

:12 Then spake Jesus again unto them, saying, I am the light of the world: he that followeth me shall not walk in darkness, but shall have the light of life.

13 The Pharisees therefore said unto him, Thou bearest record of thyself; thy record is not true.

14 Jesus answered and said unto them, Though I bear record of myself, yet my record is true: for I know whence I came, and whither I go; but ye cannot tell whence I come, and whither I go.

⁴Luke 9:11	*them of the kingdom of God,* and . . . to teach them many things, ⁴*and healed them that had need of healing.*

THE FEEDING OF THE FIVE THOUSAND

MARK 6	:35 And when the day was now far spent, his disciples came unto him, and said, this is a desert place, and now the time is far passed:
¹Luke 9:12	36 Send them away, that they may go into the country round about, and into the villages, ¹*and lodge,* and buy themselves bread: for they have nothing to eat.
JOHN 6	:4 And the passover, a feast of the Jews, was nigh.
²Matt. 14:16	5 . . . Jesus then . . . saith unto Philip, ²*They need not depart,* ³*Give ye them to eat.*
³Mark 6:37	6 And this he said to prove him: for he himself knew what he would do.
	7 Philip answered him, Two hundred pennyworth of bread is not sufficient for them, that every one of them may take a little.
MARK 6	:38 He saith unto them, How many loaves have ye? go and see.
JOHN 6	:8 One of his disciples, Andrew, Simon Peter's brother, saith unto him.
⁴Luke 9:13	9 There is a lad here, which hath five barley loaves, and two small fishes: but what are they among so many? ⁴*except we should* go and buy meat for all this people.
MARK 6	:39 And he commanded them to make all sit down by companies upon the green grass.
	40 And they sat down in ranks, by hundreds, and by fifties.
⁵Luke 9:16	41 And when he had taken the five loaves and the two fishes, he looked up to heaven, and blessed, and brake the loaves, and gave them to his disciples to set before them: and the two fishes divided he among the ⁵*disciples to set before the multitude.*
⁶Luke 9:17	42 And they did all eat, and were filled: [Then] ⁶*he said unto his disciples, Gather up the fragments that remain, that nothing be lost.*

JOHN 6	13 Therefore they gathered them together, and filled twelve baskets with the fragments of the five barley loaves, which remained over and above unto them that had eaten.
MATT. 14	:21 And they that had eaten were about five thousand men, beside women and children.
JOHN 6	:14 Then those men, when they had seen the miracle that Jesus did, said, This is of a truth that Prophet that should come into the world.
	15 Jesus therefore perceived that they would come and take him by force, to make him a king . . .
MATT. 14	:22 And straightway Jesus constrained his disciples to get into a ship, and to go before him into
[7]John 6:17 [8]Mark 6:45	the other side, [7]*toward Caper'na-um*, [8]*unto Bethsai'da*, while he sent the multitudes away.
	23 And when he had sent the multitudes away, he went up into a mountain apart to pray, and when the
[9]Mark 6:47	evening was come, he was there alone [9]*on the land*.

JESUS WALKS ON THE SEA

MATT. 14	:24 But the ship was now in the midst of the sea
[1]John 6:18 great	tossed with waves: for the wind was [1]contrary, [2]*and it was now dark, and Jesus was not come to them.*
[2]John 6:17	[3]*And he saw them toiling in rowing;*
[3]Mark 6:48	25 And in the fourth watch of the night, [4]*when*
[4]John 6:19	*they had rowed about five and twenty or thirty furlongs, they see Jesus walking on the sea, and drawing nigh unto the ship:* [3]*and would have passed by them*, they were troubled, saying, It is a spirit;
[5]Mark 6:50	and they cried out for fear, [5]*for they all saw him.*
MATT. 14	:27 But straightway Jesus spake unto them, saying, Be of good cheer: it is I; be not afraid.
	28 And Peter answered him and said, Lord, if it be thou, bid me come unto thee on the water.
	29 And he said, Come. And when Peter was come down out of the ship, he walked on the water, to go to Jesus.
	30 And when he saw the wind boisterous, he was afraid; and beginning to sink, he cried, saying, Lord, save me.
	31 And immediately Jesus stretched forth his

hand, and caught him, and said unto him, O thou of little faith, wherefore didst thou doubt?

32 And when they were come, *⁶they willingly received him* into the ship, the wind ceased, *⁷and they were sore amazed in themselves* and wondered, *⁸for their heart was hardened;* and immediately the ship was at the land whither they went.

⁶John 6:21
⁷Mark 6:51
⁸Mark 6:52

33 Then they that were in the ship came and worshipped him, saying, Of a truth thou art the Son of God.

JESUS HEALS THE SICK IN GENNESARET

MARK 6 :53 And when they had passed over, they came into the land of Gennes'aret, and drew to the shore.

54 And when they were come out of the ship, straightway they knew him,

55 And ran through that whole region round about, and began to carry about in beds *¹and brought unto him all* those that were sick, where they heard he was.

¹Matt. 14:35

56 And whithersoever he entered, into villages, or cities, or country, they laid the sick in the streets, and besought him that they might touch if it were but the border of his garment: and as many as touched him were made whole.

THE PEOPLE SEEK JESUS

JOHN 6 :22 The day following, when the people, which stood on the other side of the sea, saw that there was none other boat there, save that one whereinto his disciples were entered, and that Jesus went not with his disciples into the boat, but that his disciples were gone away alone;

23 (Howbeit there came other boats from Tibe'rias nigh unto the place where they did eat bread, after that the Lord had given thanks:)

24 When the people therefore saw that Jesus was not there, neither his disciples, they also took shipping, and came to Caper'na-um, seeking for Jesus.

25 And when they had found him on the other side

JOHN 6

of the sea, they said unto him, Rabbi, when camest thou hither?

26 Jesus answered them and said, Verily, verily, I say unto you, Ye seek me, not because ye saw the miracles, but because ye did eat of the loaves, and were filled.

27 Labor not for the meat which perisheth, but for that meat which endureth unto everlasting life, which the Son of man shall give unto you: for him hath God the father sealed.

28 Then said they unto him, What shall we do, that we might work the works of God?

29 Jesus answered and said unto them, This is the work of God, that ye believe on him whom he hath sent.

JESUS THE BREAD OF LIFE

JOHN 6

:30 They said therefore unto him, What sign shewest thou then, that we may see, and believe thee? what dost thou work?

31 Our fathers did eat manna in the desert; as it is written, He gave them bread from heaven to eat.

32 Then Jesus said unto them, Verily, verily, I say unto you, Moses gave you not that bread from heaven; but my Father giveth you the true bread from heaven.

33 For the bread of God is he which cometh down from heaven, and giveth life unto the world.

34 Then said they unto him, Lord, evermore give us this bread.

35 And Jesus said unto them, I am the bread of life: he that cometh to me shall never hunger; and he that believeth on me shall never thirst.

36 But I said unto you, That ye also have seen me, and believe not.

37 All that the Father giveth me shall come to me; and him that cometh to me I will in no wise cast out.

38 For I came down from heaven, not to do mine own will, but the will of him that sent me.

39 And this is the Father's will which hath sent me, that of all which he hath given me I should lose nothing, but should raise it up again at the last day.

JOHN 6

40 And this is the will of him that sent me, that every one which seeth the Son, and believeth on him, may have everlasting life: and I will raise him up at the last day.

41 The Jews then murmured at him, because he said, I am the bread which came down from heaven.

42 And they said, Is not this Jesus, the son of Joseph, whose father and mother we know? how is it then that he saith, I came down from heaven?

43 Jesus therefore answered and said unto them, Murmur not among yourselves.

44 No man can come to me, except the Father which hath sent me draw him: and I will raise him up at the last day.

45 It is written in the prophets, And they shall be all taught of God. Every man therefore that hath heard, and hath learned of the Father, cometh unto me.

46 Not that any man hath seen the Father, save he which is of God, he hath seen the Father.

47 Verily, verily, I say unto you, He that believeth on me hath everlasting life.

48 I am the bread of life.

49 Your fathers did eat manna in the wilderness, and are dead.

50 This is the bread which cometh down from heaven, that a man may eat thereof, and not die.

51 I am the living bread which came down from heaven: if any man eat of this bread, he shall live for ever: and the bread that I will give is my flesh, which I will give for the life of the world.

52 The Jews therefore strove among themselves, saying, How can this man give us his flesh to eat?

53 Then Jesus said unto them, Verily, verily, I say unto you, Except ye eat the flesh of the Son of man, and drink his blood, ye have no life in you.

54 Whoso eateth my flesh, and drinketh my blood, hath eternal life; and I will raise him up at the last day.

55 For my flesh is meat indeed, and my blood is drink indeed.

JOHN 6

56 He that eateth my flesh, and drinketh my blood, dwelleth in me, and I in him.

57 As the living Father hath sent me, and I live by the Father; so he that eateth me, even he shall live by me.

58 This is that bread which came down from heaven: not as your fathers did eat manna, and are dead: he that eateth of this bread shall live for ever.

59 These things said he in the synagogue, as he taught in Caper'na-um.

JOHN 6

THE WORDS OF ETERNAL LIFE

:60 Many therefore of his disciples, when they had heard this, said, This is a hard saying; who can hear it?

61 When Jesus knew in himself that his disciples murmured at it, he said unto them, Doth this offend you?

62 What and if ye shall see the Son of man ascend up where he was before?

63 It is the Spirit that quickeneth; the flesh profiteth nothing: the words that I speak unto you, they are spirit, and they are life.

64 But there are some of you that believe not. For Jesus knew from the beginning who they were that believed not, and who should betray him.

65 And he said, Therefore said I unto you, that no man can come unto me, except it were given unto him of my Father.

66 From that time many of his disciples went back, and walked no more with him.

67 Then said Jesus unto the twelve, Will ye also go away?

68 Then Simon Peter answered him, Lord, to whom shall we go? thou hast the words of eternal life.

69 And we believe and are sure that thou art that Christ, the Son of the living God.

70 Jesus answered them, Have not I chosen you twelve, and one of you is a devil?

71 He spake of Judas Iscar'i-ot the son of Simon: for he it was that should betray him, being one of the twelve.

THE UNBELIEF OF JESUS' BRETHREN

JOHN 7

:1 After these things Jesus walked in Galilee: for he would not walk in Jewry, because the Jews sought to kill him.

2 Now the Jews' feast of tabernacles was at hand.

3 His brethren therefore said unto him, Depart hence, and go into Judea, that thy disciples also may see the works that thou doest.

4 For there is no man that doeth any thing in secret, and he himself seeketh to be known openly. If thou do these things, show thyself to the world.

5 For neither did his brethren believe in him.

6 Then Jesus said unto them, My time is not yet come: but your time is always ready.

7 The world cannot hate you; but me it hateth, because I testify of it, that the works thereof are evil.

8 Go ye up unto this feast: I go not up yet unto this feast; for my time is not yet full come.

9 When he had said these words unto them, he abode still in Galilee.

THINGS THAT DEFILE

MARK 7

:1 Then came together unto him the Pharisees, and certain of the scribes, which came from Jerusalem.

2 And when they saw some of his disciples eat bread with defiled, that is to say, with unwashen hands, they found fault.

3 For the Pharisees, and all the Jews, except they wash their hands oft, eat not, holding the tradition of the elders.

4 And when they come from the market except they wash, they eat not. And many other things there be, which they have received to hold, as the washing of cups, and pots, brazen vessels, and of tables.

[1]Matt. 15:2 transgress the tradition of the elders

5 Then the Pharisees and scribes asked him, Why [1]walk not thy disciples according to the tradition of the elders, but eat bread with unwashen hands?

MARK 7

[2]Matt. 15:3
Why do ye transgress the commandment of God by your tradition?

[3]Matt. 15:8
draweth nigh

6 He answered and said unto them, [2]Well hath Isaiah prophesied of you hypocrites, as it is written, This people [3]honoreth me with their lips but their heart is far from me.

7 Howbeit in vain do they worship me, teaching for doctrines the commandments of men.

8 For laying aside the commandment of God, ye hold the tradition of men, as the washing of pots and cups: and many other such like things ye do.

9 And he said unto them, Full well ye reject the commandment of God, that ye may keep your own tradition.

10 For Moses said, Honor thy father and thy mother; and, whoso curseth father or mother, let him die the death:

11 But ye say, If a man shall say to his father or mother, It is Corban, that is to say, a gift, by whatsoever thou mightest be profited by me [4]*And honor not his father or his mother, he shall be free.*

[4]Matt. 15:6

MARK 7

12 And ye suffer him no more to do aught for his father or his mother;

13 Making the word of God of none effect through your tradition, which ye have delivered: and many such like things do ye.

14 And when he had called all the [5]people unto him, he said unto them, Hearken unto me every one of you, and understand:

[5]Matt. 15:10
multitude

15 There is nothing from without a man, that entering into him can defile him: but the things which come out of him, those are they that defile the man.

16 If any man have ears to hear, let him hear.

17 And when he was entered into the house from the people, [6]*his disciples . . . said unto him, Knowest thou that the Pharisees were offended, after they heard this saying?*

[6]Matt. 15:12

MATT. 15

:13 But he answered and said, Every plant, which my heavenly Father hath not planted, shall be rooted up.

14 Let them alone: they be blind, both shall fall into the ditch.

ARRANGED AS A SINGLE NARRATIVE

MATT. 15
[7]Mark 7:17
disciples
MARK 7

15 Then answered [7]Peter and said unto him, Declare unto us this parable.

:18 And he saith unto them, Are ye so without understanding also? Do ye not perceive, that whatsoever thing from without entereth it cannot defile him;

19 Because it entereth not into his heart, and goeth out into the draught, purging all meats?

[8]Matt. 15:18

20 And he said, That which cometh out of [8]*the mouth of the man,* [8]*come forth from the heart,* that defileth the man.

21 For from within, out of the heart of men, proceed evil thoughts, adulteries, fornications,

[9]Matt. 15:19

murders, [9]*false witnesses.*

22 Thefts, covetousness, wickedness, deceit, lasciviousness, an evil eye, blasphemy, pride, foolishness:

[10]Matt. 15:20

23 All these evil things come from within, and defile the man. [10]*But to eat with unwashen hands defileth not a man.*

THE SYROPHOENICIAN WOMAN'S FAITH

MARK 7

:24 And from thence he arose, and went into the borders of Tyre and Sidon, and entered into a house, and would have no man know it: but he could not be hid.

[1]Matt. 15:22

25 [1]*Behold* a certain woman [1]*of Canaan came out of the same coasts,* whose young daughter had an unclean spirit, heard of him, and came and fell at his feet: [1]*and cried unto him, saying, Have mercy on me, O Lord, thou son of David; my daughter is grievously vexed with a devil.*

26 The woman was a Greek, a Syrophoeni'cian by nation; and she besought him that he would cast forth the devil out of her daughter.

MATT. 15

:23 But he answered her not a word. And his disciples came and besought him, saying, Send her away; for she crieth after us.

24 But he answered and said, I am not sent but unto the lost sheep of the house of Israel.

25 Then came she and worshipped him, saying, Lord, help me.

MARK 7 :27 But Jesus said unto her, Let the children first be filled: for it is not meet to take the children's bread, and to cast it unto the dogs.

28 And she answered and said unto him, Yes, Lord: yet the dogs under the ²*masters'* table eat of the children's crumbs.

²Matt. 15:27

³Matt. 15:28

29 And he said unto her ³*O Woman, great is thy faith.* For this saying go thy way; ³*be it unto thee even as thou wilt. And her daughter was made whole from that very hour.*

30 And when she was come to her house, she found the devil gone out, and her daughter laid upon the bed.

JESUS HEALS A DEAF AND DUMB MAN

MARK 7 :31 And again, departing from the coasts of Tyre and Sidon, he came unto the sea of Galilee, through the midst of the coasts of Decap'olis, ¹*and went up into a mountain, and sat down there.*

¹Matt. 15:29

MATT. 15 :30 And great multitudes came unto him, having with them those that were lame, blind, dumb, maimed, and many others, and cast them down at Jesus' feet; and he healed them:

MARK 7 :32 And they bring unto him one that was deaf, and had an impediment in his speech; and they beseech him to put his hand upon him.

33 And he took him aside from the multitude, and put his fingers into his ears, and he spit, and touched his tongue;

34 And looking up to heaven, he sighed, and saith unto him, Eph'phatha, that is, Be opened.

35 And straightway his ears were opened, and the string of his tongue was loosed, and he spake plain.

36 And he charged them that they should tell no man: the more he charged them, so much the more a great deal they published it;

37 And were beyond measure astonished, saying, He hath done all things well: he maketh both the deaf to hear, and the dumb to speak.

THE FEEDING OF THE FOUR THOUSAND

MARK 8 :1 In those days the multitude being very great, and having nothing to eat, Jesus called his disciples unto him, and saith unto them,

2 I have compassion on the multitude, because they have now been with me three days and have had nothing to eat:

[1]Matt. 15:32

3 And . . . I [1]*will not* send them away fasting to their own houses, they will faint by the way: for divers of them came from far.

4 And his disciples answered him, From whence can a man [2]satisfy these [3]men with bread here in the wilderness?

[2]Matt. 14:33 fill
[3]Multitude
[4]Matt. 15:34

5 And he asked them, How many loaves have ye? And they said, Seven [4]*and a few little fishes*.

[5]Matt. 15:35 multitude

6 And he commanded the [5]people to sit down on the ground: and he took the seven loaves, and gave thanks, and brake, and gave to his disciples to set before them; and they did set them before the people.

7 And they had a few small fishes: and he blessed, and commanded to set them also before them.

[6]Matt. 15:37

8 So they did [6]*all* eat, and were filled: and they took up of the broken meat that was left seven baskets [6]*full*.

[7]Matt. 15:38
[8]Matt. 15:39

9 And they that had eaten were about four thousand men, [7]*beside women and children*, and he sent [8]*the multitude away*.

10 And straightway he entered into a ship with his disciples, and came into the parts of [9]Dalmanu'tha.

[9]Matt. 15:39 Mag'-dala

THE DEMAND FOR A SIGN

MATT. 16 :1 The Pharisees also with the Sadducees came [1]*forth and began to question with him,* and tempting desired him that he would show them a sign from heaven.

[1]Mark 8:11

MARK 8 :12 And he sighed deeply in his spirit, and saith, Why doth this generation seek after a sign?

MATT. 16 :2 He answered and said unto them, When it is evening, ye say, It will be fair weather: for the sky is red.

MATT. 16	3 And in the morning, It will be foul weather today: for the sky is red and lowering. O ye hypocrites, ye can discern the face of the sky; but can ye not discern the signs of the times?

4 A wicked and adulterous generation seeketh after a sign; verily I say unto you, there shall no sign be given unto it, but the sign of the prophet Jonas. |
| ²Mark 8:13 | And he left them, ²*and entering into the ship again departed to the other side.* |

THE LEAVEN OF THE PHARISEES

MARK 8
¹Matt. 16:5	:14 Now the disciples ¹*were come to the other side,* and had forgotten to take bread, neither had they in the ship with them more than one loaf.
²Matt. 16:6	15 And he, ²*Jesus,* charged them, saying, Take heed, beware of the leaven of the Pharisees, ²*and of the Sadducees,* and of the leaven of Herod.

16 And they reasoned among themselves, saying, It is because we have no bread. |
| ³Matt. 16:8
perceived
⁴Matt. 16:8 | 17 And when Jesus ³knew it, he saith unto them, ⁴*O ye of little faith, why reason ye among yourselves, because ye have brought no bread?* perceive ye not yet, neither understand? have ye your heart yet hardened?

18 Having eyes, see ye not? and having ears, hear ye not? and do ye not remember?

19 When I brake the five loaves among five thousand, how many baskets full of fragments took ye up? They say unto him, Twelve.

20 And when the seven among four thousand, how many baskets full of fragments took ye up? And they said, Seven. |
| ⁵Matt. 16:11 | 21 And he said unto them, How is it that ye do not understand? ⁵*I spake it not to you concerning bread, that ye should beware of the leaven of the Pharisees and of the Sadducees?* |
| MATT. 16 | :12 Then understood they how that he bade them not beware of the leaven of bread, but of the doctrine of the Pharisees and of the Sadducees. |

A BLIND MAN HEALED AT BETHSAIDA

MARK 8

:22 And he cometh to Bethsai'da; and they bring a blind man unto him, and besought him to touch him.

23 And he took the blind man by the hand, and led him out of the town; and when he had spit on his eyes, and put his hands upon him, he asked him if he saw aught.

24 And he looked up, and said, I see men as trees, walking.

25 After that he put his hands again upon his eyes, and made him look up; and he was restored, and saw every man clearly.

26 And he sent him away to his house, saying, Neither go into the town, nor tell it to any in the town.

PETER'S CONFESSION

MATT. 16
¹Mark 8:27
²Mark 8:27
  towns
³Luke 9:18
⁴Luke 9:18
  the people
⁵Luke 9:19

:13 When Jesus ¹*went out* with his disciples, and came into the ²coasts of Caesare'a Phil'ippi, ³*as he was alone praying,* ¹*by the way,* ³*his disciples were with him,* he asked his disciples, saying, Whom do ⁴men say that I, the Son of man am?

14 And they said, Some say that thou art John the Baptist; some, Eli'jah; and others, Jeremiah or one of the ⁵*old* prophets ⁵*is risen again.*

15 He saith unto them, But whom say ye that I am?

16 And Simon Peter answered and said, Thou art the Christ, the Son of the living God.

17 And Jesus answered and said unto him, Blessed art thou, Simon Bar-jona: for flesh and blood hath not revealed it unto thee, but my Father which is in heaven.

18 And I say also unto thee, that thou art Peter, and upon this rock I will build my church; and the gates of hell shall not prevail against it.

19 And I will give unto thee the keys of the kingdom of heaven; and whatsoever thou shalt bind on earth shall be bound in heaven; and whatsoever thou shalt loose on earth shall be loosed in heaven.

MATT. 16	20 Then charged he his disciples that they should tell no man that he was Jesus the Christ.
	## JESUS FORETELLS HIS DEATH
MARK 8 [1]Matt. 16:21	:31 [1]*From that time forth began Jesus* to teach [1]*his disciples, how that he must go unto Jerusalem, and* that the Son of man must suffer many things, and be rejected of the elders, and of the chief priests,
[2]Luke 9:22 slain	and scribes, and be [2]killed, and after three days rise up again.
	32 And he spake that saying openly. And Peter took him, and began to rebuke him, [3]*saying, Be it far*
[3]Matt. 16:22	*from thee, Lord: this shall not be unto thee.*
	33 But when he had turned about and looked on his disciples, he rebuked Peter, saying, Get thee
[4]Matt. 16:23	behind me, Satan: [4]*Thou art an offense unto me* for thou savorest not the things that be of God, but the things that be of men.
	34 And when he had called the people unto him
[5]Matt. 16:24 If any man	with his disciples also, he said unto them, [5]Whosoever will come after me, let him deny himself,
[6]Luke 9:23	and take up his cross [6]*daily,* and follow me.
	35 For whosoever will save his life shall lose it; but whosoever shall lose his life for my sake and the
[7]Matt. 16:25 find it	gospel's, the same shall [7]save it.
	36 For what shall it profit a man, if he shall gain the whole world, and lose his own soul?
	37 Or what shall a man give in exchange for his soul?
	38 Whosoever therefore shall be ashamed of me and of my words, in this adulterous and sinful generation, of him also shall the Son of man be ashamed, when he cometh in the glory of his Father
[8]Matt. 16:27	with the holy angels, [8]*and then he shall reward every man according to his works.*
MARK 9 see the Son of man coming in his kingdom	:1 And he said unto them, Verily I say unto you, That there be some of them that stand here, which shall not taste of death, till they have [9]seen the kingdom of God come with power.

THE TRANSFIGURATION

MARK 9
¹Luke 9:28 about eight days after these sayings
²Luke 9:28
³Luke 9:29
⁴Luke 9:29 the fashion of his countenance was altered
⁵Matt. 17:2
⁶Matt. 17:2 light
⁷Matt. 17:3
⁸Luke 9:31

:2 And after ¹six days Jesus taketh with him Peter, and James, and John, and leadeth them up into a high mountain apart by themselves: ²*to pray,* ³*and as he prayed,* ⁴he was transfigured before them, ⁵*and his face did shine as the sun.*

3 And his raiment became shining, exceeding white as ⁶snow; so as no fuller on earth can white them.

4 And ⁷*behold,* there appeared unto them Eli'jah with Moses; and they were talking with Jesus ⁸*who appeared in glory, and spake of his decease which he should accomplish at Jerusalem.*

LUKE 9

:32 And Peter and they that were with him were heavy with sleep: and when they were awake, they saw his glory, and the two men that stood with him.

33 And it came to pass, as they departed from him, . . .

MARK 9
⁹Matt. 17:4

:5 . . . Peter answered and said to Jesus, Master, it is good for us to be here: ⁹*if thou wilt* . . . let us make three tabernacles; one for thee, and one for Moses and one for Eli'jah.

¹⁰Luke 9:33 not knowing what to say

6 For ¹⁰he wist not what to say; for they were sore afraid.

MATT. 17
¹¹Luke 9:34
¹²Mark 9:7

:5 While he yet spake, behold, a bright cloud overshadowed them ¹¹*and they feared as they entered into the cloud* ¹²*and a voice came out of the cloud, saying, This is my beloved Son,* in whom I am well pleased; hear ye him.

6 And when the disciples heard it, they fell on their face, and were sore afraid,

7 And Jesus came and touched them and said, Arise, and be not afraid.

MARK 9	:8 And suddenly, when [13]*the voice was past* and they had looked round about, they saw no man any more, save Jesus only with themselves.
[13]Luke 9:36	
	9 And as they came down from the [14]mountain, he charged them that they should tell no man which things they had seen, till the Son of man were risen [15]*again* from the dead.
[14]Luke 9:37 hill	
[15]Matt. 17:9	
[16]Luke 9:36 kept it close	10 And they [16]kept that saying with themselves, [17]*and told no man in those days any of those things which they had seen*, questioning one with another what the rising from the dead should mean.
[17]Luke 9:36	
	11 And they asked him, saying, Why say the scribes that Eli'jah must first come [18]*and restore all things?*
[18]Matt. 17:11	
	12 And he answered and told them, Eli'jah verily cometh first, and restoreth all things; and how it is written of the Son of man, that he must suffer many things, and be set at nought.
	13 But I say unto you, That Eli'jah is indeed come, and they have done unto him whatsoever they listed, as it is written of him. [19]*Likewise shall also the Son of man suffer of them.*
[19]Matt. 17:12	
MATT. 17	:13 Then the disciples understood that he spake unto them of John the Baptist.

JESUS HEALS A BOY WITH AN UNCLEAN SPIRIT

MARK 9	:14 [1]*And it came to pass, that on the next day, when they were come down from the hill, much people met him.* And when he came to his disciples, he saw a great multitude about them, and the scribes questioning with them.
[1]Luke 9:37	
	15 And straightway all the people, when they beheld him, were greatly amazed, and running to him saluted him.
	16 And he asked the scribes, What question ye with them?
[2]Matt. 17:14	17 And [2]*there came to him a certain man*, of the multitude, [2]*kneeling down to him*, and said, Master, I have brought unto thee my [3]*lunatic* son [3]*and he is sore vexed* [4]*for he is mine only child*. [3]*Have mercy on my son*, which hath a dumb spirit;
[3]Matt. 17:15	
[4]Luke 9:38	

MARK 9	18 And wheresoever he taketh him, he teareth him; and he foameth, and gnasheth with his teeth and pineth away, [and] ⁵*hardly departeth from him*, and I ⁶spake to thy disciples that they should cast him out; and they could not.
⁵Luke 9:39	
⁶Matt. 17:16 brought him	
⁷Luke 9:41	19 He answereth him, and saith, O faithless ⁷*and perverse* generation, how long shall I be with you? how long shall I suffer you? bring him unto me.
⁸Luke 9:42	20 And they brought him unto him, and when he saw him, straightway ⁸*as he was yet coming* the ⁸*devil threw him down, and tare him;* and he fell on the ground, and wallowed foaming.

21 And he asked his father, How long is it ago since this came unto him? And he said, Of a child.

22 And ofttimes it hath cast him into the fires and into the waters, to destroy him: but if thou canst do anything, have compassion on us, and help us.

23 Jesus said unto him, If thou canst believe, all things are possible to him that believeth.

24 And straightway the father of the child cried out, and said with tears, Lord, I believe; help thou mine unbelief.

⁹Luke 9:42 unclean spirit	25 When Jesus saw that the people came running together, he rebuked the foul spirit, saying unto him, ⁹Thou dumb and deaf spirit, I charge thee, come out of him, and enter no more into him.

26 And the spirit cried and rent him sore, and came out of him: and he was as one dead, insomuch that many said, He is dead.

¹⁰Luke 9:42	27 But Jesus took him by the hand, and lifted him up: ¹⁰*and delivered him again to his father*, ¹¹*and the child was cured from that very hour*.
¹¹Matt. 17:18	
LUKE 9	:43 And they were all amazed at the mighty power of God.
MARK 9	:28 And when he was come into the house, his disciples asked him privately, Why could not we cast him out? ¹²*Because of your unbelief: for verily I say unto you, If ye have faith as a grain of mustard seed, ye shall say unto this mountain, Remove hence to yonder place; and it shall remove: and nothing shall be impossible unto you.*
¹²Matt. 17:20	

MARK 9

:29 And he said unto them, This kind can come forth by nothing, but by prayer and fasting.

JESUS AGAIN FORETELLS HIS DEATH

MARK 9

:30 And they departed thence, and ²*passed through Galilee; and he would not that any man should know it.* ¹*But while they wondered every one at all things which Jesus did,*

¹Luke 9:43
²Matt. 17:22
While he abode in

LUKE 9

31 For he taught his disciples, and said unto them,

:44 Let these sayings sink down into your ears: ³*The Son of man is* ⁴*delivered into the hands of men, and they shall kill him; and after that he is killed, he shall rise the third day.* ⁵*And they were exceeding sorry.*

³Mark 9:31
⁴Matt. 17:22 betrayed
⁵Matt. 17:23

45 But they understood not this saying, and it was hid from them, that they perceived it not: and they feared to ask him of that saying.

WHO IS THE GREATEST?

LUKE 9

:46 Then there arose a reasoning among them, which of them should be greatest.

PAYMENT OF THE TRIBUTE MONEY

MATT. 17

:24 And when they were come to Caper'na-um, they that received tribute money came to Peter, and said, Doth not your master pay tribute?

25 He saith, Yes. And when he was come into the house, Jesus prevented him, saying; What thinkest thou, Simon? of whom do the kings of the earth take custom or tribute? of their own children, or of strangers?

26 Peter saith unto him Of strangers. Jesus saith unto him, Then are the children free.

27 Notwithstanding, lest we should offend them, go thou to the sea, and cast a hook, and take up the fish that first cometh up; and when thou hast opened his mouth, thou shalt find a piece of money: that take, and give unto them for me and thee.

WHICH OF THE APOSTLES SHOULD BE THE GREATEST

MARK 9
¹Luke 9:47
²Mark 9:33

:33 ¹*Jesus perceiving the thoughts of their hearts, and being in the house [at]* ²*Caper'na-um* asked them, What was it that ye disputed among yourselves by the way?

34 But they held their peace: for by the way they had disputed among themselves, who should be the greatest.

35 And he sat down, and called the twelve, and saith unto them, If any man desire to be first, the same shall be the last of all, and servant of all.

³Luke 9:47
by him

36 And he took a child, and set him ³in the midst of them: and when he had taken him in his arms, he said unto them,

⁴Luke 9:48

37 Whosoever shall receive one of such children in my name, receiveth me; and whosoever shall receive me, receiveth not me, but him that sent me, ⁴*for he that is least among you the same shall be great.*

WHO IS THE GREATEST IN THE KINGDOM OF HEAVEN?*

MATT. 18

:1 At the same time came the disciples unto Jesus, saying, Who is the greatest in the kingdom of heaven?

2 And Jesus called a little child unto him, and set him in the midst of them,

:3 And said, Verily I say unto you, Except ye be converted, and become as little children, ye shall not enter into the kingdom of heaven.

5 And whoso shall receive one such little child in my name receiveth me.

---

*The questions, though apparently about the same time and in the same place, are quite different. They first reasoned among themselves which of *them should be the greatest*. (Luke 9:46) When they arrive at Capernaum Jesus asks them what the disputation was which they had along the way. (Mark 9:34). This illustration of greatness was given to the twelve, (Mark 9:35). In Matthew 18, other disciples came and asked, Who is greatest in *the kingdom of heaven*? Here the disciples ask, Who, and in the above the twelve argue among themselves and Jesus, without their acknowledging their problem, gives them the object lesson.

HE THAT IS NOT AGAINST US IS FOR US

MARK 9

:38 And John answered him, saying, Master, we saw one casting out devils in thy name, and he followeth not us; and we forbade him, because he followeth not us.

39 But Jesus said, Forbid him not: for there is no man which shall do a miracle in my name, that can lightly speak evil of me.

40 For he that is not against us [1]is on our part.

41 For whosoever shall give you a cup of water to drink in my name, because ye belong to Christ, verily I say unto you, he shall not lose his reward.

[1]Luke 9:50 is for us

OFFENCES

MARK 9

:42 And whosoever shall offend one of these little ones that believe in me, it is better for him that a millstone were hanged about his neck, and he were *drowned in the depths of the sea.*

[1]Matt. 18:6

MATT. 18

:7 Woe unto the world because of offences! for it must needs be that offences come; but woe to that man by whom the offence cometh!

MARK 9
[2]Matt. 18:8

:43 And if thy hand offend thee, cut it off: it is better for thee to enter into life [2]*halt or* maimed, *rather* than having two hands to go into hell, into the *everlasting* fire that never shall be quenched:

44 Where their worm dieth not, and the fire is not quenched.

45 And if thy foot offend thee, cut it off: it is better for thee to enter halt into life, than having two feet to be cast into hell, into the fire that never shall be quenched:

46 Where their worm dieth not, and the fire is not quenched.

[3]Matt. 18:9
[4]Matt. 18:9 life

47 And if thine eye offend thee, pluck it out [3]*and cast it from thee:* it is better for thee to enter into the [4]*kingdom of God* with one eye, than having two eyes to be cast into hell fire:

48 Where their worm dieth not, and the fire is not quenched.

49 For every one shall be salted with fire, and every sacrifice shall be salted with salt.

MARK 9

50 Salt is good: but if the salt have lost his saltness, wherewith will ye season it? Have salt in yourselves, and have peace one with another.

MATT. 18

:10 Take heed that ye despise not one of these little ones; for I say unto you, That in heaven their angels do always behold the face of my Father which is in heaven.

11 For the Son of man is come to save that which was lost.

THE LOST SHEEP

MATT. 18

:12 How think ye? if a man have a hundred sheep, and one of them be gone astray, doth he not leave the ninety and nine, and goeth into the mountains, and seeketh that which is gone astray?

13 And if so be that he find it, verily I say unto you, he rejoiceth more of that sheep, than of the ninety and nine which went not astray.

14 Even so it is not the will of your Father which is in heaven, that one of these little ones should perish.

IF A BROTHER SINS AGAINST THEE

MATT. 18
[1]See Luke 17:3-4 P. 149 Many of the same truths are repeated in Luke but from Luke 17 on seems to be at a later date.

:15 Moreover if thy [1]brother shall trespass against thee, go and tell him his fault between thee and him alone: if he shall hear thee, thou hast gained thy brother.

16 But if he will not hear thee, then take with thee one or two more, that in the mouth of two or three witnesses every word may be established.

17 And if he shall neglect to hear them, tell it unto the church: but if he neglect to hear the church, let him be unto thee as a heathen man and a publican.

18 Verily I say unto you, Whatsoever ye shall bind on earth shall be bound in heaven; and whatsoever ye shall loose on earth shall be loosed in heaven.

19 Again I say unto you, That if two of you shall agree on earth as touching any thing that they shall ask, it shall be done for them of my Father which is in heaven.

20 For where two or three are gathered together in my name, there am I in the midst of them.

THE UNFORGIVING SERVANT

MATT. 18

:21 Then came Peter to him, and said, Lord, how oft shall my brother sin against me, and I forgive him? till seven times?

22 Jesus saith unto him, I say not unto thee, Until seven times: but, Until seventy times seven.

23 Therefore is the kingdom of heaven likened unto a certain king, which would take account of his servants.

24 And when he had begun to reckon, one was brought unto him, which owed him ten thousand talents.

25 But forasmuch as he had not to pay, his lord commanded him to be sold, and his wife, and children, and all that he had, and payment to be made.

26 The servant therefore fell down, and worshipped him, saying, Lord have patience with me, and I will pay thee all.

27 Then the lord of that servant was moved with compassion, and loosed him, and forgave him the debt.

28 But the same servant went out, and found one of his fellow servants, which owed him a hundred pence: and he laid hands on him, and took him by the throat, saying, Pay me that thou owest.

29 And his fellow servant fell down at his feet, and besought him, saying, Have patience with me, and I will pay thee all.

30 And he would not: but went and cast him into prison, till he should pay the debt.

31 So when his fellow servants saw what was done, they were very sorry, and came and told unto their lord all that was done.

32 Then his lord, after that he had called him, said unto him, O thou wicked servant, I forgave thee all that debt, because thou desiredst me:

33 Shouldest not thou also have had compassion on thy fellow servant, even as I had pity on thee?

34 And his lord was wroth, and delivered him to the tormentors till he should pay all that was due unto him.

MATT. 18   35 So likewise shall my heavenly Father do also unto you, if ye from your hearts forgive not every one his brother their trespasses.

JESUS REBUKES JAMES AND JOHN

LUKE 9   :51 And it came to pass, when the time was come that he should be received up, *he steadfastly set his face to go to Jerusalem,**

52 And sent messengers before his face: and they went, and entered into a village of the Samaritans, to make ready for him.

53 And they did not receive him, because his face was as though he would go to Jerusalem.

54 And when his disciples James and John saw this, they said, Lord, wilt thou that we command fire to come down from heaven, and consume them, even as Eli'jah did?

55 But he turned, and rebuked them, and said, Ye know not what manner of spirit ye are of.

56 For the Son of man is not come to destroy men's lives, but to save them. And they went to another village.

THE COST OF DISCIPLESHIP

LUKE 9   :57 And it came to pass, that, as they went in the way, a certain man said unto him, Lord, I will follow thee whithersoever thou goest.

58 And Jesus said unto him, Foxes have holes, and birds of the air have nests; but the Son of man hath not where to lay his head.

59 And he said unto another, Follow me. But he said, Lord, suffer me first to go and bury my father.

60 Jesus said unto him, Let the dead bury their dead: but go thou and preach the kingdom of God.

61 And another also said, Lord, I will follow thee; but let me first go bid them farewell, which are at home at my house.

62 And Jesus said unto him, No man, having put his hand to the plow, and looking back, is fit for the kingdom of God.

---

*Although this is nearing the end of His ministry, this is not his last journey to Jerusalem. See Luke 18:31-34.

JESUS' TEACHING ON DIVORCE*

MATT. 19 :1 And it came to pass, that when Jesus had finished these sayings, he departed from Galilee, and came into the coasts of Judea beyond Jordan; ¹*and the people resort unto him again; and, as he was wont, he taught them again.*

¹Mark 10:1

2 And great multitudes followed him; and he healed them there.

3 The Pharisees also came unto him, tempting him, and saying unto him, Is it lawful for a man to put away his wife for every cause?

4 And he answered and said unto them, Have ye not read, that he which made them at the beginning made them male and female,

5 And said, For this cause shall a man leave father and mother, and shall cleave to his wife: and they twain shall be one flesh?

6 Wherefore they are no more twain, but one flesh. What therefore God hath joined together, let not man put asunder.

MARK 10 :3 And he answered and said unto them, What did Moses command you?

MATT. 19 :7 They say unto him, Why did Moses then command to give a writing of divorcement, and to put her away?

²Mark 10:5 wrote you this precept
³Mark 10:6

8 He saith unto them, Moses because of the hardness of your hearts ²suffered you to put away your wives: but from the beginning ³*of creation* it was not so.

MATT. 19 :9 And I say unto you, Whosoever shall put away his wife, except it be for fornication, and shall marry another, committeth adultery: and whoso marrieth her which is put away doth commit adultery.

MARK 10 :10 And in the house his disciples asked him again of the same matter.

11 And he saith unto them, Whosoever shall put away his wife, and marry another, committeth adultery against her.

12 And if a woman shall put away her husband, and be married to another, she committeth adultery.

---

*Mark 10 and Matthew 19 seem to be parallel passages. But there are other passages on this subject which were given on different occasions.

MATT. 19 :10 His disciples say unto him, If the case of the man be so with his wife, it is not good to marry.

11 But he said unto them, All men cannot receive this saying, save they to whom it is given.

12 For there are some eunuchs, which were so born from their mother's womb: and there are some eunuchs, which were made eunuchs of men: and there be eunuchs, which have made themselves eunuchs for the kingdom of heaven's sake. He that is able to receive it, let him receive it.

THE SEVENTY SENT FORTH*

LUKE 10** :1 After these things the Lord appointed other seventy also, and sent them two and two before his face into every city and place, whither he himself would come.

2 Therefore said he unto them, The harvest truly is great, but the laborers are few: pray ye therefore the Lord of the harvest, that he would send forth laborers into his harvest.

3 Go your ways: behold, I send you forth as lambs among wolves.

4 Carry neither purse, nor scrip, nor shoes: and salute no man by the way.

5 And into whatsoever house ye enter, first say, Peace be to this house.

6 And if the son of peace be there, your peace shall rest upon it: if not, it shall turn to you again.

---

*The directive given to the seventy is very similar to those given to the twelve apostles (Matt. 10:1-16 and Luke 9:2). The ordination address was given to the twelve, months before. The mission which the twelve made was very near the end of Christ's earthly ministry. Much of the same message is repeated after Christ's resurrection (Mark 16:18).

**It is amazing how each writes about so much which is not mentioned by the others. The recording of Luke 10:1 - 18:14 falls between the healing of the lunatic boy just after the transfiguration as recorded by all three gospels and the narrative of the rich young ruler which is preceeded each time by blessing little children: Matt. 19:16-26, 19:13-15, Mark 10:17-31 and 10:13-17, respectively. Therefore it appears that all of Luke, ch. 10:1-18:14 should be placed in this order. It is admitted that he speaks of many things which are repeated at other places by the other writers. He also repeats some of the same truths later in his gospel. Therefore it should be considered as another sermon when great truths are given needed emphasis. These were now the last few weeks of our Lord's earthly ministry. All the recorded events from all writers from the transfiguration on seem to fit into the same chronological order although not all the events are recorded by any one of the writers.

LUKE 10

7 And in the same house remain, eating and drinking such things as they give: for the laborer is worthy of his hire. Go not from house to house.

8 And into whatsoever city ye enter, and they receive you, eat such things as are set before you:

9 And heal the sick that are therein, and say unto them, The kingdom of God is come nigh unto you.

10 But into whatsoever city ye enter, and they receive you not, go your ways out into the streets of the same and say,

11 Even the very dust of your city, which cleaveth on us, we do wipe off against you: notwithstanding, be ye sure of this, that the kingdom of God is come nigh unto you.

12 But I say unto you, that it shall be more tolerable in that day for Sodom, than for that city.

13 Woe unto thee, Chora'zin! woe unto thee, Bethsai'da for if the mighty works had been done in Tyre and Sidon, which have been done in you, they had a great while ago repented, sitting in sackcloth and ashes.

14 But it shall be more tolerable for Tyre and Sidon at the judgment, than for you.

15 And thou, Caper'na-um, which are exalted to heaven, shalt be thrust down to hell.

16 He that heareth you heareth me; and he that despiseth you despiseth me; and he that despiseth me despiseth him that sent me.

THE SUCCESS OF THE SEVENTY

LUKE 10

:17 And the seventy returned again with joy, saying, Lord, even the devils are subject unto us through thy name,

18 And he said unto them, I beheld Satan as lightning fall from heaven.

19 Behold, I give unto you power to tread on serpents and scorpions, and over all the power of the enemy; and nothing shall by any means hurt you.

20 Notwithstanding, in this rejoice not, that the spirits are subject unto you; but rather rejoice, because your names are written in heaven.

JESUS REJOICES IN SPIRIT

LUKE 10 :21 In that hour Jesus rejoiced in spirit, and said, I thank thee, O Father, Lord of heaven and earth, that thou hast hid these things from the wise and prudent, and hast revealed them unto babes: even so, Father; for so it seemed good in thy sight.

22 All things are delivered to me of my father: and no man knoweth who the Son is, but the Father and who the Father is, but the Son, and he to whom the Son will reveal him.

23 And he turned him unto his disciples, and said privately, Blessed are the eyes which see the things that ye see:

24 For I tell you, that many prophets and kings have desired to see those things which ye see, and have not seen them; and to hear those things which ye hear, and have not heard them.

THE GOOD SAMARITAN

LUKE 10 :25 And, behold, a certain lawyer stood up, and tempted him, saying, Master, what shall I do to inherit eternal life?

26 He said unto him, What is written in the law? how readest thou?

27 And he answering said, Thou shalt love the Lord thy God with all thy heart, and with all thy soul, and with all thy strength, and with all thy mind; and thy neighbor as thyself.

28 And he said unto him, Thou hast answered right: this do, and thou shalt live.

29 But he, willing to justify himself, said unto Jesus, And who is my neighbor?

30 And Jesus answering said, A certain man went down from Jerusalem to Jericho, and fell among thieves, which stripped him of his raiment, and wounded him, and departed, leaving him half dead.

31 And by chance there came down a certain priest that way; and when he saw him, he passed by on the other side.

32 And likewise a Levite, when he was at the place, came and looked on him, and passed by on the other side.

LUKE 10

33 But a certain Samaritan, as he journeyed, came where he was; and when he saw him, he had compassion on him.

34 And went to him, and bound up his wounds, pouring in oil and wine, and set him on his own beast, and brought him to an inn, and took care of him.

35 And on the morrow when he departed, he took out two pence, and gave them to the host, and said unto him, Take care of him: and whatsoever thou spendest more, when I come again, I will repay thee.

36 Which now of these three, thinkest thou, was neighbor unto him that fell among the thieves?

37 And he said, He that showed mercy on him. Then said Jesus unto him, Go, and do thou likewise.

JESUS VISITS MARTHA AND MARY

LUKE 10

38 Now it came to pass, as they went, that he entered into a certain village: and a certain woman named Martha received him into her house.

39 And she had a sister called Mary, which also sat at Jesus' feet, and heard his word.

40 But Martha was cumbered about much serving, and came to him, and said, Lord, dost thou not care that my sister hath left me to serve alone? bid her therefore that she help me.

41 And Jesus answered and said unto her, Martha, Martha, thou art careful and troubled about many things:

42 But one thing is needful; and Mary hath chosen that good part, which shall not be taken away from her.

JESUS AT THE FEAST
OF TABERNACLES

JOHN 7

:10 *But when his brethren were gone up, then went he also up unto the feast, not openly, but as it were in secret.

11 Then the Jews sought him at the feast, and said, Where is he?

12 And there was much murmuring among the people concerning him: for some said, He is a good man: others said, Nay; but he deceiveth the people.

---
*See footnote on next page.

ARRANGED AS A SINGLE NARRATIVE

JOHN 7

13 Howbeit no man spake openly of him for fear of the Jews.

14 Now about the midst of the feast Jesus went up into the temple, and taught.

15 And the Jews marveled, saying, How knoweth this man letters, having never learned?

16 Jesus answered them, and said, My doctrine is not mine, but his that sent me.

17 If any man will do his will, he shall know of the doctrine, whether it be of God, or whether I speak of myself.

18 He that speaketh of himself seeketh his own glory: but he that seeketh his glory that sent him, the same is true, and no unrighteousness is in him.

:19 Did not Moses give you the law, and yet none of you keepeth the law? Why go ye about to kill me?

20 The people answered and said, Thou hast a devil: who goeth about to kill thee?

21 Jesus answered and said unto them, I have done one work, and ye all marvel.

22 Moses therefore gave unto you circumcision; (not because it is of Moses, but of the fathers;) and ye on the sabbath day circumcise a man.

23 If a man on the sabbath day receive circumcision, that the law of Moses should not be broken; are ye angry at me, because I have made a man every whit whole on the sabbath day?

24 Judge not according to the appearance, but judge righteous judgment.

Many events have taken place between John 7:9 and 7:10. In verse 9 he is in Galilee, vs. 10 in Jerusalem. In Luke 9:51-53 we see Christ on his way to Jerusalem, Luke 10:38 he is in Bethany very near Jerusalem. In Luke 13:22 we see him journeying again toward Jerusalem. It seems quite probable that John 7:10-10:42 was given at this time when he went out from Jerusalem into beyond Jordan (10:40). Where he was praying in Luke, ch. 11 does not say, but he must have left the vicinity, because we see him again on the way to Jerusalem in Luke 13:22. In Luke 13:31-35 Christ is evidently in Herod's jurisdiction, not Jerusalem. In Luke 17:11 it says *it came to pass as he went to Jerusalem*. He had not yet arrived for we have the narrative of Christ blessing the young children followed by the narrative of the rich young ruler. The last parallel account of John is the feeding of the 5,000 and the following is that of the triumphal entry. This makes it very difficult where John 7:10-11:57 should be placed in the narrative.

IS THIS THE CHRIST?

JOHN 7

:25 Then said some of them of Jerusalem, Is not this he, whom they seek to kill?

26 But, lo, he speaketh boldly, and they say nothing unto him. Do the rulers know indeed that this is the very Christ?

27 Howbeit we know this man whence he is: but when Christ cometh, no man knoweth whence he is.

28 Then cried Jesus in the temple as he taught, saying, Ye both know me, and ye know whence I am: and I am not come of myself, but he that sent me is true, whom ye know not.

29 But I know him; for I am from him, and he hath sent me.

30 Then they sought to take him: but no man laid hands on him, because his hour was not yet come.

31 And many of the people believed on him, and said, When Christ cometh, will he do more miracles than these which this man hath done?

OFFICERS SENT TO ARREST JESUS

JOHN 7

:32 The Pharisees heard that the people murmured such things concerning him; and the Pharisees and the chief priests sent officers to take him.

33 Then said Jesus unto them, Yet a little while am I with you, and then I go unto him that sent me.

34 Ye shall seek me, and shall not find me: and where I am, thither ye cannot come.

35 Then said the Jews among themselves, Whither will he go, that we shall not find him? will he go unto the dispersed among the Gentiles, and teach the Gentiles?

36 What manner of saying is this that he said, Ye shall seek me, and shall not find me: and where I am, thither ye cannot come?

RIVERS OF LIVING WATER

JOHN 7

:37 In the last day, that great day of the feast, Jesus stood and cried, saying, If any man thirst, let him come unto me, and drink.

JOHN 7 — 38 He that believeth on me, as the Scripture hath said, out of his belly shall flow rivers of living water.

39 (But this spake he of the Spirit, which they that believe on him should receive: for the Holy Ghost was not yet given; because that Jesus was not yet glorified.)

DIVISION AMONG THE PEOPLE

JOHN 7 — 40 Many of the people therefore, when they heard this saying, said, Of a truth this is the Prophet.

41 Others said, This is the Christ. But some said, Shall Christ come out of Galilee?

42 Hath not the Scripture said, That Christ cometh of the seed of David, and out of the town of Bethlehem, where David was?

43 So there was a division among the people because of him.

44 And some of them would have taken him; but no man laid hands on him.

THE UNBELIEF OF THOSE IN AUTHORITY

JOHN 7 — :45 Then came the officers to the chief priests and Pharisees; and they said unto them, Why have ye not brought him?

46 The officers answered, Never man spake like this man.

47 Then answered them the Pharisees, Are ye also deceived?

48 Have any of the rulers of the Pharisees believed on him?

49 But this people who knoweth not the law are cursed.

50 Nicode'mus saith unto them, (he that came to Jesus by night, being one of them,)

51 Doth our law judge any man, before it hear him, and know what he doeth?

52 They answered and said unto him, Art thou also of Galilee? Search, and look: for out of Galilee ariseth no prophet.

53 And every man went unto his own house.

THE WOMAN CAUGHT IN ADULTERY

JOHN 8 :1 Jesus went unto the mount of Olives.

2 And early in the morning he came again into the temple, and all the people came unto him; and he sat down, and taught them.

3 And the scribes and Pharisees brought unto him a woman taken in adultery; and when they had set her in the midst,

4 They say unto him, Master, this woman was taken in adultery, in the very act.

5 Now Moses in the law commanded us, that such should be stoned: but what sayest thou?

6 This they said, tempting him, that they might have to accuse him. But Jesus stooped down, and with his finger wrote on the ground, as though he heard them not.

7 So when they continued asking him, he lifted up himself, and said unto them, He that is without sin among you, let him first cast a stone at her.

8 And again he stooped down, and wrote on the ground.

9 And they which heard it, being convicted by their own conscience, went out one by one, beginning at the eldest, even unto the last: and Jesus was left alone, and the woman standing in the midst.

10 When Jesus had lifted up himself, and saw none but the woman, he said unto her, Woman, where are those thine accusers? hath no man condemned thee?

11 She said, No man, Lord. And Jesus said unto her, Neither do I condemn thee: go, and sin no more.

JESUS THE LIGHT OF THE WORLD

JOHN 8 :12 Then spake Jesus again unto them, saying, I am the light of the world: he that followeth me shall not walk in darkness, but shall have the light of life.

13 The Pharisees therefore said unto him, Thou bearest record of thyself; thy record is not true.

14 Jesus answered and said unto them, Though I bear record of myself, yet my record is true: for I know whence I came, and whither I go; but ye cannot tell whence I come, and whither I go.

JOHN 8

15 Ye judge after the flesh; I judge no man.
16 And yet if I judge, my judgment is true: for I am not alone, but I and the Father that sent me.
17 It is also written in your law, that the testimony of two men is true.
18 I am one that bear witness of myself, and the Father that sent me beareth witness of me.
19 Then said they unto him, Where is thy Father? Jesus answered, Ye neither know me, nor my Father: if ye had known me, ye should have known my Father also.
20 These words spake Jesus in the treasury, as he taught in the temple: and no man laid hands on him; for his hour was not yet come.

WHITHER I GO YE CANNOT COME

JOHN 8

:21 Then said Jesus again unto them, I go my way, and ye shall seek me, and shall die in your sins: whither I go, ye cannot come.
22 Then said the Jews, Will he kill himself? because he saith, Whither I go, ye cannot come.
23 And he said unto them, Ye are from beneath; I am from above: ye are of this world; I am not of this world.
24 I said therefore unto you, that ye shall die in your sins: for if ye believe not that I am he, ye shall die in your sins.
25 Then said they unto him, Who art thou? And Jesus saith unto them, Even the same that I said unto you from the beginning.
26 I have many things to say and to judge of you: but he that sent me is true; and I speak to the world those things which I have heard of him.
27 They understood not that he spake to them of the Father.
28 Then said Jesus unto them, When ye have lifted up the Son of man, then shall ye know that I am he, and that I do nothing of myself; but as my Father hath taught me, I speak these things.
29 And he that sent me is with me: the Father hath not left me alone; for I do always those things that please him.

JOHN 8

30 As he spake these words, many believed on him.

THE TRUTH SHALL MAKE YOU FREE

JOHN 8

:31 Then said Jesus to those Jews which believed on him, If ye continue in my word, then are ye my disciples indeed;

32 And ye shall know the truth, and the truth shall make you free.

33 They answered him, We be Abraham's seed, and were never in bondage to any man: how sayest thou, Ye shall be made free?

34 Jesus answered them, Verily, verily, I say unto you, Whosoever committeth sin is the servant of sin.

35 And the servant abideth not in the house for ever: but the Son abideth ever.

36 If the Son therefore shall make you free, ye shall be free indeed.

37 I know that ye are Abraham's seed; but ye seek to kill me, because my word hath no place in you.

38 I speak that which I have seen with my Father: and ye do that which ye have seen with your father.

YOUR FATHER THE DEVIL

JOHN 8

:39 They answered and said unto him, Abraham is our father. Jesus saith unto them, If ye were Abraham's children, ye would do the works of Abraham.

40 But now ye seek to kill me, a man that hath told you the truth, which I have heard of God: this did not Abraham.

41 Ye do the deeds of your father. Then said they to him, We be not born of fornication; we have one Father, even God.

42 Jesus said unto them, If God were your Father, ye would love me: for I proceeded forth and came from God; neither came I of myself, but he sent me.

JOHN 8

43 Why do ye not understand my speech? even because ye cannot hear my word.

44 Ye are of your father the devil, and the lusts of your father ye will do: he was a murderer from the beginning, and abode not in the truth, because there is no truth in him. When he speaketh a lie, he speaketh of his own: for he is a liar, and the father of it.

45 And because I tell you the truth, ye believe me not.

46 Which of you convinceth me of sin? And if I say the truth, why do ye not believe me?

47 He that is of God heareth God's words: ye therefore hear them not, because ye are not of God.

BEFORE ABRAHAM WAS, I AM

JOHN 8

:48 Then answered the Jews, and said unto him, Say we not well that thou art a Samaritan, and hast a devil?

49 Jesus answered, I have not a devil; but I honor my Father, and ye do dishonor me.

50 And I seek not mine own glory: there is one that seeketh and judgeth.

51 Verily, verily, I say unto you, If a man keep my saying, he shall never see death.

52 Then said the Jews unto him, Now we know that thou hast a devil. Abraham is dead, and the prophets; and thou sayest, If a man keep my saying, he shall never taste of death.

53 Art thou greater than our father Abraham, which is dead? and the prophets are dead: whom makest thou thyself?

54 Jesus answered, If I honor myself, my honor is nothing: it is my Father that honoreth me; of whom ye say, that he is your God:

55 Yet ye have not known him; but I know him: and if I should say, I know him not, I shall be a liar like unto you: but I know him, and keep his saying.

56 Your father Abraham rejoiced to see my day: and he saw it, and was glad.

57 Then said the Jews unto him, Thou art not yet fifty years old, and hast thou seen Abraham?

JOHN 8

58 Jesus said unto them, Verily, verily, I say unto you, Before Abraham was, I am.

59 Then took they up stones to cast at him: but Jesus hid himself, and went out of the temple, going through the midst of them, and so passed by.

JESUS HEALS THE MAN
BORN BLIND

JOHN 9

:1 And as Jesus passed by, he saw a man which was blind from his birth.

2 And his disciples asked him, saying, Master, who did sin, this man, or his parents, that he was born blind?

3 Jesus answered, Neither hath this man sinned, nor his parents: but that the works of God should be made manifest in him.

4 I must work the works of him that sent me, while it is day: the night cometh, when no man can work.

5 As long as I am in the world, I am the light of the world.

6 When he had thus spoken, he spat on the ground, and made clay of the spittle, and he anointed the eyes of the blind man with the clay,

7 And said unto him, Go, wash in the pool of Silo'am, (which is by interpretation, Sent.) He went his way therefore, and washed, and came seeing.

8 The neighbors therefore, and they which before had seen him that he was blind, said, Is not this he that sat and begged?

9 Some said, This is he: others said, He is like him: but he said, I am he.

10 Therefore said they unto him, How were thine eyes opened?

11 He answered and said, A man that is called Jesus made clay, and anointed mine eyes, and said unto me, Go to the pool of Silo'am, and wash: and I went and washed, and I received sight.

12 Then said they unto him, Where is he? He said, I know not.

THE PHARISEES INVESTIGATE
THE HEALING

JOHN 9

:13 They brought to the Pharisees him that aforetime was blind.

14 And it was the sabbath day when Jesus made the clay, and opened his eyes.

15 Then again the Pharisees also asked him how he had received his sight. He said unto them, He put clay upon mine eyes, and I washed, and do see.

16 Therefore said some of the Pharisees, This man is not of God, because he keepeth not the sabbath day. Others said, How can a man that is a sinner do such miracles? And there was a division among them.

17 They say unto the blind man again, What sayest thou of him, that he hath opened thine eyes? He said, He is a prophet.

18 But the Jews did not believe concerning him, that he had been blind, and received his sight, until they called the parents of him that had received his sight.

19 And they asked them, saying, Is this your son, who ye say was born blind? how then doth he now see?

20 His parents answered them and said, We know that this is our son, and that he was born blind:

21 But by what means he now seeth, we know not; or who hath opened his eyes, we know not: he is of age; ask him: he shall speak for himself.

22 These words spake his parents, because they feared the Jews: for the Jews had agreed already, that if any man did confess that he was Christ, he should be put out of the synagogue.

23 Therefore said his parents, He is of age; ask him.

24 Then again called they the man that was blind, and said unto him, Give God the praise: we know that this man is a sinner.

25 He answered and said, Whether he be a sinner or no, I know not: one thing I know, that, whereas I was blind, now I see.

JOHN 9

26 Then said they to him again, What did he to thee? how opened he thine eyes?

27 He answered them, I have told you already, and ye did not hear: wherefore would ye hear it again? will ye also be his disciples?

28 Then they reviled him, and said, Thou art his disciple; but we are Moses' disciples.

29 We know that God spake unto Moses: as for this fellow, we know not from whence he is.

30 The man answered and said unto them, Why herein is a marvelous thing, that ye know not from whence he is, and yet he hath opened mine eyes.

31 Now we know that God heareth not sinners: but if any man be a worshipper of God, and doeth his will, him he heareth.

32 Since the world began was it not heard that any man opened the eyes of one that was born blind.

33 If this man were not of God, he could do nothing.

34 They answered and said unto him, Thou wast altogether born in sins, and dost thou teach us? And they cast him out.

SPIRITUAL BLINDNESS

JOHN 9

:35 Jesus heard that they had cast him out; and when he had found him, he said unto him, Dost thou believe on the Son of God?

36 He answered and said, Who is he, Lord, that I might believe on him?

37 And Jesus said unto him, Thou hast both seen him, and it is he that talketh with thee.

38 And he said, Lord, I believe. And he worshipped him.

39 And Jesus said, For judgment I am come into this world, that they which see not might see; and that they which see might be made blind.

40 And some of the Pharisees which were with him heard these words, and said unto him, Are we blind also?

41 Jesus said unto them, If ye were blind, ye should have no sin: but now ye say, We see; therefore your sin remaineth.

THE PARABLE OF THE SHEEPFOLD

JOHN 10

:1 Verily, verily, I say unto you, He that entereth not by the door into the sheepfold, but climbeth up some other way, the same is a thief and a robber.

2 But he that entereth in by the door is the shepherd of the sheep.

3 To him the porter openeth; and the sheep hear his voice: and he calleth his own sheep by name, and leadeth them out.

4 And when he putteth forth his own sheep, he goeth before them, and the sheep follow him: for they know his voice.

5 And a stranger will they not follow, but will flee from him; for they know not the voice of strangers.

6 This parable spake Jesus unto them; but they understood not what things they were which he spake unto them.

JESUS THE GOOD SHEPHERD

JOHN 10

7 Then said Jesus unto them again, Verily, verily, I say unto you, I am the door of the sheep.

8 All that ever came before me are thieves and robbers: but the sheep did not hear them.

9 I am the door: by me if any man enter in, he shall be saved, and shall go in and out and find pasture.

10 The thief cometh not, but for to steal, and to kill, and to destroy: I am come that they might have life, and that they might have it more abundantly.

11 I am the good shepherd: the good shepherd giveth his life for the sheep.

12 But he that is a hireling, and not the shepherd, whose own the sheep are not, seeth the wolf coming, and leaveth the sheep, and fleeth; and the wolf catcheth them, and scattereth the sheep.

13 The hireling fleeth, because he is a hireling, and careth not for the sheep.

14 I am the good shepherd, and know my sheep, and am known of mine.

15 As the Father knoweth me, even so know I the Father: and I lay down my life for the sheep.

16 And other sheep I have, which are not of this

JOHN 10

fold: them also I must bring, and they shall hear my voice; and there shall be one fold, and one shepherd.

17 Therefore doth my Father love me, because I lay down my life, that I might take it again.

18 No man taketh it from me, but I lay it down of myself. I have power to lay it down, and I have power to take it again. This commandment have I received of my Father.

19 There was a division therefore again among the Jews for these sayings.

20 And many of them said, He hath a devil, and is mad; why hear ye him?

21 Others said, These are not the words of him that hath a devil. Can a devil open the eyes of the blind?

22 And it was at Jerusalem the feast of the dedication, and it was winter.

23 And Jesus walked in the temple in Solomon's porch.

24 Then came the Jews round about him, and said unto him, How long dost thou make us to doubt? If thou be the Christ, tell us plainly.

25 Jesus answered them, I told you, and ye believed not: the works that I do in my Father's name, they bear witness of me.

26 But ye believe not, because ye are not of my sheep, as I said unto you.

27 My sheep hear my voice, and I know them, and they follow me:

28 And I give unto them eternal life; and they shall never perish, neither shall any man pluck them out of my hand.

29 My Father, which gave them me, is greater than all; and no man is able to pluck them out of my Father's hand.

30 I and my Father are one.

31 Then the Jews took up stones again to stone him.

32 Jesus answered them, Many good works have I showed you from my Father; for which of those works do ye stone me?

33 The Jews answered him, saying, For a good

JOHN 10

work we stone thee not; but for blasphemy; and because that thou, being a man, makest thyself God.

34 Jesus answered them, Is it not written in your law, I said, Ye are gods?

35 If he called them gods, unto whom the word of God came, and the Scripture cannot be broken;

36 Say ye of him, whom the Father hath sanctified, and sent into the world, Thou blasphemest; because I said, I am the Son of God?

37 If I do not the works of my Father, believe me not.

38 But if I do, though ye believe not me, believe the works; that ye may know, and believe, that the Father is in me, and I in him.

39 Therefore they sought again to take him; but he escaped out of their hand,

40 And went away again beyond Jordan into the place where John at first baptized; and there he abode.

41 And many resorted unto him and said, John did no miracle: but all things that John spake of this man were true.

42 And many believed on him there.

THE MODEL PRAYER

LUKE 11

:1 And it came to pass, that, as he was praying in a certain place, when he ceased, one of his disciples said unto him, Lord, teach us to pray, as John also taught his disciples.

2 And he said unto them, When ye pray, say, Our Father which art in heaven, Hallowed be thy name. Thy kingdom come. Thy will be done, as in heaven, so in earth.

3 Give us day by day our daily bread.

4 And forgive us our sins; for we also forgive every one that is indebted to us. And lead us not into temptation; but deliver us from evil.

EARNEST PRAYING

LUKE 11

:5 And he said unto them, Which of you shall have a friend, and shall go unto him at midnight, and say unto him, Friend, lend me three loaves;

LUKE 11

:6 For a friend of mine in his journey is come to me, and I have nothing to set before him?

7 And he from within shall answer and say, Trouble me not: the door is now shut, and my children are with me in bed; I cannot rise and give thee.

8 I say unto you, Though he will not rise and give him, because he is his friend, yet because of his importunity he will rise and give him as many as he needeth.

9 And I say unto you, Ask, and it shall be given you; seek and ye shall find; knock, and it shall be opened unto you.

10 For every one that asketh receiveth; and he that seeketh findeth; and to him that knocketh it shall be opened.

11 If a son shall ask bread of any of you that is a father, will he give him a stone? or if he ask a fish, will he for a fish give him a serpent?

12 Or if he shall ask an egg, will he offer him a scorpion?

13 If ye then, being evil, know how to give good gifts unto your children; how much more shall your heavenly Father give the Holy Spirit to them that ask him?

CHRIST VS. BEELZEBUB*

LUKE 11

:14 And he was casting out a devil, and it was dumb. And it came to pass, when the devil was gone out, the dumb spake; and the people wondered.

15 But some of them said, He casteth out devils through Beel'zebub the chief of the devils.

16 And others, tempting him, sought of him a sign from heaven.

17 But he, knowing their thoughts, said unto them, Every kingdom divided against itself is brought to desolation; and a house divided against a house falleth.

18 If Satan also be divided against himself, how

---

*The context makes it clear that this is a repetition of the same truth as given in Matt. 12:22-23 and Mark 3:22-30, but given at another time.

shall his kingdom stand? because ye say that I cast out devils through Beel'zebub.

LUKE 11

19 And if I by Beel'zebub cast out devils, by whom do your sons cast them out? therefore shall they be your judges.

20 But if I with the finger of God cast out devils, no doubt the kingdom of God is come upon you.

21 When a strong man armed keepeth his palace, his goods are in peace:

22 But when a stronger than he shall come upon him, and overcome him, he taketh from him all his armor wherein he trusted, and divideth his spoils.

23 He that is not with me is against me; and he that gathereth not with me scattereth.

THE RETURN OF THE UNCLEAN SPIRIT

LUKE 11

:24 When the unclean spirit is gone out of a man, he walketh through dry places, seeking rest; and finding none, he saith, I will return unto my house whence I came out.

25 And when he cometh, he findeth it swept and garnished.

26 Then goeth he, and taketh to him seven other spirits more wicked than himself; and they enter in, and dwell there: and the last state of that man is worse than the first.

27 And it came to pass, as he spake these things, a certain woman of the company lifted up her voice and said unto him, Blessed is the womb that bare thee, and the paps which thou has sucked.

28 But he said, Yea, rather, blessed are they that hear the word of God, and keep it.

JONAH, A SIGN TO NINEVITES

LUKE 11
Matt. 12:38
Matt. 12:39
Matt. 12:39

:29 And when the people were gathered thick together, *¹certain of the scribes and of the Pharisees answered, saying, Master, we would see a sign from thee. ²But he answered and said unto them,* This is an evil ³*and adulterous* generation: they seek a sign; and there shall no sign be given it, but the sign of Jonah the prophet.

LUKE 11

30 For as Jonah was a sign unto the Nin'-evites, so shall also the Son of man be to this generation.

MATT. 12

:40 For as Jonah was three days and three nights in the whale's belly; so shall the Son of man be three days and three nights in the heart of the earth.

LUKE 11

:31 The queen of the south shall rise up in the judgment with the men of this generation, and condemn them: for she came from the utmost parts of the earth to hear the wisdom of Solomon; and behold, a greater than Solomon is here.

32 The men of Nin'eveh shall rise up in the judgment with this generation, and shall condemn it: for they repented at the preaching of Jonah; and behold, a greater than Jonah is here.

THE EYE SHOULD BE SINGLE

LUKE 11

:33 No man, when he hath lighted a candle, putteth it in a secret place, neither under a bushel, but on a candlestick, that they which come in may see the light.

34 The light of the body is the eye: therefore when thine eye is single, thy whole body also is full of light; but when thine eye is evil, thy body also is full of darkness.

35 Take heed therefore, that the light which is in thee be not darkness.

36 If thy whole body therefore be full of light, having no part dark, the whole shall be full of light, as when the bright shining of a candle doth give thee light.

JESUS DINES WITH A PHARISEE

LUKE 11

:37 And as he spake, a certain Pharisee besought him to dine with him: and he went in, and sat down to meat.

38 And when the Pharisee saw it, he marveled that he had not first washed before dinner.

39 And the Lord said unto him, Now do ye Pharisees make clean the outside of the cup and the platter; but your inward part is full of ravening and wickedness.

LUKE 11

40 Ye fools, did not he, that made that which is without, make that which is within also?

41 But rather give alms of such things as ye have; and, behold, all things are clean unto you.

42 But woe unto you, Pharisees! for ye tithe mint and rue and all manner of herbs, and pass over judgment and the love of God: these ought ye to have done, and not to leave the other undone.

43 Woe unto you, Pharisees! for ye love the uppermost seats in the synagogues, and greetings in the markets.

44 Woe unto you, scribes and Pharisees, hypocrites! for ye are as graves which appear not, and the men that walk over them are not aware of them.

45 Then answered one of the lawyers, and said unto him, Master, thus saying thou reproachest us also.

46 And he said, Woe unto you also, ye lawyers! for ye lade men with burdens grievous to be borne, and ye yourselves touch not the burdens with one of your fingers.

47 Woe unto you! for ye build the sepulchres of the prophets, and your fathers killed them.

48 Truly ye bear witness that ye allow the deeds of your fathers: for they indeed killed them, and ye build their sepulchres.

49 Therefore also said the wisdom of God, I will send them prophets and apostles, and some of them they shall slay and persecute:

50 That the blood of all the prophets, which was shed from the foundation of the world, may be required of this generation;

51 From the blood of Abel unto the blood of Zechari'ah, which perished between the altar and the temple: verily I say unto you, It shall be required of this generation.

52 Woe unto you, lawyers! for ye have taken away the key of knowledge: ye entered not in yourselves, and them that were entering in ye hindered.

53 And as he said these things unto them, the scribes and the Pharisees began to urge him

LUKE 11

vehemently, and to provoke him to speak of many things:

54 Laying wait for him, and seeking to catch something out of his mouth, that they might accuse him.

BEWARE OF HYPOCRISY

LUKE 12

:1 In the mean time, when there were gathered together an innumerable multitude of people, insomuch that they trode one upon another, he began to say unto his disciples first of all, Beware ye of the leaven of the Pharisees, which is hypocrisy.

2 For there is nothing covered, that shall not be revealed; neither hid, that shall not be known.

3 Therefore, whatsoever ye have spoken in darkness shall be heard in the light; and that which ye have spoken in the ear in closets shall be proclaimed upon the housetops.

WHOM TO FEAR

LUKE 12

:4 And I say unto you my friends, Be not afraid of them that kill the body, and after that have no more that they can do.

5 But I will forewarn you whom ye shall fear: Fear him, which after he hath killed hath power to cast into hell; yea, I say unto you, Fear him.

6 Are not five sparrows sold for two farthings, and not one of them is forgotten before God?

7 But even the very hairs of your head are all numbered. Fear not therefore: ye are of more value than many sparrows.

CONFESSING CHRIST AND TRUSTING THE LEADERSHIP OF THE HOLY SPIRIT

LUKE 12

:8 Also I say unto you, Whosoever shall confess me before men, him shall the Son of man also confess before the angels of God:

9 But he that denieth me before men shall be denied before the angels of God.

10 And whosoever shall speak a word against the Son of man, it shall be forgiven him: but unto him

that blasphemeth against the Holy Ghost it shall not be forgiven.

11 And when they bring you unto the synagogues, and unto magistrates, and powers, take ye no thought how or what thing ye shall answer, or what ye shall say:

12 For the Holy Ghost shall teach you in the same hour what ye ought to say.

THE RICH FOOL

LUKE 12

:13 And one of the company said unto him, Master, speak to my brother, that he divide the inheritance with me.

14 And he said unto him, Man, who made me a judge or a divider over you?

15 And he said unto them, Take heed, and beware of covetousness; for a man's life consisteth not in the abundance of the things which he possesseth.

16 And he spake a parable unto them, saying, The ground of a certain rich man brought forth plentifully:

17 And he thought within himself, saying, What shall I do, because I have no room where to bestow my fruits?

18 And he said, This will I do: I will pull down my barns, and build greater; and there will I bestow all my fruits and my goods.

19 And I will say to my soul, Soul, thou hast much goods laid up for many years; take thine ease, eat, drink, and be merry.

20 But God said unto him, Thou fool, this night thy soul shall be required of thee: then whose shall those things be, which thou hast provided?

21 So is he that layeth up treasure for himself, and is not rich toward God.

SEEK FIRST THE KINGDOM OF GOD

LUKE 12

:22 And he said unto his disciples, Therefore I say unto you, Take no thought for your life, what ye shall eat; neither for the body, what ye shall put on.

23 The life is more than meat, and the body is more than raiment.

LUKE 12

24 Consider the ravens: for they neither sow nor reap; which neither have storehouse nor barn; and God feedeth them: how much more are ye better than the fowls?

25 And which of you with taking thought can add to his stature one cubit?

26 If ye then be not able to do that thing which is least, why take ye thought for the rest?

27 Consider the lilies how they grow: they toil not, they spin not; and yet I say unto you, that Solomon in all his glory was not arrayed like one of these.

28 If then God so clothe the grass, which is today in the field, and tomorrow is cast into the oven; how much more will he clothe you, O ye of little faith?

29 And seek not ye what ye shall eat, or what ye shall drink, neither be ye of doubtful mind.

30 For all these things do the nations of the world seek after: and your Father knoweth that ye have need of these things.

31 But rather seek ye the kingdom of God; and all these things shall be added unto you.

WHERE IS YOUR TREASURE?

LUKE 12

:32 Fear not, little flock; for it is your Father's good pleasure to give you the kingdom.

33 Sell that ye have, and give alms; provide yourselves bags which wax not old, a treasure in the heavens that faileth not, where no thief approacheth, neither moth corrupteth.

34 For where your treasure is, there will your heart be also.

BE READY FOR CHRIST'S RETURN

LUKE 12

:35 Let your loins be girded about, and your lights burning;

36 And ye yourselves like unto men that wait for their lord, when he will return from the wedding; that, when he cometh and knocketh, they may open unto him immediately.

37 Blessed are those servants, whom the lord when he cometh shall find watching: verily I say

LUKE 12

unto you, that he shall gird himself, and make them to sit down to meat, and will come forth and serve them.

38 And if he shall come in the second watch, or come in the third watch, and find them so, blessed are those servants.

39 And this know, that if the goodman of the house had known what hour the thief would come, he would have watched, and not have suffered his house to be broken through.

40 Be ye therefore ready also: for the Son of man cometh at an hour when ye think not.

PERSONAL RESPONSIBILITY

LUKE 12

41 Then Peter said unto him, Lord, speakest thou this parable unto us, or even to all?

42 And the Lord said, Who then is that faithful and wise steward, whom his lord shall make ruler over his household, to give them their portion of meat in due season?

43 Blessed is that servant, whom his lord when he cometh shall find so doing.

44 Of a truth I say unto you, that he will make him ruler over all that he hath.

45 But and if that servant say in his heart, My lord delayeth his coming; and shall begin to beat the menservants and maidens, and to eat and drink, and to be drunken;

46 The lord of that servant will come in a day when he looketh not for him, and at an hour when he is not aware, and will cut him in sunder, and will appoint him his portion with the unbelievers.

47 And that servant, which knew his lord's will, and prepared not himself, neither did according to his will, shall be beaten with many stripes.

48 But he that knew not, and did commit things worthy of stripes, shall be beaten with few stripes. For unto whomsoever much is given, of him shall be much required; and to whom men have committed much, of him they will ask the more.

CHRISTIAN CONVICTIONS CAUSE DIVISIONS

LUKE 12 :49 I am come to send fire on the earth; and what will I, if it be already kindled?

50 But I have a baptism to be baptized with; and how am I straitened till it be accomplished!

51 Suppose ye that I am come to give peace on earth? I tell you, Nay; but rather division:

52 For from henceforth there shall be five in one house divided, three against two, and two against three.

53 The father shall be divided against the son, and the son against the father; the mother against the daughter, and the daughter against the mother; the mother-in-law against her daughter-in-law, and the daughter-in-law against her mother-in-law.

DISCERNING THE TIMES

LUKE 12 :54 And he said also to the people, When ye see a cloud rise out of the west, straightway ye say, There cometh a shower; and so it is.

55 And when ye see the south wind blow, ye say, There will be heat; and it cometh to pass.

56 Ye hypocrites, ye can discern the face of the sky and of the earth; but how is it that ye do not discern this time?

57 Yea, and why even of yourselves judge ye not what is right?

58 When thou goest with thine adversary to the magistrate, as thou art in the way, give diligence that thou mayest be delivered from him; lest he hale thee to the judge, and the judge deliver thee to the officer, and the officer cast thee into prison.

59 I tell thee, thou shalt not depart thence, till thou hast paid the very last mite.

REPENT OR PERISH

LUKE 13 :1 There were present at that season some that told him of the Galileans, whose blood Pilate had mingled with their sacrifices.

2 And Jesus answering said unto them, Suppose

LUKE 13
ye that these Galileans were sinners above all the Galileans, because they suffered such things?

3 I tell you, Nay: but, except ye repent, ye shall all likewise perish.

4 Or those eighteen, upon whom the tower in Silo'am fell, and slew them, think ye that they were sinners above all men that dwelt in Jerusalem?

5 I tell you, Nay: but, except ye repent, ye shall all likewise perish.

THE FRUITLESS FIG TREE

LUKE 13
:6 He spake also this parable; A certain man had a fig tree planted in his vineyard; and he came and sought fruit thereon, and found none.

7 Then said he unto the dresser of his vineyard, Behold, these three years I come seeking fruit on this fig tree, and find none: cut it down; why cumbereth it the ground?

8 And he answering said unto him, Lord, let it alone this year also, till I shall dig about it, and dung it:

9 And if it bear fruit, well: and if not, then after that thou shalt cut it down.

CHRIST'S ADVERSARIES ASHAMED

LUKE 13
:10 And he was teaching in one of the synagogues on the sabbath.

11 And, behold, there was a woman which had a spirit of infirmity eighteen years, and was bowed together, and could in no wise lift up herself.

12 And when Jesus saw her, he called her to him, and said unto her, Woman, thou art loosed from thine infirmity.

13 And he laid his hands on her: and immediately she was made straight, and glorified God.

14 And the ruler of the synagogue answered with indignation, because that Jesus had healed on the sabbath day, and said unto the people, There are six days in which men ought to work: in them therefore come and be healed, and not on the sabbath day.

15 The Lord then answered him, and said, Thou hypocrite, doth not each one of you on the sabbath

LUKE 13

loose his ox or his ass from the stall, and lead him away to watering?

16 And ought not this woman, being a daughter of Abraham, whom Satan hath bound, lo, these eighteen years, be loosed from this bond on the sabbath day?

17 And when he had said these things, all his adversaries were ashamed: and all the people rejoiced for all the glorious things that were done by him.

THE PARABLE OF THE MUSTARD SEED

LUKE 13

:18 Then said he, Unto what is the kingdom of God like? and whereunto shall I resemble it?

19 It is like a grain of mustard seed, which a man took and cast into his garden; and it grew, and waxed a great tree; and the fowls of the air lodged in the branches of it.

THE PARABLE OF THE LEAVEN

LUKE 13

:20 And again he said, Whereunto shall I liken the kingdom of God?

21 It is like leaven, which a woman took and hid in three measures of meal, till the whole was leavened.

TWO WAYS

LUKE 13

:22 And he went through the cities and villages, teaching, and journeying toward Jerusalem.

23 Then said one unto him, Lord, are there few that be saved? And he said unto them,

24 Strive to enter in at the strait gate: for many, I say unto you, will seek to enter in, and shall not be able.

25 When once the master of the house is risen up, and hath shut to the door, and ye begin to stand without, and to knock at the door, saying, Lord, Lord, open unto us; and he shall answer and say unto you, I know you not whence ye are:

26 Then shall ye begin to say, We have eaten and drunk in thy presence, and thou hast taught in our streets.

LUKE 13

27 But he shall say, I tell you, I know you not whence ye are; depart from me, all ye workers of iniquity.

28 There shall be weeping and gnashing of teeth, when ye shall see Abraham, and Isaac, and Jacob, and all the prophets, in the kingdom of God, and you yourselves thrust out.

29 And they shall come from the east, and from the west, and from the north, and from the south, and shall sit down in the kingdom of God.

30 And, behold, there are last which shall be first; and there are first which shall be last.

O JERUSALEM, JERUSALEM

LUKE 13

:31 The same day there came certain of the Pharisees, saying unto him, Get thee out, and depart hence; for *Herod will kill thee.

32 And he said unto them, Go ye, and tell that fox, Behold, I cast out devils, and I do cures today and tomorrow, and the third day I shall be perfected.

33 Nevertheless I must walk today, and tomorrow, and the day following: for it cannot be that a prophet perish out of Jerusalem.

34 O Jerusalem, Jerusalem, which killest the prophets, and stonest them that are sent unto thee; how often would I have gathered thy children together, as a hen doth gather her brood under her wings, and ye would not!

35 Behold, your house is left unto you desolate: and verily I say unto you, Ye shall not see me, until the time come when ye shall say, Blessed is he that cometh in the name of the Lord.

---

*Evidently he was still beyond Jordan, in Herod's jurisdiction after having left Jerusalem (John 10:40) and is now on his way toward Jerusalem again in Luke 13:22. At some juncture on his way to Jerusalem he is called to the home of Mary and Martha to pray for Lazarus. In John 11:7 he says Let us go up again into Judea. Whether he went on to Jerusalem which is just over Olivet and the Cedron Valley from Bethany, we do not know. But we do know that after raising Lazarus from the dead he departed into the city of Ephraim near the wilderness (John 11:54). In Luke 17:11 he passed through the midst of Samaria and Galilee. This could logically follow John 11:54 where he was in a city called Ephraim.

THE DEATH OF LAZARUS

JOHN 11 :1 Now a certain man was sick, named Lazarus, of Bethany, the town of Mary and her sister Martha.

2 (It was that Mary which anointed the Lord with ointment, and wiped his feet with her hair, whose brother Lazarus was sick.)

3 Therefore his sisters sent unto him, Saying, Lord, behold he whom thou lovest is sick.

4 When Jesus heard that, he said, This sickness is not unto death, but for the glory of God, that the Son of God might be glorified thereby.

5 Now Jesus loved Martha, and her sister, and Lazarus.

6 When he had heard therefore that he was sick, he abode two days still in the same place where he was.

7 Then after that saith he to his disciples, Let us go into Judea again.

8 His disciples say unto him, Master, the Jews of late sought to stone thee; and goest thou thither again?

9 Jesus answered, Are there not twelve hours in the day? If any man walk in the day, he stumbleth not, because he seeth the light of this world.

10 But if a man walk in the night, he stumbleth, because there is no light in him.

11 These things said he: and after that he saith unto them, Our friend Lazarus sleepeth; but I go, that I may awake him out of sleep.

12 Then said his disciples, Lord, if he sleep, he shall do well.

13 Howbeit Jesus spake of his death: but they thought that he had spoken of taking of rest in sleep.

14 Then said Jesus unto them plainly, Lazarus is dead.

15 And I am glad for your sakes that I was not there, to the intent ye may believe; nevertheless let us go unto him.

16 Then said Thomas, which is called Did'ymus, unto his fellow disciples, Let us also go, that we may die with him.

JESUS THE RESURRECTION AND THE LIFE

JOHN 11

:17 Then when Jesus came, he found that he had lain in the grave four days already.

18 Now Bethany was nigh unto Jerusalem, about fifteen furlongs off:

19 And many of the Jews came to Martha and Mary, to comfort them concerning their brother.

20 Then Martha, as soon as she heard that Jesus was coming, went and met him: but Mary sat still in the house.

21 Then said Martha unto Jesus, Lord, if thou hadst been here, my brother had not died.

22 But I know, that even now, whatsoever thou wilt ask of God, God will give it thee.

23 Jesus saith unto her, Thy brother shall rise again.

24 Martha saith unto him, I know that he shall rise again in the resurrection at the last day.

25 Jesus said unto her, I am the resurrection, and the life: he that believeth in me, though he were dead, yet shall he live.

26 And whosoever liveth and believeth in me shall never die. Believest thou this?

27 She saith unto him, Yea, Lord: I believe that thou art the Christ, the Son of God, which should come into the world.

JESUS WEEPS

JOHN 11

:28 And when she had so said, she went her way, and called Mary her sister secretly, saying, The Master is come, and calleth for thee.

29 As soon as she heard that, she arose quickly, and came unto him.

30 Now Jesus was not yet come into the town, but was in that place where Martha met him.

31 The Jews then which were with her in the house, and comforted her, when they saw Mary, that she rose up hastily and went out, followed her, saying, She goeth unto the grave to weep there.

32 Then when Mary was come where Jesus was, and saw him, she fell down at his feet, saying unto

JOHN 11

him, Lord, if thou hadst been here, my brother had not died.

33 When Jesus therefore saw her weeping, and the Jews also weeping which came with her, he groaned in the spirit, and was troubled,

34 And said, Where have ye laid him? They say unto him, Lord, come and see.

35 Jesus wept.

36 Then said the Jews, Behold how he loved him!

37 And some of them said, Could not this man, which opened the eyes of the blind, have caused that even this man should not have died?

LAZARUS BROUGHT TO LIFE

JOHN 11

:38 Jesus therefore again groaning in himself cometh to the grave. It was a cave, and a stone lay upon it.

39 Jesus said, Take ye away the stone. Martha, the sister of him that was dead, saith unto him, Lord, by this time he stinketh: for he hath been dead four days.

40 Jesus saith unto her, Said I not unto thee, that, if thou wouldest believe, thou shouldest see the glory of God?

41 Then they took away the stone from the place where the dead was laid. And Jesus lifted up his eyes, and said, Father, I thank thee that thou hast heard me.

42 And I knew that thou hearest me always: but because of the people which stand by I said it, that they may believe that thou hast sent me.

43 And when he thus had spoken, he cried with a loud voice, Lazarus, come forth.

44 And he that was dead came forth, bound head and foot with graveclothes; and his face was bound about with a napkin. Jesus saith unto them, Loose him, and let him go.

45 Then many of the Jews which came to Mary, and had seen the things which Jesus did, believed on him.

46 But some of them went their ways to the Pharisees, and told them what things Jesus had done.

CAIAPHAS PROPHESIES THAT ONE SHOULD DIE FOR THE NATION

JOHN 11

:47 Then gathered the chief priests and the Pharisees a council, and said, What do we? for this man doeth many miracles.

48 If we let him thus alone, all men will believe on him; and the Romans shall come and take away both our place and nation.

49 And one of them, named Cai'aphas, being the high priest that same year, said unto them, Ye know nothing at all,

50 Nor consider that it is expedient for us, that one man should die for the people, and that the whole nation perish not.

51 And this spake he not of himself: but being high priest that year, he prophesied that Jesus should die for that nation;

52 And not for that nation only, but that also he should gather together in one the children of God that were scattered abroad.

53 Then from that day forth they took counsel together for to put him to death.

54 Jesus therefore walked no more openly among the Jews; but went thence unto a country near to the wilderness, into a city called E'phra-im, and there continued with his disciples.

55 And the Jews' passover was nigh at hand: and many went out of the country up to Jerusalem before the passover, to purify themselves.

56 Then sought they for Jesus, and spake among themselves, as they stood in the temple, What think ye, that he will not come to the feast?

57 Now both the chief priests and the Pharisees had given a commandment, that, if any man knew where he were, he should show it, that they might take him.

THE MAN WHO HAD DROPSY HEALED

LUKE 14

:1 And it came to pass, as he went into the house of one of the chief Pharisees to eat bread on the sabbath day, that they watched him.

2 And, behold, there was a certain man before him which had the dropsy.

LUKE 14

3 And Jesus answering spake unto the lawyers and Pharisees, saying, Is it lawful to heal on the sabbath day?

4 And they held their peace. And he took him, and healed him, and let him go;

5 And answered them, saying, Which of you shall have an ass or an ox fallen into a pit, and will not straightway pull him out on the sabbath day?

6 And they could not answer him again to these things.

A LESSON ON HUMILITY

LUKE 14

:7 And he put forth a parable to those which were bidden, when he marked how they chose out the chief rooms; saying unto them,

8 When thou art bidden of any man to a wedding, sit not down in the highest room; lest a more honorable man than thou be bidden of him;

9 And he that bade thee and him come and say to thee, Give this man place; and thou begin with shame to take the lowest room.

10 But when thou art bidden, go and sit down in the lowest room; that when he that bade thee cometh, he may say unto thee, Friend, go up higher: then shalt thou have worship in the presence of them that sit at meat with thee.

11 For whosoever exalteth himself shall be abased; and he that humbleth himself shall be exalted.

12 Then said he also to him that bade him, When thou makest a dinner or a supper, call not thy friends, nor thy brethren, neither thy kinsmen, nor thy rich neighbors; lest they also bid thee again, and a recompense be made thee.

13 But when thou makest a feast, call the poor, the maimed, the lame, the blind:

14 And thou shalt be blessed; for they cannot recompense thee: for thou shalt be recompensed at the resurrection of the just.

THE PARABLE OF THE GREAT SUPPER

LUKE 14

:15 And when one of them that sat at meat with

LUKE 14

him heard these things, he said unto him, Blessed is he that shall eat bread in the kingdom of God.

16 Then said he unto him, A certain man made a great supper, and bade many:

17 And sent his servant at supper time to say to them that were bidden, Come; for all things are now ready.

18 And they all with one consent began to make excuse. The first said unto him, I have bought a piece of ground, and I must needs go and see it: I pray thee have me excused.

19 And another said, I have bought five yoke of oxen, and I go to prove them: I pray thee have me excused.

20 And another said, I have married a wife, and therefore I cannot come.

21 So that servant came, and showed his lord these things. Then the master of the house being angry said to his servant, Go out quickly into the streets and lanes of the city, and bring in hither the poor, and the maimed, and the halt, and the blind.

22 And the servant said, Lord, it is done as thou hast commanded, and yet there is room.

23 And the lord said unto the servant, Go out into the highways and hedges, and compel them to come in, that my house may be filled.

24 For I say unto you, That none of those men which were bidden shall taste of my supper.

COUNTING THE COST

LUKE 14

:25 And there went great multitudes with him: and he turned, and said unto them,

26 If any man come to me, and hate not his father, and mother, and wife, and children, and brethren, and sisters, yea, and his own life also, he cannot be my disciple.

27 And whosoever doth not bear his cross, and come after me, cannot be my disciple.

28 For which of you, intending to build a tower, sitteth not down first, and counteth the cost, whether he have sufficient to finish it?

29 Lest haply, after he hath laid the foundation,

LUKE 14

and is not able to finish it, all that behold it begin to mock him,

30 Saying, This man began to build, and was not able to finish.

31 Or what king, going to make war against another king, sitteth not down first, and consulteth whether he be able with ten thousand to meet him that cometh against him with twenty thousand?

32 Or else, while the other is yet a great way off, he sendeth an ambassage, and desireth conditions of peace.

33 So likewise, whosoever he be of you that forsaketh not all that he hath, he cannot be my disciple.

LUKE 14

SALT CAN LOSE ITS SAVOR

:34 Salt is good: but if the salt have lost his savor, wherewith shall it be seasoned?

35 It is neither fit for the land, nor yet for the dunghill; but men cast it out. He that hath ears to hear, let him hear.

THE LOST SHEEP

LUKE 15

:1 Then drew near unto him all the publicans and sinners for to hear him.

2 And the Pharisees and scribes murmured, saying, This man receiveth sinners, and eateth with them.

3 And he spake this parable unto them, saying,

4 What man of you, having a hundred sheep, if he lose one of them, doth not leave the ninety and nine in the wilderness, and go after that which is lost, until he find it?

5 And when he hath found it, he layeth it on his shoulders, rejoicing.

6 And when he cometh home, he calleth together his friends and neighbors, saying unto them, Rejoice with me; for I have found my sheep which was lost.

7 I say unto you, that likewise joy shall be in heaven over one sinner that repenteth, more than over ninety and nine just persons, which need no repentance.

THE LOST COIN

LUKE 15 :8 Either what woman having ten pieces of silver, if she lose one piece, doth not light a candle, and sweep the house, and seek diligently till she find it?

9 And when she hath found it, she calleth her friends and her neighbors together, saying, Rejoice with me; for I have found the piece which I had lost.

10 Likewise, I say unto you, there is joy in the presence of the angels of God over one sinner that repenteth.

THE PRODIGAL SON

LUKE 15 :11 And he said, A certain man had two sons:

12 And the younger of them said to his father, Father, give me the portion of goods that falleth to me. And he divided unto them his living.

13 And not many days after the younger son gathered all together, and took his journey into a far country, and there wasted his substance with riotous living.

14 And when he had spent all, there arose a mighty famine in that land; and he began to be in want.

15 And he went and joined himself to a citizen of that country; and he sent him into his fields to feed swine.

16 And he would fain have filled his belly with the husks that the swine did eat: and no man gave unto him.

17 And when he came to himself, he said, How many hired servants of my father's have bread enough and to spare, and I perish with hunger!

18 I will arise and go to my father, and will say unto him, Father, I have sinned against heaven, and before thee,

19 And am no more worthy to be called thy son: make me as one of thy hired servants.

20 And he arose, and came to his father. But when he was yet a great way off, his father saw him, and had compassion, and ran, and fell on his neck, and kissed him.

21 And the son said unto him, Father, I have

sinned against heaven, and in thy sight, and am no more worthy to be called thy son.

22 But the father said to his servants, Bring forth the best robe, and put it on him; and put a ring on his hand, and shoes on his feet:

23 And bring hither the fatted calf, and kill it; and let us eat, and be merry:

24 For this my son was dead, and is alive again; he was lost, and is found. And they began to be merry.

25 Now his elder son was in the field: and as he came and drew nigh to the house, he heard music and dancing.

26 And he called one of the servants, and asked what these things meant.

27 And he said unto him, Thy brother is come; and thy father hath killed the fatted calf, because he hath received him safe and sound.

28 And he was angry, and would not go in: therefore came his father out, and entreated him.

29 And he answering said to his father, Lo, these many years do I serve thee, neither transgressed I at any time thy commandment; and yet thou never gavest me a kid, that I might make merry with my friends:

30 But as soon as this thy son was come, which hath devoured thy living with harlots, thou hast killed for him the fatted calf.

31 And he said unto him, Son, thou art ever with me, and all that I have is thine.

32 It was meet that we should make merry, and be glad: for this thy brother was dead, and is alive again; and was lost, and is found.

THE PARABLE OF THE DISHONEST STEWARD

:1 And he said also unto his disciples, There was a certain rich man, which had a steward; and the same was accused unto him that he had wasted his goods.

2 And he called him, and said unto him, How is it that I hear this of thee? give an account of thy stewardship; for thou mayest be no longer steward.

3 Then the steward said within himself, What

LUKE 16

shall I do? for my lord taketh away from me the stewardship: I cannot dig, to beg I am ashamed.

4 I am resolved what to do, that when I am put out of the stewardship, they may receive me into their houses.

5 So he called every one of his lord's debtors unto him, and said unto the first, How much owest thou unto my lord?

6 And he said, A hundred measures of oil. And he said unto him, Take thy bill, and sit down quickly, and write fifty.

7 Then said he to another, And how much owest thou? and he said, A hundred measures of wheat. And he said unto him, Take thy bill, and write fourscore.

8 And the lord commended the unjust steward, because he had done wisely: for the children of this world are in their generation wiser than the children of light.

9 And I say unto you, Make to yourselves friends of the mammon of unrighteousness; that, when ye fail, they may receive you into everlasting habitations.

10 He that is faithful in that which is least is faithful also in much: and he that is unjust in the least is unjust also in much.

11 If therefore ye have not been faithful in the unrighteous mammon, who will commit to your trust the true riches?

12 And if ye have not been faithful in that which is another man's, who shall give you that which is your own?

13 No servant can serve two masters: for either he will hate the one, and love the other; or else he will hold to the one, and despise the other. Ye cannot serve God and mammon.

14 And the Pharisees also, who were covetous, heard all these things: and they derided him.

15 And he said unto them, Ye are they which justify yourselves before men; but God knoweth your hearts: for that which is highly esteemed among men is abomination in the sight of God.

THE LAW AND THE KINGDOM OF GOD

LUKE 16 :16 The law and the prophets were until John: since that time the kingdom of God is preached, and every man presseth into it.

17 And it is easier for heaven and earth to pass, than one tittle of the law to fail.

DIVORCE AND REMARRIAGE

LUKE 16 :18 Whosoever putteth away his wife, and marrieth another, committeth adultery: and whosoever marrieth her that is put away from her husband committeth adultery.

THE RICH MAN AND LAZARUS

LUKE 16 :19 There was a certain rich man, which was clothed in purple and fine linen, and fared sumptuously every day:

20 And there was a certain beggar named Lazarus, which was laid at his gate, full of sores,

21 And desiring to be fed with the crumbs which fell from the rich man's table: moreover the dogs came and licked his sores.

22 And it came to pass, that the beggar died, and was carried by the angels into Abraham's bosom: the rich man also died, and was buried;

23 And in hell he lifted up his eyes, being in torments, and seeth Abraham afar off, and Lazarus in his bosom.

24 And he cried and said, Father Abraham, have mercy on me, and send Lazarus, that he may dip the tip of his finger in water, and cool my tongue; for I am tormented in this flame.

25 But Abraham said, Son, remember that thou in thy lifetime receivedst thy good things, and likewise Lazarus evil things: but now he is comforted, and thou art tormented.

26 And beside all this, between us and you there is a great gulf fixed: so that they which would pass from hence to you cannot; neither can they pass to us, that would come from thence.

27 Then he said, I pray thee therefore, father, that thou wouldest send him to my father's house:

LUKE 16

28 For I have five brethren; that he may testify unto them, lest they also come into this place of torment.

29 Abraham saith unto him, They have Moses and the prophets; let them hear them.

30 And he said, Nay, father Abraham: but if one went unto them from the dead, they will repent.

31 And he said unto him, If they hear not Moses and the prophets, neither will they be persuaded, though one rose from the dead.

OFFENSE WILL COME

LUKE 17

:1 Then said he unto the disciples, It is impossible but that offenses will come: but woe unto him, through whom they come!

2 It were better for him that a millstone were hanged about his neck, and he cast into the sea, than that he should offend one of these little ones.

3 Take heed to yourselves: If thy brother trespass against thee, rebuke him; and if he repent, forgive him.

4 And if he trespass against thee seven times in a day, and seven times in a day turn again to thee, saying, I repent; thou shalt forgive him.

MUSTARD SEED

LUKE 17

:5 And the apostles said unto the Lord, Increase our faith.

6 And the Lord said, If ye had faith as a grain of mustard seed, ye might say unto this sycamine tree, Be thou plucked up by the root, and be thou planted in the sea; and it should obey you.

WE ARE UNPROFITABLE SERVANTS

LUKE 17

:7 But which of you, having a servant plowing or feeding cattle, will say unto him by and by, when he is come from the field, Go and sit down to meat?

8 And will not rather say unto him, Make ready wherewith I may sup, and gird thyself, and serve me, till I have eaten and drunken; and afterward thou shalt eat and drink?

9 Doth he thank that servant because he did the things that were commanded him? I trow not.

LUKE 17

10 So likewise ye, when ye shall have done all those things which are commanded you, say, We are unprofitable servants: we have done that which was our duty to do.

JESUS CLEANSES TEN LEPERS

LUKE 17

:11 And it came to pass, as he went to Jerusalem, that he passed through the midst of Samaria and Galilee.

12 And as he entered into a certain village, there met him ten men that were lepers, which stood afar off:

13 And they lifted up their voices, and said, Jesus, Master, have mercy on us.

14 And when he saw them, he said unto them, Go show yourselves unto the priests. And it came to pass, that as they went, they were cleansed.

15 And one of them, when he saw that he was healed, turned back, and with a loud voice glorified God,

16 And fell down on his face at his feet, giving him thanks: and he was a Samaritan.

17 And Jesus answering said, Were there not ten cleansed? but where are the nine?

18 There are not found that returned to give glory to God, save this stranger.

19 And he said unto him, Arise, go thy way: thy faith hath made thee whole.

THE KINGDOM OF GOD IS WITHIN YOU

LUKE 17

:20 And when he was demanded of the Pharisees, when the kingdom of God should come, he answered them and said, The kingdom of God cometh not with observation:

21 Neither shall they say, Lo here! or, lo there! for, behold, the kingdom of God is within you.

22 And he said unto the disciples, The days will come, when ye shall desire to see one of the days of the Son of man, and ye shall not see it.

23 And they shall say to you, See here; or, see there: go not after them, nor follow them.

24 For as the lightning, that lighteneth out of the

Arranged As a Single Narrative

one part under heaven, shineth unto the other part under heaven; so shall also the Son of man be in his day.

LUKE 17

25 But first must he suffer many things, and be rejected of this generation.

AS IN THE DAYS OF NOAH

LUKE 17

:26 And as it was in the days of Noah, so shall it be also in the days of the Son of man.

27 They did eat, they drank, they married wives, they were given in marriage, until the day that Noah entered into the ark, and the flood came, and destroyed them all.

28 Likewise also as it was in the days of Lot; they did eat, they drank, they bought, they sold, they planted, they builded;

29 But the same day that Lot went out of Sodom it rained fire and brimstone from heaven, and destroyed them all.

30 Even thus shall it be in the day when the Son of man is revealed.

31 In that day, he which shall be upon the housetop, and his stuff in the house, let him not come down to take it away: and he that is in the field, let him likewise not return back.

32 Remember Lot's wife.

33 Whosoever shall seek to save his life shall lose it; and whosoever shall lose his life shall preserve it.

34 I tell you, in that night there shall be two men in one bed; the one shall be taken, and the other shall be left.

35 Two women shall be grinding together; the one shall be taken, and the other left.

36 Two men shall be in the field; the one shall be taken, and the other left.

[1]See Matt. 24:28 p. 180

37 And they answered and said unto him, Where, Lord? And he said unto them, [1]Wheresoever the body is, thither will the eagles be gathered together.

THE WIDOW AND THE UNJUST JUDGE

LUKE 18

:1 And he spake a parable unto them to this end, that men ought always to pray, and not to faint;

LUKE 18

2 Saying, There was in a city a judge, which feared not God, neither regarded man:

3 And there was a widow in that city; and she came unto him, saying, Avenge me of mine adversary.

4 And he would not for a while: but afterward he said within himself, Though I fear not God, nor regard man;

5 Yet because this widow troubleth me, I will avenge her, lest by her continual coming she weary me.

6 And the Lord said, Hear what the unjust judge saith.

7 And shall not God avenge his own elect, which cry day and night unto him, though he bear long with them?

8 I tell you that he will avenge them speedily. Nevertheless, when the Son of man cometh, shall he find faith on the earth?

THE PHARISEE AND THE PUBLICAN

LUKE 18

:9 And he spake this parable unto certain which trusted in themselves that they were righteous, and despised others:

10 Two men went up into the temple to pray; the one a Pharisee, and the other a publican.

11 The Pharisee stood and prayed thus with himself, God, I thank thee, that I am not as other men are, extortioners, unjust, adulterers, or even as this publican.

12 I fast twice in the week, I give tithes of all that I possess.

13 And the publican, standing afar off, would not lift up so much as his eyes unto heaven, but smote upon his breast, saying, God be merciful to me a sinner.

14 I tell you, this man went down to his house justified rather than the other: for every one that exalteth himself shall be abased; and he that humbleth himself shall be exalted.

JESUS BLESSES LITTLE CHILDREN

MARK 10
[1] Luke 18:15 infants
[2] Matt. 19:13

:13 And they brought young [1]*children to him,* [2]*that he should put his hands on them, and pray:* that he should touch them; and his disciples rebuked those that brought them.

[3] Luke 18:16

14 But when Jesus saw it, he was much displeased, [and] [3]*called them unto him,* and said unto them, Suffer the little children to come unto me

[4] Matt. 19:14
[5] Matt. 19:14 heaven

and forbid them not [4]*to come unto me;* for of such is the kingdom of [5]God.

15 Verily I say unto you, Whosoever shall not receive the kingdom of God as a little child, he shall

[6] Luke 18:17 in no wise
[7] Matt. 19:15

[6]not enter therein.

16 And he took them up in his arms, put his hands upon them, and blessed them, [7]*and departed thence.*

THE RICH YOUNG RULER

MATT. 19
[1] Mark 10:17

:16 And, [1]*when he was gone forth into the way,* behold [1]*there came one running, and kneeling to him* said unto him, Good Master, What good thing shall I do, that I may [2]*have eternal life?*

[2] Luke 18:18 inherit

17 And he said unto him, Why callest thou me good? there is none good but one, that is, God: but if thou wilt enter into life, keep the commandments.

[3] Luke 18:20

18 He saith unto him, Which? Jesus said, [3]*Thou knowest the commandments.* Thou shalt do no murder, Thou shalt not commit adultery, Thou shalt not steal, Thou shalt not bear false witness.

19 Honor thy father and thy mother: and, Thou shalt love thy neighbor as thyself.

[4] Mark 10:20 observed
[5] Luke 18:22
[6] Mark 10:21

20 The young man saith unto him, All these things have I [4]kept from my youth up: what lack I yet? [5]*Now when Jesus heard these things,* [6]*Then Jesus beholding him loved him, and said unto him, One thing thou lackest.*

[7] Mark 10:21

21 ... If thou wilt be perfect, go [7]*thy way* and sell [7]*whatsoever* thou hast, and give to the poor, and thou shalt have treasure in heaven: and come [7]*take up the cross* and follow me.

[8] Mark 10:22
[9] Mark 10:22 grieved

22 But when the young man heard that saying, [8]*was sad,* and he went away [9]sorrowful: for he had great possessions.

MATT. 19
[10]Luke 18:24
[11]Mark 10:23
[12]Luke 18:24
they that have riches
[13]Mark 10:24

23 [10]*And when Jesus saw that he was very sorrowful,* [11]*Jesus looked round about, and saith,* unto his disciples, Verily I say unto you [12]that a rich man shall hardly enter into the kingdom of heaven. [13]*And the disciples were astonished at his words. But Jesus answereth again, and saith unto them, Children, how hard is it for them that* [12]*trust*[13] *in riches to enter into the kingdom of God!*

24 And again I say unto you, It is easier for a camel to go through the eye of a needle, than for a rich man to enter into the kingdom of God.

[14]Mark 10:26
astonished
out of
measure
[15]Mark 10:27

26 When his disciples heard it, they were exceedingly [14]amazed, saying, Who then can be saved?

26 But Jesus beheld them, and said unto them, With men this is impossible; but [15]*not* with God, [15]*for with God* all things are possible.

27 Then answered Peter and said unto him, Behold, we have forsaken all, and followed thee; what shall we have therefore?

28 And Jesus said unto them, Verily I say unto you, That ye which have followed me, in the regeneration when the Son of man shall sit in the throne of his glory, ye also shall sit upon twelve thrones, judging the twelve tribes of Israel.

[16]Mark 10:29
[17]Luke 18:30
manifold more
[18]Mark 10:30

29 And every one that hath forsaken houses, or brethren, or sisters, or father, or mother, or wife, or children, or lands, for my name's sake, [16]*and the gospel's,* shall receive [17]a hundredfold, [18]*now in this time, houses, and brethren, and sisters, and mothers, and children, and lands, with persecutions; and in the world to come* inherit everlasting life.

30 But many that are first shall be last; and the last shall be first.

LABORERS IN THE VINEYARD

MATT. 20

:1 For the kingdom of heaven is like unto a man that is a householder, which went out early in the morning to hire laborers into his vineyard.

2 And when he had agreed with the laborers for a penny a day, he sent them into his vineyard.

3 And he went out about the third hour, and saw others standing idle in the market place,

MATT. 20

4 And said unto them; Go ye also into the vineyard, and whatsoever is right I will give you. And they went their way.

5 Again he went out about the sixth and ninth hour, and did likewise.

6 And about the eleventh hour he went out, and found others standing idle, and saith unto them, Why stand ye here all the day idle?

7 They say unto him, Because no man hath hired us. He saith unto them, Go ye also into the vineyard; and whatsoever is right, that shall ye receive.

8 So when even was come the lord of the vineyard saith unto his steward, Call the laborers, and give them their hire, beginning from the last unto the first.

9 And when they came that were hired about the eleventh hour, they received every man a penny.

10 But when the first came, they supposed that they should have received more; and they likewise received every man a penny.

11 And when they had received it, they murmured against the goodman of the house.

12 Saying, These last have wrought but one hour, and thou hast made them equal unto us, which have borne the burden and heat of the day.

13 But he answered one of them, and said, Friend, I do thee no wrong: didst not thou agree with me for a penny?

14 Take that thine is, and go thy way: I will give unto this last, even as unto thee.

15 Is it not lawful for me to do what I will with mine own? Is thine eye evil, because I am good?

16 So the last shall be first, and the first last: for many be called, but few are chosen.

JESUS FORETELLS HIS DEATH
A THIRD TIME

MARK 10

:32 And they were in the way going up to Jerusalem; and Jesus went before them: and they were amazed; and as they followed, they were afraid. And he took again the twelve, and began to tell them

[1]Luke 18:31 what things should happen unto him, [1]*all things that*

are written by the prophets concerning the Son of man shall be accomplished.

MARK 10
[2] Matt. 20:18
betrayed

33 Saying, Behold, we go up to Jerusalem; and the Son of man shall be [2]delivered unto the chief priests, and unto the scribes; and they shall condemn him to death, and shall deliver him to the Gentiles:

[3] Luke 18:32
[4] Luke 18:33
put him to death
Matt. 20:19
crucify
[5] Luke 18:34

34 And they shall mock him, [3]*and be spitefully entreated* and shall scourge him, and shall spit upon him, and shall [4]kill him; and the third day he shall rise again. [5]*And they understood none of these things: and this saying was hid from them, neither knew they the things which were spoken.*

THE REQUEST OF JAMES AND JOHN

MATT. 20

:20 Then came to him the mother of Zeb'edee's children with her sons, worshipping him, and desiring a certain thing of him.

21 And he said unto her, What wilt thou? She saith unto him, grant that these my two sons may sit, the one on thy right hand, and the other on the left, in thy kingdom. [1]*And James and John* [also said,] [1]*Master, we would that thou shouldest do for us whatsoever we shall desire.* [2]*And he said unto them, What would ye that I should do for you?* [3]*They said unto him, Grant unto us that we may sit, one on thy right hand, and the other on thy left hand, in thy glory.*

[1] Mark 10:35

[2] Mark 10:36

[3] Mark 10:37

22 But Jesus answered and said, Ye know not what ye ask. Are ye able to drink of the cup that I shall drink of, and to be baptized with the baptism that I am baptized with? They say unto him, [4]We are able.

[4] Mark 10:39
We Can

23 And he saith unto them, Ye shall drink indeed of my cup, and be baptized with the baptism that I am baptized with: but to sit on my right hand, and on my left, is not mine to give, but it shall be given to them for whom it is prepared of my Father.

[5] Mark 10:41
much displeased with James and John

24 And when the ten heard it, they were moved with [5]indignation against the two brethren.

25 But Jesus called them unto him, and said, Ye

ARRANGED AS A SINGLE NARRATIVE

MATT. 20
⁶Mark 10:42
they which are accounted to rule over
⁷lordship
⁸Mark 10:42
⁹Mark 10:44
servant of all

know that ⁶the princes of the Gentiles exercise ⁷dominion over them, and they that are great ⁸*ones* exercise authority upon them.

26 But it shall not be so among you: but whosoever will be great among you, let him be your minister;

27 And whosoever will be chief among you, let him be your ⁹servant:

28 Even as the Son of man came not to be ministered unto, but to minister, and to give his life a ransom for many.

A BLIND BEGGAR HEALED NEAR JERICHO*

LUKE 18

:35 And it came to pass, that as he was come nigh unto Jericho, a certain blind man sat by the wayside begging:

36 And hearing the multitude pass by, he asked what it meant.

37 And they told him, that Jesus of Nazareth passeth by.

38 And he cried, saying, Jesus, thou Son of David, have mercy on me.

39 And they which went before rebuked him, that he should hold his peace: but he cried so much the more, Thou Son of David, have mercy on me.

40 And Jesus stood, and commanded him to be brought unto him: and when he was come near, he asked him,

41 Saying, What wilt thou that I shall do unto thee? And he said, Lord, that I may receive my sight.

42 And Jesus said unto him, Receive thy sight: thy faith hath saved thee.

---

*On this journey to Jerusalem we have three recordings of Jesus healing the blind as follows: Luke 18:25-43, a blind beggar is healed near Jericho; Matt. 20:29-34, two blind men sitting by the wayside as they "departed from Jericho", and Mark 10:46-52 gives the account of blind Bartimeus. There can be no question about the account given by Luke that this man was not the one mentioned by Mark and Matthew. These accounts are followed in Luke 19:1-28 by the narrative of Zacchaeus and the parable of the nobleman who went into a far country. It is my opinion that all these are different accounts of healing. The scripture is consistent in each case, in the account of healing of the two blind men Matthew speaks of them always in the plural, as "they, them, us, our, and their". Mark always speaks of blind Bartimeus in the singular: "he, me, him, his, the blind man, I and my."

LUKE 18

¹Mark 10:46

43 And immediately he received his sight, and followed him, glorifying God: and all the people, when they saw it, gave praise unto God. ¹*And they came to Jericho.*

TWO BLIND MEN RECEIVE SIGHT

MATT. 20

:29 And as they departed from Jericho, a great multitude followed him.

30 And, behold, two blind men sitting by the wayside, when they heard that Jesus passed by, cried out, saying, Have mercy on us, O Lord, thou Son of David.

31 And the multitude rebuked them, because they should hold their peace: but they cried the more, saying, Have mercy on us, O Lord, thou Son of David.

32 And Jesus stood still, and called them and said, What will ye that I shall do unto you?

33 They say unto him, Lord, that our eyes may be opened.

34 So Jesus had compassion on them, and touched their eyes: and immediately their eyes received sight, and they followed him.

BLIND BARTIMEUS RECEIVES SIGHT

MARK 10

:46 . . . and as he went out of Jericho with his disciples and a great number of people, blind Bartime'us, the son of Time'us, sat by the highway side begging.

47 And when he heard that it was Jesus of Nazareth, he began to cry out, and say, Jesus, thou Son of David, have mercy on me.

48 And many charged him that he should hold his peace: but he cried the more a great deal, Thou Son of David, have mercy on me.

49 And Jesus stood still, and commanded him to be called. And they call the blind man, saying unto him, Be of good comfort, rise; he calleth thee.

50 And he, casting away his garment, rose, and came to Jesus.

51 And Jesus answered and said unto him, What

MARK 10

wilt thou that I should do unto thee? The blind man said unto him, Lord, that I might receive my sight.

52 And Jesus said unto him, Go thy way; thy faith hath made thee whole. And immediately he received his sight, and followed Jesus in the way.

JESUS AND ZACCHEUS

LUKE 19

:1 And Jesus entered and passed through Jericho.

2 And, behold, there was a man named Zacche'us, which was the chief among the publicans, and he was rich.

3 And he sought to see Jesus who he was; and could not for the press, because he was little of stature.

4 And he ran before, and climbed up into a sycamore tree to see him; for he was to pass that way.

5 And when Jesus came to the place, he looked up, and saw him, and said unto him, Zacche'us, make haste, and come down; for today I must abide at thy house.

6 And he made haste, and came down, and received him joyfully.

7 And when they saw it, they all murmured, saying, That he was gone to be guest with a man that is a sinner.

8 And Zacche'us stood, and said unto the Lord; Behold, Lord, the half of my goods I give to the poor; and if I have taken anything from any man by false accusation, I restore him fourfold.

9 And Jesus said unto him, This day is salvation come to this house, forasmuch as he also is a son of Abraham.

10 For the Son of man is come to seek and to save that which was lost.

THE PARABLE OF THE NOBLEMAN AND THE TEN SERVANTS

LUKE 19

:11 And as they heard these things, he added and spake a parable, because he was nigh to Jerusalem, and because they thought that the kingdom of God should immediately appear.

LUKE 19

12 He said therefore, A certain nobleman went into a far country to receive for himself a kingdom, and to return.

13 And he called his ten servants, and delivered them ten pounds, and said unto them, Occupy till I come.

14 But his citizens hated him, and sent a message after him, saying, We will not have this man to reign over us.

15 And it came to pass, that when he was returned, having received the kingdom, then he commanded these servants to be called unto him, to whom he had given the money, that he might know how much every man had gained by trading.

16 Then came the first, saying, Lord thy pound hath gained ten pounds.

17 And he said unto him, Well, thou good servant: because thou hast been faithful in a very little, have thou authority over ten cities.

18 And the second came, saying, Lord, thy pound hath gained five pounds.

19 And he said likewise to him, Be thou also over five cities.

20 And another came, saying, Lord, behold, here is thy pound, which I have kept laid up in a napkin:

21 For I feared thee, because thou art an austere man: thou takest up that thou layedst not down, and reapest that thou didst not sow.

22 And he saith unto him, Out of thine own mouth will I judge thee, thou wicked servant. Thou knewest that I was an austere man, taking up that I laid not down, and reaping that I did not sow:

23 Wherefore then gavest not thou my money into the bank, that at my coming I might have required mine own with usury?

24 And he said unto them that stood by, Take from him the pound, and give it to him that hath ten pounds.

25 (And they said unto him, Lord, he hath ten pounds.)

26 For I say unto you, That unto every one which hath shall be given; and from him that hath not, even that he hath shall be taken away from him.

ARRANGED AS A SINGLE NARRATIVE

LUKE 19

27 But those mine enemies, which would not that I should reign over them, bring hither, and slay them before me.

28 And when he had thus spoken, he went before, ascending up to Jerusalem.

JESUS ANOINTED AT BETHANY*

JOHN 12

:1 Then Jesus six days before the passover came to Bethany, where Lazarus was which had been dead, whom he raised from the dead.

2 There they made him a supper; and Martha served: but Lazarus was one of them that sat at the table with him.

3 Then took Mary a pound of ointment of spikenard, very costly, and anointed the feet of Jesus, and wiped his feet with her hair: and the house was filled with the odor of the ointment.

4 Then saith one of his disciples, Judas Iscar'i-ot, Simon's son, which should betray him,

5 Why was not this ointment sold for three hundred pence, and given to the poor?

6 This he said, not that he cared for the poor; but because he was a thief, and had the bag, and bare that was put therein.

7 Then said Jesus, Let her alone: against the day of my burying hath she kept this.

8 For the poor always ye have with you; but me ye have not always.

---

* The account of Jesus being anointed at Bethany in Mark and Matthew is so similar to this account in John that they would appear to be the same, but there are statements which make it clear that they are not the same. Mark and Matthew clearly state that the one they refer to was in the house of Simon, the leper, and that it was two days before the passover. They do not state who the woman was. John does not positively say where, but the context seems to imply that it took place in the home of Mary and Martha, and clearly declares it was Mary who anointed His feet, while Mark and Matthew say the anointing was on the head. Furthermore, John declares the time to be six days before the feast and in chapter 12, verse 12, he says "the next day" was the triumphal entry. The dating of the two events would necessarily make them different anointings.

THE PLOT AGAINST LAZARUS

JOHN 12

:9 Much people of the Jews therefore knew that he was there: and they came not for Jesus' sake only, but that they might see Lazarus also, whom he had raised from the dead.

10 But the chief priests consulted that they might put Lazarus also to death;

11 Because that by reason of him many of the Jews went away, and believed on Jesus.

THE TRIUMPHAL ENTRY INTO JERUSALEM

LUKE 19
[1] John 12:12
[2] Mark 11:1

:29 [1]*On the next day,* it came to pass, when he was come nigh to [2]*Jerusalem unto* Bethphage and Bethany, at the mount called the mount of Olives, he sent two of his disciples,

[3] Mark 11:2
[4] Matt. 21:2

30 Saying, [3]*Go your way,* into the village over against you; in the which at your entering ye [4]*shall find an ass tied and* a colt tied [4]*with her,* whereon yet never man sat: loose him, and bring [5]him hither.

[5] Matt. 21:2 them

[6] Mark 11:3

31 And if any man ask you, Why do ye loose him? thus shall ye say unto him, Because the Lord hath need of him, [6]*and straightway he will send him hither.*

[7] Mark 11:4

32 And they that were sent went their way, and found [7]*the colt tied by the door without in a place where two ways met;* even as he had said unto them.

[8] Mark 11:5 and certain of them that stood there

[9] Mark 11:6

[10] Matt. 21:7

33 And as they were loosing the colt, the [8]owners thereof said unto them, Why loose ye the colt?

34 And they said [9]*unto them even as Jesus had commanded* The Lord hath need of him: [9]*and they let them go.*

35 And they brought [10]*the ass and the colt* to Jesus: and they cast their garments upon the colt, and they set Jesus thereon,

JOHN 12

:12 . . . *Much people that were come to the feast, when they heard that Jesus was coming to Jerusalem,

13 Took branches of palm trees and went forth to

---

*Note John 12:12. This was before Christ begins his Triumphal Entry. John 12:37-38 is during the procession.

meet him, and cried, Hosanna: Blessed is the King of Israel that cometh in the name of the Lord.

MATT. 21

:4 All this was done, that it might be fulfilled which was spoken by the prophet, saying,

5 Tell ye the daughter of Zion, Behold, thy King cometh unto thee, meek, and sitting upon an ass, and a colt the foal of an ass.

JOHN 12

:16 These things understood not his disciples at the first: but when Jesus was glorified, then remembered they that these things were written of him, and that they had done these things unto him.

17 The people therefore that was with him when he called Lazarus out of his grave, and raised him from the dead, bare record.

18 For this cause the people also met him, for that they heard that he had done this miracle.

LUKE 19
[11]Mark 11:8
many
[12]garments
[13]Mark 11:8

[14]Matt. 2:19

[15]Mark 11:9
[16]John 12:13
[17]Mark 11:10

:36 ... as he went, [11]they spread their [12]clothes in the way [13]*and others cut down branches off the trees, and strewed them in the way.*

37 And when he was come nigh, even now at the descent of the mount of Olives, the whole multitude of the disciples, [14]*that went before and that followed*, began to rejoice and praise God with a loud voice for all the mighty works that they had seen;

38 Saying, [15]*Hosanna*, Blessed be the King [16]*of Israel* that cometh in the name of the Lord: [17]*Blessed be the kingdom of our Father David, that cometh in the name of the Lord: Hosanna in the highest*, peace in heaven, and glory in the highest.

39 And some of the Pharisees from among the multitude said unto him, Master, rebuke thy disciples.

40 And he answered and said unto them, I tell you that if these should hold their peace, the stones would immediately cry out.

41 And when he was come near, he beheld the city, and wept over it,

42 Saying, If thou hadst known, even thou, at least in this day, the things which belong unto thy peace! but now they are hid from thine eyes.

43 For the days shall come upon thee, that thine

enemies shall cast a trench about thee, and compass thee round, and keep thee in on every side,

44 And shall lay thee even with the ground, and thy children with thee; and they shall not leave in thee one stone upon another; because thou knewest not the time of thy visitation.

MATT. 21 :10 And when he was come into Jerusalem, all the city was moved, saying, Who is this?

11 And the multitude said, This is Jesus the prophet of Nazareth of Galilee.

JOHN 12 :19 The Pharisees therefore said among themselves, Perceive ye how ye prevail nothing? behold, the world is gone after him.

MARK 11 :11 And Jesus entered into Jerusalem, and into the temple: and when he had looked round about upon all things, and now the eventide was come, he went out unto Bethany with the twelve.

THE CURSING OF THE FIG TREE

MATT. 21 :18 Now in the morning, as he returned into the city, *¹from Bethany,* he hungered.
¹Mark 11:12
²Mark 11:13

19 And when he saw a fig tree *²afar off having leaves* he came to it, *²if haply he might find any thing thereon: and when he came to it,* and found nothing thereon, but leaves only, *²for the time of figs was not yet,* said unto it, ³Let no fruit grow on thee hence forward for ever. And presently the fig tree withered away.

³Mark 11:14
No man eat fruit of thee hereafter for ever.
⁴Mark 11:14

20 And when the disciples ⁴*heard it and* saw it, they marveled, saying How soon is the fig tree withered away!

21 Jesus answered and said unto them, Verily I say unto you, If ye have faith, and doubt not, ye shall not only do this which is done to the fig tree, but also if ye shall say unto this mountain, Be thou removed, and be thou cast into the sea; it shall be done.

22 And all things, whatsoever ye shall ask in prayer, believing, ye shall receive.

THE CLEANSING OF THE TEMPLE

MATT. 21

¹Mark 11:15

²Mark 11:16

³Mark 11:17 taught
⁴Mark 11:17

:12 ¹*And they come to Jerusalem,* And Jesus went into the temple of God, and ¹*began to* cast out all of them that sold and bought in the temple, and overthrew the tables of the money changers, and the seats of them that sold doves, ²*And would not suffer that any man should carry any vessel through the temple.*

13 And ³said unto them, It is written, My house shall be called ⁴*of all nations* the house of prayer; but ye have made it a den of thieves.

14 And the blind and the lame came to him in the temple; and he healed them.

15 And when the chief priests and scribes saw the wonderful things that he did, and the children crying in the temple, and saying, Hosanna to the Son of David; they were sore displeased.

16 And said unto him, Hearest thou what these say? And Jesus saith unto them, Yea; have ye never read, Out of the mouth of babes and sucklings thou hast perfected praise? ⁵*And the scribes and chief priests heard it, and sought how they might destroy him; for they feared him, because all the people was astonished at his doctrine.* ⁶*And could not find what they might do: for all the people were very attentive to hear him.*

⁵Mark 11:18

⁶Luke 19:48

17 And he left them, and went out of the city into Bethany; and he lodged there.

THE LESSON FROM THE WITHERED FIG TREE

MARK 11

:20 And in the morning, as they passed by, they saw the fig tree dried up from the roots.

21 And Peter calling to remembrance saith unto him, Master, behold, the fig tree which thou cursedst is withered away.

22 And Jesus answering saith unto them, Have faith in God.

23 For verily I say unto you, That whosoever shall say unto this mountain be thou removed, and be thou cast into the sea; and shall not doubt in his heart, but shall believe that those things which he

saith shall come to pass; he shall have whatsoever he saith.

MARK 11

24 Therefore I say unto you, What things soever ye desire, when ye pray, believe that ye receive them, and ye shall have them.

25 And when ye stand praying, forgive, if ye have aught against any; that your Father also which is in heaven may forgive you your trespasses.

26 But if ye do not forgive, neither will your Father which is in heaven forgive your trespasses.

JESUS' AUTHORITY QUESTIONED

LUKE 20
[1] Matt. 21:23
[2] Mark 11:27

:1 And *when he was come **again** into the temple*, he taught the people, and preached the gospel. *As he was walking in the temple* the chief priests and the scribes came upon him with the elders.

2 And spake unto him, saying, Tell us, by what authority doest thou these things? or who is he that gave thee this authority?

[3] Mark 11:29
[4] Matt. 21:24

3 And *Jesus* answered and said unto them, I will also ask you one thing; *which if ye tell me, I in like wise will tell you by what authority I do these things*, answer me:

[5] Matt. 21:25
[6] Mark 11:30

4 The baptism of John *whence was it?* was it from heaven, or of men? *answer me.*

5 And they reasoned with themselves, saying, If we shall say, From heaven; he will say *unto us*, Why *did ye not then believe him?*

[7] Mark 11:32
[8] Matt. 21:26

6 But and if we *shall* say, Of men; *we fear the people* will stone us: for they be persuaded that John was a prophet, *indeed*.

7 And they answered, *and said unto Jesus* that they could not tell whence it was.

[9] Mark 11:33

8 And Jesus said unto them, Neither tell I you by what authority I do these things.

THE PARABLE OF THE TWO SONS

MATT. 21

:28 But what think ye? A certain man had two sons; and he came to the first, and said, Son, go work today in my vineyard.

ARRANGED AS A SINGLE NARRATIVE   167

MATT. 21

29 He answered and said, I will not; but afterward he repented, and went.

30 And he came to the second, and said likewise. And he answered and said, I go, sir; and went not.

31 Whether of them twain did the will of his father: They say unto him, The first. Jesus saith unto them, Verily I say unto you, That the publicans and the harlots go into the kingdom before you.

32 For John came unto you in the way of righteousness, and ye believed him not; but the publicans and the harlots believed him: and ye, when ye had seen it, repented not afterward, that ye might believe him.

THE PARABLE OF THE WICKED HUSBANDMEN

MATT. 21
[1]Mark 12:1

[2]Luke 20:9

[3]Mark 12:2
 season
[4]Mark 12:2
[5]Luke 20:10
[6]Matt. 21:36
 more than
 the first
[7]Mark 12:4
[8]Mark 12:5
[9]Luke 20:12
 a third

LUKE 20
[10]Mark 12:6
[11]Matt. 21:37
 But last of
 all he sent
 his son

:33 [1]*And he began to speak unto them by parables*, and said Hear another parable: There was a certain householder, which planted a vineyard, and hedged it round about, and digged a [1]*place for the winepress* in it, and built a tower, and let it out to husbandmen, and went into a far country [2]*for a long time*.

34 And when the [3]time of the fruit drew near, he sent his servants to the husbandmen, that they might receive the fruits of [4]*the vineyard*.

35 And the husbandmen took his *servants, and beat one, [5]*and sent him away empty*, and stoned another. [7]*And again he sent unto them* [6]*another servant; and at him they cast stones, and wounded him in the head, and sent him away shamefully handled.* [8]*And again he sent* [9]*another; and him they killed, and many others; beating some, and killing some.*

:13 Then said the lord of the vineyard, [10]*having yet therefore one son*, What shall I do? [11]I will send my beloved son: it may be they will reverence him when they see him.

---

*Servants — It appears from the other gospels that there was one servant, here it is in the plural, yet followed by the singular. It could be assumed that the one spoken of was the one in charge of the mission who had several assistants.

MATT. 21
[12] Luke 20:14
[13] Mark 12:7
the inheritance will be ours

:38 But when the husbandmen saw the son, they [12]*reasoned* among themselves [12]*saying,* This is the heir; come, let us kill him, [13]and let us seize on his inheritance.

39 And they caught him, and cast him out of the vineyard, and slew him.

40 When the lord therefore of the vineyard cometh, what will he do unto those husbandmen?

41 They say unto him, He will miserably destroy those wicked men, and will let out his vineyard unto other husbandmen, which shall render him the fruits in their seasons. [14]*God forbid.*

[14] Luke 20:16
[15] Luke 20:17

42 Jesus saith unto them, [15]*What is this then that is written?* Did ye never read in the Scriptures, The stone which the builders rejected, the same is become the head of the corner: this is the Lord's doing, and it is marvelous in our eyes?

43 Therefore say I unto you, The kingdom of God shall be taken from you, and given to a nation bringing forth the fruits thereof.

44 And whosoever shall fall on this stone shall be broken: but on whomsoever it shall fall, it will grind him to powder.

45 And when the chief priests and Pharisees had heard his parables, they perceived that he spake of them.

46 But when they sought to lay hands on him, they feared the multitude, because they took him for a prophet [16]*and they left him, and went their way.*

[16] Mark 12:12

THE PARABLE OF THE MARRIAGE FEAST*

MATT. 22

:1 And Jesus answered and spake unto them again by parables, and said,

2 The kingdom of heaven is like unto a certain king, which made a marriage for his son,

3 And sent forth his servants to call them that were bidden to the wedding: and they would not come.

---

*This is not to be confused with Luke 14:16 which was given on the way to Jerusalem. This one in Matthew was given after the triumphal entry, apparently while in the Temple.

ARRANGED AS A SINGLE NARRATIVE

MATT. 22

4 Again, he sent forth other servants, saying, Tell them which are bidden, Behold, I have prepared my dinner: my oxen and my fatlings are killed, and all things are ready: come unto the marriage.

5 But they made light of it, and went their ways, one to his farm, another to his merchandise:

6 And the remnant took his servants, and entreated them spitefully, and slew them.

7 But when the king heard thereof, he was wroth: and he sent forth his armies, and destroyed those murderers, and burned up their city.

8 Then saith he to his servants, The wedding is ready, but they which were bidden were not worthy.

9 Go ye therefore into the highways, and as many as ye shall find, bid to the marriage.

10 So those servants went out into the highways, and gathered together all as many as they found, both bad and good: and the wedding was furnished with guests.

11 And when the king came in to see the guests, he saw there a man which had not on a wedding garment:

12 And he saith unto him, Friend, how camest thou in hither not having a wedding garment? And he was speechless.

13 Then said the king to the servants, Bind him hand and foot, and take him away, and cast him into outer darkness; there shall be weeping and gnashing of teeth.

14 For many are called, but few are chosen.

PAYING TAXES TO CAESAR

MATT. 22

:15 Then went the Pharisees, and took counsel how they might entangle him in his talk.

[1]Luke 20:20
[2]Luke 20:20 spies
[3]Mark 12:13

16 [1]*And they watched him,* And they sent out unto him [2]*their disciples* [and] [3]*Pharisees* with the Hero'di-ans, [1]*which should feign themselves just men, that they might take hold of his words, that so they might deliver him unto the power and authority of the governor,* saying, Master, we know that thou art true, and teachest the way of God in truth, neither carest thou for any man: for thou regardest not the person of men.

MATT. 22

[4]Mark 12:15
[5]Luke 20:23
craftiness

17 Tell us therefore, What thinkest thou? Is it lawful to give tribute unto Caesar, or not? [4]*Shall we give or shall we not give?*

18 But Jesus perceived their [5]*wickedness,* [4]*knowing their hypocrisy* and said, Why tempt ye me, ye hypocrites?

19 Show me the tribute money. And they brought him a penny.

20 And he saith unto them, Whose is this image and superscription?

21 They say unto him, Caesar's. Then saith he unto them, Render therefore unto Caesar the things which are Caesar's; and unto God the things that are God's.

[6]Luke 20:26

22 [6]*And they could not take hold of his words before the people: and they marveled at his answer, and held their peace,* and left him, and went their way.

THE QUESTION ABOUT THE RESURRECTION

LUKE 20
[1]Matt. 22:23

:27 Then came to him [1]*the same day* certain of the Sadducees, which deny that there is any resurrection; and they asked him,

28 Saying, Master, Moses wrote unto us, If any man's brother die, having a wife, and he die without children, that his brother should take his wife, and raise up seed unto his brother.

[2]Matt. 22:25

29 There were therefore seven brethren: and the first took a wife, and died without children and [2]*left his wife unto his brother.*

30 And the second took her to wife, and he died childless.

31 And the third took her; and in like manner the seven also: and they left no children, and died.

32 Last of all the woman died also.

[3]Mark 12:23

33 Therefore in the resurrection [3]*when they shall rise,* whose wife of them is she? for seven had her to wife.

[4]Matt. 22:29

34 And Jesus answering said unto them, [4]*ye do err, not knowing the Scriptures, nor the power of God.* The children of this world marry, and are given in marriage:

ARRANGED AS A SINGLE NARRATIVE

LUKE 20

⁵Matt. 22:30

⁶Mark 12:26

⁷Mark 12:27

⁸Matt. 22:33

35 But they which shall be accounted worthy to obtain that world, and the resurrection from the dead, neither marry, nor are given in marriage:

36 Neither can they die any more: for they are equal unto the angels ⁵*of God in heaven*, and are the children of God, being children of the resurrection. ⁶*And as touching the dead, that they rise; have ye not read in the book of Moses, how in the bush God spake unto him, saying, I am the God of Abraham, and the God of Isaac, and the God of Jacob?*

38 For he is not a God of the dead, but of the living: for all live unto him, ⁷*ye therefore do greatly err.*

39 Then certain of the scribes answering said, Master, thou hast well said. ⁸*And when the multitude heard this, they were astonished at his doctrine.*

40 And after that they* durst not ask him any question at all.

THE GREAT COMMANDMENT

MARK 12
¹Matt. 22:34
²Matt. 22:35

³Matt. 22:36
⁴Matt. 22:36
in the law

⁵Matt. 22:39

⁶Matt. 22:40

:28 ¹*But when the Pharisees had heard that he had put the Sadducees to silence, they were gathered together.* And one of the scribes ²*which was a lawyer* came, and having heard them reasoning together, and perceiving that he had answered them well, asked him, ²*a question, tempting him, and saying,* ³*Master,* which is the first commandment of ⁴*all?*

29 And Jesus answered him, The first of all the commandments is, Hear, O Israel; The Lord our God is one Lord:

30 And thou shalt love the Lord thy God with all thy heart, and with all thy soul, and with all thy mind, and with all thy strength: this is the first commandment.

31 And the second is like ⁵*unto it*, namely this, Thou shalt love thy neighbor as thyself. There is none other commandment greater than these. ⁶*On these two commandments hang all the law, and the prophets.*

32 And the scribe said unto him, Well, Master,

*Only the Sadducees asked him no more questions.

MARK 12

thou hast said the truth: for there is one God; and there is none other but he:

33 And to love him with all the heart, and with all the understanding, and with all the soul, and with all the strength, and to love his neighbor as himself, is more than all whole burnt offerings and sacrifices.

34 And when Jesus saw that he answered discreetly, he said unto him, Thou art not far from the kingdom of God.

THE QUESTION ABOUT DAVID'S SON

MATT. 22
¹Mark 12:35

²Mark 12:36
by the Holy Ghost
³Luke 20:42

⁴Mark 12:37

:41 While the Pharisees were gathered together, [and] ¹*he taught in the temple,* Jesus asked them,

42 Saying, What think ye of Christ? whose son is he? They say unto him, The son of David.

43 He saith unto them, How then doth David in ²spirit ³*in the book of Psalms,* call him Lord, saying,

44 The Lord said unto my Lord, Sit thou on my right hand, till I make thine enemies thy footstool?

45 If David then call him Lord, how is he his son? ⁴*And the common people heard him gladly.*

46 And no man was able to answer him a word, neither durst any man from that day forth ask him any more questions.

JESUS DENOUNCES THE SCRIBES AND PHARISEES

MATT. 23

¹Luke 20:46

²Mark 12:38

:1 Then spake Jesus to the multitude, and to his disciples,

2 Saying, ¹*Beware* the scribes and the Pharisees sit in Moses' seat:

3 All therefore whatsoever they bid you observe, that observe and do; but do not ye after their works: for they say, and do not.

4 For they bind heavy burdens and grievous to be born, and lay them on men's shoulders; but they themselves will not move them with one of their fingers.

5 But all their works they do for to be seen of men: ²*which love to go in long clothing,* they make broad

MATT. 23

their phylacteries, and enlarge the borders of their garments,

6 And love the uppermost rooms at feasts, and the chief seats in the synagogues,

7 And greetings in the markets, and to be called of men, Rabbi, Rabbi.

8 But be not ye called Rabbi: for one is your Master, even Christ; and all ye are brethren.

9 And call no man your father upon the earth: for one is your Father, which is in heaven.

10 Neither be ye called masters: for one is your Master, even Christ.

11 But he that is greatest among you shall be your servant.

12 And whosoever shall exalt himself shall be abased; and he that shall humble himself shall be exalted.

13 But woe unto you, scribes and Pharisees, hypocrites! for ye shut up the kingdom of heaven against men: for ye neither go in yourselves, neither suffer ye them that are entering to go in.

14 Woe unto you, scribes and Pharisees, hypocrites! for ye devour widows' houses, and for a pretence make long prayer: therefore ye shall receive the greater damnation.

15 Woe unto you scribes and Pharisees, hypocrites! for ye compass sea and land to make one proselyte; and when he is made, ye make him twofold more the child of hell than yourselves.

16 Woe unto you, ye blind guides, which say, Whosoever shall swear by the temple, it is nothing; but whosoever shall swear by the gold of the temple, he is a debtor!

17 Ye fools and blind: for whether is greater, the gold, or the temple that sanctifieth the gold?

18 And, Whosoever shall swear by the altar, it is nothing; but whosoever sweareth by the gift that is upon it, he is guilty.

19 Ye fools and blind: for whether is greater, the gift, or the altar that sanctifieth the gift?

20 Whoso therefore shall swear by the altar, sweareth by it, and by all things thereon.

21 And whoso shall swear by the temple, sweareth by it, and by him that dwelleth therein.

22 And he that shall swear by heaven, sweareth by the throne of God, and by him that sitteth thereon.

23 Woe unto you, scribes and Pharisees, hypocrites! for ye pay tithe of mint and anise and cummin, and have omitted the weightier matters of the law, judgment, mercy, and faith: these ought ye to have done, and not to leave the other undone.

24 Ye blind guides, which strain at a gnat, and swallow a camel.

25 Woe unto you, scribes and Pharisees, hypocrites! for ye make clean the outside of the cup and of the platter, but within they are full of extortion and excess.

26 Thou blind Pharisee, cleanse first that which is within the cup and platter, that the outside of them may be clean also.

27 Woe unto you, scribes and Pharisees, hypocrites! for ye are like unto whited sepulchres, which indeed appear beautiful outward, but are within full of dead men's bones, and of all uncleanness.

28 Even so ye also outwardly appear righteous unto men, but within ye are full of hypocrisy and iniquity.

29 Woe unto you, scribes and Pharisees, hypocrites! because ye build the tombs of the prophets, and garnish the sepulchres of the righteous,

30 And say, If we had been in the days of our fathers, we would not have been partakers with them in the blood of the prophets.

31 Wherefore ye be witnesses unto yourselves, that ye are the children of them which killed the prophets.

32 Fill ye up then the measure of your fathers.

33 Ye serpents, ye generation of vipers, how can ye escape the damnation of hell?

34 Wherefore, behold, I send unto you prophets, and wise men, and scribes: and some of them ye shall

MATT. 23

kill and crucify; and some of them shall ye scourge in your synagogues, and persecute them from city to city:

35 That upon you may come all the righteous blood shed upon the earth, from the blood of righteous Abel unto the blood of Zechari'ah son of Berechi'ah, whom ye slew between the temple and the altar.

36 Verily I say unto you, All these things shall come upon this generation.

JESUS LAMENTS OVER JERUSALEM

MATT. 23

:37 O Jerusalem, Jerusalem, thou that killest the prophets, and stonest them which are sent unto thee, how often would I have gathered thy children together, even as a hen gathereth her chickens under her wings, and ye would not!

38 Behold, your house is left unto you desolate.

39 For I say unto you, Ye shall not see me henceforth, till ye shall say, Blessed is he that cometh in the name of the Lord.

THE WIDOW'S OFFERING

MARK 12

:41 And Jesus sat over against the treasury, and beheld how the people cast money into the treasury: and many that were rich cast in much.

[1] Luke 21:2

42 And there came a certain poor widow, and she threw in [1]*thither* two mites, which make a farthing.

[2] Luke 21:3

43 And he called unto him his disciples, and saith unto them, Verily [2]*of a truth* I say unto you, That this poor widow hath cast more in, than all they which have cast into the treasury:

[3] Luke 21:4
[4] Luke 21:4 penury

44 For all they did cast in of their abundance; [3]*unto the offerings of God:* but she of her [4]want did cast in all that she had, even all her living.

SOME GREEKS WOULD SEE JESUS

JOHN 12

:20 And there were certain Greeks among them that came up to worship at the feast:

21 The same came therefore to Philip, which was of Bethsai'da of Galilee, and desire him, saying, Sir, we would see Jesus.

22 Philip cometh and telleth Andrew: and again Andrew and Philip tell Jesus.

23 And Jesus answered them, saying, The hour is come, that the Son of man should be glorified.

24 Verily, verily, I say unto you, Except a corn of wheat fall into the ground and die, it abideth alone: but if it die, it bringeth forth much fruit.

25 He that loveth his life shall lose it; and he that hateth his life in this world shall keep it unto life eternal.

26 If any man serve me, let him follow me; and where I am, there shall also my servant be: if any man serve me, him will my Father honor.

THE SON OF MAN MUST BE LIFTED UP

:27 Now is my soul troubled; and what shall I say? Father, save me from this hour: but for this cause came I unto this hour.

28 Father, glorify thy name. Then came there a voice from heaven, saying, I have both glorified it, and will glorify it again.

29 The people therefore that stood by, and heard it, said that it thundered: others said, An angel spake to him.

30 Jesus answered and said, This voice came not because of me, but for your sakes.

31 Now is the judgment of this world: now shall the prince of this world be cast out.

32 And I, if I be lifted up from the earth, will draw all men unto me.

33 This he said, signifying what death he should die.

34 The people answered him, We have heard out of the law that Christ abideth for ever: and how sayest thou, The Son of man must be lifted up? who is this Son of man?

35 Then Jesus said unto them, Yet a little while is the light with you. Walk while ye have the light, lest darkness come upon you: for he that walketh in darkness knoweth not whither he goeth.

36 While ye have light, believe in the light, that ye may be the children of light.

BELIEVING PHARISEES AFRAID
TO CONFESS HIM

JOHN 12 :36 These things spake Jesus, and departed, and did hide himself from them.

37 But though he had done so many miracles before them, yet they believed not on him:

38 That the saying of Isaiah the prophet might be fulfilled, which he spake, Lord, who hath believed our report? and to whom hath the arm of the Lord been revealed?

39 Therefore they could not believe, because that Isaiah said again,

40 He hath blinded their eyes, and hardened their heart; that they should not see with their eyes, nor understand with their heart, and be converted, and I should heal them.

41 These things said Isaiah, when he saw his glory, and spake of him.

42 Nevertheless among the chief rulers also many believed on him: but because of the Pharisees they did not confess him, lest they should be put out of the synagogue:

43 For they loved the praise of men more than the praise of God.

TO BELIEVE CHRIST IS TO BELIEVE
IN GOD THE FATHER

JOHN 12 :44 Jesus cried and said, He that believeth on me, believeth not on me, but on him that sent me.

45 And he that seeth me seeth him that sent me.

46 I am come a light into the world, that whosoever believeth on me should not abide in darkness.

47 And if any man hear my words, and believe not, I judge him not: for I came not to judge the world, but to save the world.

48 He that rejecteth me, and receiveth not my words, hath one that judgeth him: the word that I have spoken, the same shall judge him in the last day.

49 For I have not spoken of myself; but the

THE FOUR GOSPELS

JOHN 12

Father which sent me, he gave me a commandment, what I should say, and what I should speak.

50 And I know that his commandment is life everlasting: whatsoever I speak therefore, even as the Father said unto me, so I speak.

THE DESTRUCTION OF THE TEMPLE AND SIGNS BEFORE THE END

MATT. 24
¹Mark 13:1

²Luke 21:5

³Mark 13:2
⁴Luke 21:6

⁵Mark 13:3

⁶Luke 21:7

⁷Mark 13:4

⁸Luke 21:8

⁹Luke 21:9
terrified
¹⁰by and by
¹¹Luke 21:9
¹²Luke 21:11

:1 And ¹*as* Jesus went out ¹*of the temple* and departed, *¹*one of his disciples saith unto him, Master, see what manner of stones and what buildings are here!* ²*how it was adorned with goodly stones and gifts.*

2 And Jesus said unto them, See ye not all these ³*great buildings?* verily I say unto you, ⁴*As for these things which ye behold, the days will come, in the which* there shall not be left here one stone upon another, that shall not be thrown down.

3 And as he sat upon the mount of Olives, ⁵*over against the temple,* the disciples, ⁵*Peter . . . James . . . John and Andrew* came unto him privately, and ⁵*asked him* saying, Tell us, when shall these things be ⁶*and what sign will there be when these things shall come to pass?* and what shall be the sign of thy coming, and of the end of the world ⁷*when all these shall be fulfilled?*

4 And Jesus answered and said unto them, Take heed that no man deceive you.

5 For many shall come in my name, saying, I am Christ; ⁸*and the time draweth near: go ye not therefore after them,* [for they] shall deceive many.

6 And ye shall hear of wars and rumors of wars: see that ye be not ⁹troubled: for all these things must ¹¹*first* come to pass, but the end is not ¹⁰yet.

7 For nation shall rise against nation, and kingdom against kingdom: and there shall be famines, and pestilences, and earthquakes, in divers places, ¹²*and fearful sights and great signs shall there be from heaven.*

---

*Matthew uses the plural, and his "disciples came to him for to show him the buildings of the temple". Peter, as in most instances, was possibly the spokesman for the disciples.

Arranged As a Single Narrative

MATT. 24	8 All these are the beginning of sorrows. [13]*But take heed to yourselves.* [14]*But before all these, they shall lay their hands on you, and* [15]*persecute you, delivering you up to the synagogues, and into prisons, being brought before kings and rulers for my name's sake* [16]*for a testimony against them.*
[13]Mark 13:9	
[14]Luke 21:12	
[15]Mark 13:9 beaten	
[16]Mark 13:9	
MATT. 24	9 ... and shall kill you: and ye shall be hated of all nations for my name's sake.
LUKE 21	:13 And it shall turn to you for a testimony.
	14 Settle it therefore in your hearts, not to [17]meditate before ye shall answer:
[17]Mark 13:11 take no thought beforehand	15 For I will give you a mouth and wisdom, which all your adversaries shall not be able to gainsay nor resist, [18]*but whatsoever shall be given you in that hour, that speak ye: for it is not ye that speak, but the Holy Ghost.*
[18]Mark 13:11	
MATT. 24	:10 And then shall many be offended, [19]*and shall betray one another, and shall hate one another, both by parents and brethren, and kinsfolk, and friends;* [20]*Now the brother shall betray the brother to death, and the father the son; and children shall rise up against their parents, and shall cause them to be put to death.* [21]*And ye shall be hated of all men for my name's sake.* [22]*But there shall not a hair of your head perish.*
[19]Luke 21:16	
[20]Mark 13:12	
[21]Luke 21:17	
[22]Luke 21:18	
	11 And many false prophets shall rise, and shall deceive many.
	12 And because iniquity shall abound, the love of many shall wax cold.
[23]Luke 21:19	13 But he that shall endure unto the end, the same shall be saved. [23]*In your patience possess ye your souls.*
	14 And this gospel of the kingdom shall be preached in all the world for a witness unto all nations; and then shall the end come.
LUKE 21	:20 And when ye shall see Jerusalem compassed with armies, then know that the desolation thereof is nigh.
MATT. 24	:15 When ye therefore shall see the abomination of desolation, spoken of by Daniel the prophet, stand in the holy place [24]*where it ought not* (whoso readeth, let him understand,)
[24]Mark 13:14	

The FOUR GOSPELS

MATT. 24
²⁵Luke 21:21

²⁶Mark 13:15

²⁷Mark 13:16
²⁸Mark 13:16
garment
²⁹Luke 21:22
³⁰Luke 21:23

³¹Mark 13:19
affliction
³²creation
³³Luke 21:24

³⁴Mark 13:20

³⁵Mark 13:22
³⁶Mark 13:23
³⁷Mark 13:23

³⁸See Luke
17:20-37
Page 150-151

16 Then let them which be in Judea flee into the mountains ²⁵*and let them which are in the midst of it depart out;*

17 Let him which is on the housetop not ²⁶*go* down ²⁶*into the house, neither enter therein,* to take any thing out of his house.

18 Neither let him which is in the field return back ²⁷*again* to take his ²⁸*clothes,* ²⁹*for these be the days of vengeance, that all things which are written may be fulfilled.*

19 And woe unto them that are with child and to them that give suck in those days! ³⁰*for there shall be great distress in the land, and wrath upon this people.*

20 But pray ye that your flight be not in the winter, neither on the sabbath day:

21 For then shall be great ³¹tribulation, such as was not since the beginning of the ³²world to this time, no, nor ever shall be. ³³*And they shall fall by the edge of the sword, and shall be led away captive into all nations: and Jerusalem shall be trodden down of the Gentiles, until the times of the Gentiles be fulfilled.*

22 And except those days should be shortened, there should no flesh be saved: but for the elect's sake, ³⁴*whom he hath chosen,* those days shall be shortened.

23 Then if any man shall say unto you, Lo, here is Christ, or there; believe it not.

24 For there shall arise false Christs, and false prophets, and shall show great signs and wonders ³⁵*to seduce,* insomuch that, if it were possible, they shall deceive the very elect. ³⁶*But take ye heed.*

25 Behold, I have ³⁷*foretold you all things.*

26 Wherefore if they shall say unto you, Behold, he is in the desert; go not forth: behold, he is in the secret chambers; believe it not.

27 For as the lightning cometh out of the east, and shineth even unto the west; so shall also the coming of the Son of man be.

28 ³⁸For wheresoever the carcass is, there will the eagles be gathered together.

THE SIGN OF THE COMING OF
THE SON OF MAN

MATT. 24
¹Luke 21:25

:29 Immediately after the tribulation of those days ¹*there shall be signs in the sun, and in the moon, and in the stars,* the sun [shall] be darkened, and the moon shall not give her light, and the stars shall fall from heaven, and the powers of the heavens shall be shaken: ¹*and upon the earth distress of nations, with perplexity; the sea and waves roaring;*

²Luke 21:26

²*Men's hearts failing them for fear and for looking after those things which are coming on the earth: for*

³Luke 21:28

the powers of heaven shall be shaken. ³*And when these things begin to come to pass, then look up, and lift up your heads; for your redemption draweth nigh.*

30 And then shall appear the sign of the Son of man in heaven: and then shall all the tribes of the earth mourn, and they shall see the Son of man coming in the clouds of heaven with power and great glory.

31 And he shall send his angels with a great sound of a trumpet, and they shall gather together his elect

⁴Mark 13:27

from the four winds, ⁴*from the uttermost part of the earth* from one end of heaven to the other.

⁵Luke 21:29

32 Now learn a parable of the fig tree ⁵*and all the trees;* When his branch is yet tender, and putteth

⁶Luke 21:30
⁷Mark 13:29
⁸Luke 21:31

forth leaves, ye know that summer is nigh ⁶*at hand.*

33 So ⁷*ye in like manner,* when ye shall see all these things ⁸*come to pass* know ⁸*ye that the kingdom of God is nigh at hand,* even at the doors.

34 Verily I say unto you, This generation shall not pass, till all these things be fulfilled.

35 Heaven and earth shall pass away, but my words shall not pass away.

IN SUCH AN HOUR AS
YE THINK NOT

LUKE 21

:34 And take heed to yourselves, lest at any time your hearts be overcharged with surfeiting, and drunkenness, and cares of this life, and so that day come upon you unawares.

LUKE 21

35 For as a snare shall it come on all them that dwell on the face of the whole earth.

36 Watch ye therefore, and pray always, that ye may be accounted worthy to escape all these things that shall come to pass, and to stand before the Son of man.

MATT. 24
[1]**Mark 13:32**

:36 But of that day and hour knoweth no man, no, not the angels of heaven, [1]*neither the Son,* but my Father only.

37 But as the days of Noah were, so shall also the coming of the Son of man be.

38 For as in the days that were before the flood they were eating and drinking, marrying and giving in marriage, until the day that Noah entered into the ark,

39 And knew not until the flood came, and took them all away; so shall also the coming of the Son of man be.

40 Then shall two be in the field; the one shall be taken, and the other left.

41 Two women shall be grinding at the mill; the one shall be taken, the other left.

MARK 13

:34 For the Son of man is as a man taking a far journey, who left his house, and gave authority to his servants, and to every man his work, and commanded the porter to watch.

35 Watch ye therefore: for ye know not when the master of the house cometh, at even, or at midnight, or at the cockcrowing, or in the morning:

36 Lest coming suddenly he find you sleeping.

MATT. 24

:42 Watch therefore; for ye know not what hour your Lord doth come.

43 But know this, that if the goodman of the house had known in what watch the thief would come, he would have watched, and would not have suffered his house to be broken up.

44 Therefore be ye also ready: for in such an hour as ye think not the Son of man cometh. [2]*And what I*

[2]**Mark 13:37**
say unto you I say unto all, Watch.

THE FAITHFUL SERVANT WATCHES

MATT. 24
:45 Who then is a faithful and wise servant, whom

MATT. 24

his lord hath made ruler over his household, to give them meat in due season?

46 Blessed is that servant, whom his lord when he cometh shall find so doing.

47 Verily I say unto you, That he shall make him ruler over all his goods.

48 But and if that evil servant shall say in his heart, My lord delayeth his coming;

49 And shall begin to smite his fellow servants, and to eat and drink with the drunken;

50 The lord of that servant shall come in a day when he looketh not for him, and in an hour that he is not aware of,

51 And shall cut him asunder, and appoint him his portion with the hypocrites: there shall be weeping and gnashing of teeth.

THE VIRGINS—WISE AND FOOLISH

MATT. 25

:1 Then shall the kingdom of heaven be likened unto ten virgins, which took their lamps, and went forth to meet the bridegroom.

2 And five of them were wise, and five were foolish.

3 They that were foolish took their lamps, and took no oil with them.

4 But the wise took oil in their vessels with their lamps.

5 While the bridegroom tarried, they all slumbered and slept.

6 And at midnight there was a cry made, Behold the bridegroom cometh, go ye out to meet him.

7 Then all those virgins arose, and trimmed their lamps.

8 And the foolish said unto the wise, Give us of your oil; for our lamps are gone out.

9 But the wise answered saying, Not so; lest there be not enough for us and you: but go ye rather to them that sell, and buy for yourselves.

10 And while they went to buy, the bridegroom came; and they that were ready went in with him to the marriage: and the door was shut.

11 Afterward came also the other virgins, saying, Lord, Lord, open to us.

MATT. 25

12 But he answered and said, Verily I say unto you, I know you not.

13 Watch therefore; for ye know neither the day nor the hour wherein the Son of man cometh.

THE PARABLE OF THE TALENTS

MATT. 25

:14 For the kingdom of heaven is as a man traveling into a far country, who called his own servants, and delivered unto them his goods.

15 And unto one he gave five talents, to another two, and to another one; to every man according to his several ability; and straightway took his journey.

16 Then he that had received the five talents went and traded with the same, and made them other five talents.

17 And likewise he that had received two, he also gained other two.

18 But he that had received one went and digged in the earth, and hid his lord's money.

19 After a long time the lord of those servants cometh, and reckoneth with them.

20 And so he that had received five talents came and brought other five talents, saying, Lord, thou deliveredst unto me five talents: behold, I have gained beside them five talents more.

21 His lord said unto him, Well done, thou good and faithful servant: thou hast been faithful over a few things, I will make thee ruler over many things: enter thou into the joy of thy lord.

22 He also that had received two talents came and said, Lord, thou deliveredst unto me two talents: behold, I have gained two other talents beside them.

23 His lord said unto him, Well done, good and faithful servant; thou hast been faithful over a few things, I will make thee ruler over many things: enter thou into the joy of thy lord.

24 Then he which had received the one talent came and said, Lord, I knew thee that thou art a hard man, reaping where thou hast not sown, and gathering where thou hast not strawed:

25 And I was afraid, and went and hid thy talent in the earth: lo, there thou hast that is thine.

MATT. 25

26 His lord answered and said unto him, Thou wicked and slothful servant, thou knewest that I reap where I sowed not, and gather where I have not strawed:

27 Thou oughtest therefore to have put my money to the exchangers, and then at my coming I should have received mine own with usury.

28 Take therefore the talent from him, and give it unto him which hath ten talents.

29 For unto every one that hath shall be given, and he shall have abundance: but from him that hath not shall be taken away even that which he hath.

30 And cast ye the unprofitable servant into outer darkness: there shall be weeping and gnashing of teeth.

THE JUDGMENT OF NATIONS

MATT. 25

:31 When the Son of man shall come in his glory, and all the holy angels with him, then shall he sit upon the throne of his glory:

32 And before him shall be gathered all nations: and he shall separate them one from another, as a shepherd divideth his sheep from the goats:

33 And he shall set the sheep on his right hand, but the goats on the left.

34 Then shall the King say unto them on his right hand, Come, ye blessed of my Father, inherit the kingdom prepared for you from the foundation of the world:

35 For I was ahungered, and ye gave me meat: I was thirsty, and ye gave me drink: I was a stranger, and ye took me in:

36 Naked, and ye clothed me: I was sick, and ye visited me: I was in prison, and ye came unto me.

37 Then shall the righteous answer him, saying, lord, when saw we thee ahungered, and fed thee? or thirsty, and gave thee drink?

38 When saw we thee a stranger, and took thee in? or naked, and clothed thee?

39 Or when saw we thee sick, or in prison, and came unto thee?

40 And the King shall answer and say unto them,

MATT. 25

Verily I say unto you, Inasmuch as ye have done it unto one of the least of these my brethren, ye have done it unto me.

41 Then shall he say also unto them on the left hand, Depart from me, ye cursed, into everlasting fire, prepared for the devil and his angels:

42 For I was ahungered, and ye gave me no meat: I was thirsty and ye gave me no drink:

43 I was a stranger, and ye took me not in: naked, and ye clothed me not: sick, and in prison, and ye visited me not.

44 Then shall they also answer him, saying, Lord, when saw we thee ahungered, or athirst, or a stranger, or naked, or sick, or in prison and did not minister unto thee?

45 Then shall he answer them, saying, Verily I say unto you, Inasmuch as ye did it not to one of the least of these, ye did it not to me.

46 And these shall go away into everlasting punishment: but the righteous into life eternal.

LUKE 21

:37 And in the daytime he was teaching in the temple; and at night he went out, and abode in the mount that is called the mount of Olives.

38 And all the people came early in the morning to him in the temple, for to hear him.

THE LEADERS PLOT AGAINST JESUS

MATT. 26

:1 And it came to pass, when Jesus had finished all these sayings, he said unto his disciples.

[1]Luke 22:1

2 Ye know that after two days is the feast [1]*of unleavened bread . . . which is called* the passover, and the Son of man is betrayed to be crucified.

3 Then assembled together the chief priests, and the scribes, and the elders of the people, unto the palace of the high priest, who was called Cai'aphas,

4 And consulted that they might take Jesus by [2]subtilty, and kill him,

[2]Mark 14:1 craft

5 But they said, Not on the feast day, lest there be an uproar among the people, [3]*for they feared the people.*

[3]Luke 22:2

JESUS ANOINTED AT BETHANY THE THIRD TIME*

MATT. 26 :6 Now when Jesus was in Bethany, in the house of Simon the leper,

7 There came unto him a woman having an alabaster box of very precious ointment ¹*of spikenard . . . and she brake the box,* and poured it on his head, as he sat at meat.

¹Mark 14:3

8 But when his disciples saw it, they had indignation ²*within* themselves, saying, To what purpose is this ²*waste of the ointment* made?

²Mark 14:4

9 For this ointment might have been sold ³*for more than three hundred pence,* and given to the poor, ³*and they murmured against her.*

³Mark 14:5

10 When Jesus understood it, he said unto them, Why trouble ye the woman? ⁴*Let her alone;* for she hath wrought a good work upon me.

⁴Mark 14:6

11 For ye have the poor always with you ⁵*and whensoever ye will ye may do them good:* but me ye have not always. ⁶*She hath done what she could.*

⁵Mark 14:7
⁶Mark 14:8

12 For in that she hath ⁶*come aforehand* and poured this ointment on my body, she did it for my burial.

13 Verily I say unto you, Wheresoever this gospel shall be preached in the whole world, ⁷*this also that she hath done shall be spoken of for a memorial of her.*

⁷Mark 14:9

SATAN ENTERS INTO JUDAS

LUKE 22 :3 Then entered Satan into Judas surnamed Iscar'i-ot, being of the number of the twelve.

4 And he went his way, and communed with the chief priests and captains, how he might betray him unto them.

¹Mark 14:11
²Matt. 26:15

5 And ¹*when they heard it* they were glad, ²*And he said unto them, What will ye give me, and I will deliver him unto you? And they covenanted with him for thirty pieces of silver.*

---

*First anointing (Luke 7:37-38) — in the house of a Pharisee by a woman who was a sinner. Second anointing (John 12:1-3 and 12) — Mary at Bethany six days before the Passover, and the day before the Triumphal Entry. Third anointing (Matt. 26:2; Mark 14:1) — at Bethany, in the house of Simon the leper, two days before the feast.

LUKE 22 ³Mark 14:11 ⁴Matt. 26:16	6 And he promised, and sought opportunity ³*how he might conveniently* betray him unto them in the absence of the multitude. ⁴*And from that time he sought opportunity to betray him.*

JESUS EATS THE PASSOVER
WITH HIS DISCIPLES

JOHN 13	:1 Now before the feast of the passover, when Jesus knew that his hour was come that he should depart out of this world unto the Father, having loved his own which were in the world, he loved them unto the end.
MATT. 26 ¹Luke 22:7 ²Mark 14:12	:17 Now the first day of the feast of unleavened bread ¹*when the passover must be killed* the disciples came to Jesus, saying unto him, Where wilt thou that we prepare for thee ²*that thou mayest* eat the passover?
³Luke 22:8	18 And he said to ³*Peter and John . . . Go and prepare us the passover, that we may eat.*
LUKE 22	:10 And he said unto them, Behold, when ye are entered into the city, there shall a man meet you, bearing a pitcher of water; follow him into the house where he entereth in.
⁴Matt. 26:18	11 And ye shall say unto the goodman of the house. The Master saith unto thee ⁴*My time is at hand; I will keep the passover at thy house with my disciples.* Where is the guest chamber, where I shall eat the passover with my disciples?
⁵Mark 14:15	12 And he shall show you a large upper room furnished ⁵*and prepared:* there make ready ⁵*for us.*
MARK 14	:16 And his disciples went forth, and came into the city, and found as he had said unto them, and they made ready the passover.
MATT. 26	:20 Now when the even was come, he sat down with the twelve.
LUKE 22	:15 And he said unto them, With desire I have desired to eat this passover with you before I suffer: 16 For I say unto you, I will not any more eat thereof, until it be fulfilled in the kingdom of God.
MATT. 26 ⁶Mark 14:18	:21 And as they did eat, he said, Verily I say unto you, that one of you ⁶*which eateth with me* shall betray me.

Arranged As a Single Narrative

MATT. 26
[7]Mark 14:19

22 And they were exceeding sorrowful, and began every one of them to say unto him, [7]*one by one*, Lord, is it I?

[8]Mark 14:20
It is one of the twelve.

23 And he answered and said, [8]He that dippeth his hand with me in the dish, the same shall betray me.

24 The Son of man goeth as it is written of him: but woe unto that man by whom the Son of man is betrayed! it had been good for that man if he had not been born.

25 Then Judas, which betrayed him, answered and said, Master, is it I? He said unto him, Thou hast said.

LUKE 22
[9]Matt. 22:26
[10]Matt. 26:27
Drink ye all of it
[11]Mark 14:23
[12]Matt. 26:28
[13]Mark 14:25
[14]Matt. 26:29
My Father

:17 [9]*As they were eating,* . . . He took the cup, and gave thanks and said, Take this, [10]*divide it among yourselves:* [11]*and they all drank of it.* [12]*For this is my blood of the New Testament which is shed for many for the remission of sins.* [13]*Verily I say unto you, I will drink no more of the fruit of the vine, until that day that I drink it new in the kingdom of* [14]*God.*

LUKE 22
[15]Matt. 26:26

:19 And he took bread, and gave thanks, and brake it, and gave unto them, Saying, [15]*Take, eat,* This is my body which is given for you: this do in remembrance of me.

20 Likewise also the *cup after supper, saying, This is the new testament in my blood, which is shed for you.

JOHN 13

:21 But behold the hand of him that betrayeth me is with me on the table.

23 And they began to inquire among **themselves, which of them it was that should do this thing.

---

*From the account given here in Luke in verse 17 and 20 it appears that the cup was given both before and after the bread.

**At first they ask, "Lord, is it I?" Here they inquire among themselves. Also after Jesus had washed their feet, Peter beckons to John to ask who it should be of whom Jesus spake.

JESUS WASHES HIS DISCIPLES' FEET

JOHN 13

2 And supper being ended, the devil having now put into the heart of Judas Iscar'i-ot, Simon's son to betray him;

3 Jesus knowing that the Father had given all things into his hands, and that he was come from God, and went to God;

4 He riseth from supper, and laid aside his garments; and took a towel, and girded himself.

5 After that he poureth water into a basin, and began to wash the disciples' feet, and to wipe them with the towel wherewith he was girded.

6 Then cometh he to Simon Peter: and Peter saith unto him, Lord, dost thou wash my feet?

7 Jesus answered and said unto him, What I do thou knowest not now; but thou shalt know hereafter.

8 Peter saith unto him, Thou shalt never wash my feet. Jesus answered him, If I wash thee not, thou hast no part with me.

9 Simon Peter saith unto him, Lord, not my feet only, but also my hands and my head.

10 Jesus saith to him, He that is washed needeth not save to wash his feet, but is clean every whit: and ye are clean, but not all.

11 For he knew who should betray him; therefore said he, Ye are not all clean.

12 So after he had washed their feet, and had taken his garments, and was set down again, he said unto them, Know ye what I have done to you?

13 Ye call me Master and Lord: and ye say well; for so I am.

14 If I then, your Lord and Master, have washed your feet; ye also ought to wash one another's feet.

15 For I have given you an example, that ye should do as I have done to you.

16 Verily, verily, I say unto you, The servant is not greater than his lord; neither he that is sent greater than he that sent him.

17 If ye know these things, happy are ye if ye do them.

18 I speak not of you all: I know whom I have

chosen: but that the Scripture may be fulfilled, He that eateth bread with me hath lifted up his heel against me.

JOHN 13

19 Now I tell you before it come, that, when it is come to pass, ye may believe that I am he.

20 Verily, verily, I say unto you, He that receiveth whomsoever I send receiveth me; and he that receiveth me receiveth him that sent me.

JESUS FORETELLS HIS BETRAYAL

JOHN 13

:21 When Jesus had thus said, he was troubled in spirit, and testified, and said, Verily, verily, I say unto you, that one of you shall betray me.

22 Then the disciples looked one on another, doubting of whom he spake.

23 Now there was leaning on Jesus' bosom one of his disciples, whom Jesus loved.

24 Simon Peter therefore beckoned to him, that he should ask who it should be of whom he spake.

25 He then lying on Jesus' breast saith unto him, Lord, who is it?

26 Jesus answered, He it is, to whom I shall give a sop, when I have dipped it. And when he had dipped the sop, he gave it to Judas Iscar'i-ot, the son of Simon.

27 And after the sop Satan *entered into him. Then said Jesus unto him, That thou doest, do quickly.

28 Now no man at the table knew for what intent he spake this unto him.

29 For some of them thought, because Judas had the bag, that Jesus had said unto him, Buy those things that we have need of against the feast; or, that he should give something to the poor.

30 He then, having received the sop, went immediately out; and it was night.

THE NEW COMMANDMENT

JOHN 13

:31 Therefore, when he was gone out, Jesus said,

John 13:2 The devil succeeds in tempting Judas; here Satan enters him and takes command of him.

JOHN 13

Now is the Son of man glorified, and God is glorified in him.

32 If God be glorified in him, God shall also glorify him in himself, and shall straightway glorify him.

33 Little children, yet a little while I am with you. Ye shall seek me; and as I said unto the Jews, Whither I go, ye cannot come; so now I say to you.

34 A new commandment I give unto you, That ye love one another; as I have loved you, that ye also love one another.

35 By this shall all men know that ye are my disciples, if ye have love one to another.

THE THIRD DISPUTE ABOUT GREATNESS

LUKE 22

:24 And there was also a strife among them, which of them should be accounted the greatest.

25 And he said unto them, The kings of the Gentiles exercise lordship over them; and they that exercise authority upon them are called benefactors.

26 But ye shall not be so: but he that is greatest among you, let him be as the younger; and he that is chief, as he that doth serve.

27 For whether is greater, he that sitteth at meat, or he that serveth? is not he that sitteth at meat? but I am among you as he that serveth.

28 Ye are they which have continued with me in my temptations.

29 And I appoint unto you a kingdom, as my Father hath appointed unto me;

30 That ye may eat and drink at my table in my kingdom, and sit on thrones judging the twelve tribes of Israel.

PETER'S DENIAL FORETOLD

JOHN 13

:36 Simon Peter said unto him, Lord, whither goest thou? Jesus answered him, Whither I go, thou canst not follow me now; but thou shalt follow me afterward.

37 Peter said unto him, Lord, why cannot I follow thee now? I will lay down my life for thy sake.

JOHN 13   38 Jesus answered him, Wilt thou lay down thy life for my sake?

LUKE 22   :31 And the Lord said, Simon, Simon, behold, Satan hath desired to have you, that he may sift you as wheat:

32 But I have prayed for thee, that thy faith fail not: and when thou art converted, strengthen thy brethren.

33 And he said unto him, Lord, I am ready to go with thee, both into prison, and to death.

34 And he said, I tell thee, Peter, the cock shall not crow this day, before that thou shalt thrice deny that thou knowest me.

JESUS THE WAY, THE TRUTH AND THE LIFE

JOHN 14   :1 Let not your heart be troubled: ye believe in God, believe also in me.

2 In my Father's house are many mansions: if it were not so, I would have told you. I go to prepare a place for you.

3 And if I go and prepare a place for you, I will come again, and receive you unto myself; that where I am, there ye may be also.

4 And whither I go ye know, and the way ye know.

5 Thomas saith unto him, Lord, we know not whither thou goest; and how can we know the way?

6 Jesus saith unto him, I am the way, the truth, and the life; no man cometh unto the Father, but by me.

7 If ye had known me, ye should have known my father also: and from henceforth ye know him, and have seen him.

8 Philip saith unto him, Lord, show us the Father, and it sufficeth us.

9 Jesus saith unto him, Have I been so long time with you, and yet hast thou not known me, Philip? he that hath seen me hath seen the Father; and how sayest thou then, Show us the Father?

10 Believest thou not that I am in the Father, and the Father in me? the words that I speak unto you I

JOHN 14

speak not of myself: but the Father that dwelleth in me, he doeth the works.

11 Believe me that I am in the Father, and the Father in me: or else believe me for the very works sake.

12 Verily, verily, I say unto you, He that believeth on me, the works that I do shall he do also; and greather works than these shall he do; because I go unto my Father.

13 And whatsoever ye shall ask in my name, that will I do, that the Father may be glorified in the Son.

14 If ye shall ask any thing in my name, I will do it.

THE PROMISE OF THE HOLY SPIRIT

JOHN 14

:15 If ye love me, keep my commandments.

16 And I will pray the Father, and he shall give you another Comforter, that he may abide with you for ever;

17 Even the Spirit of truth; whom the world cannot receive, because it seeth him not, neither knoweth him: but ye know him; for he dwelleth with you, and shall be in you.

18 I will not leave you comfortless: I will come to you.

19 Yet a little while, and the world seeth me no more; but ye see me: because I live, ye shall live also.

20 At that day ye shall know that I am in my Father, and ye in me, and I in you.

21 He that hath my commandments, and keepeth them, he it is that loveth me: and he that loveth me shall be loved of my Father, and I will love him, and will manifest myself to him.

22 Judas saith unto him, not Iscar'i-ot, Lord, how is it that thou wilt manifest thyself unto us, and not unto the world?

23 Jesus answered and saith unto him, If a man love me, he will keep my words; and my Father will love him, and we will come unto him, and make our abode with him.

24 He that loveth me not keepeth not my sayings: and the word which ye hear is not mine, but the Father's which sent me.

JOHN 14

25 These things have I spoken unto you, being yet present with you.

26 But the Comforter, which is the Holy Ghost, whom the Father will send in my name, he shall teach you all things, and bring all things to your remembrance, whatsoever I have said unto you.

27 Peace I leave with you, my peace I give unto you: not as the world giveth, give I unto you. Let not your heart be troubled, neither let it be afraid.

28 Ye have heard how I said unto you, I go away, and come again unto you. If ye loved me, ye would rejoice, because I said, I go unto the Father: for my Father is greater than I.

29 And now I have told you before it come to pass, that, when it is come to pass, ye might believe.

30 Hereafter I will not talk much with you: for the prince of this world cometh, and hath nothing in me.

31 But that the world may know that I love the Father; and as the Father gave me commandment, even so I do. Arise, let us go hence.

JESUS THE TRUE VINE

JOHN 15

:1 I am the true vine, and my Father is the husbandman.

2 Every branch in me that beareth not fruit he taketh away: and every branch that beareth fruit, he purgeth it, that it may bring forth more fruit.

3 Now ye are clean through the word which I have spoken unto you.

4 Abide in me, and I in you. As the branch cannot bear fruit of itself, except it abide in the vine; no more can ye, except ye abide in me.

5 I am the vine, ye are the branches. He that abideth in me, and I in him, the same bringeth forth much fruit; for without me ye can do nothing.

6 If a man abide not in me, he is cast forth as a branch, and is withered; and men gather them, and cast them into the fire, and they are burned.

7 If ye abide in me, and my words abide in you, ye shall ask what ye will, and it shall be done unto you.

8 Herein is my Father glorified, that ye bear much fruit; so shall ye be my disciples.

9 As the Father hath loved me, so have I loved you: continue ye in my love.

10 If ye keep my commandments, ye shall abide in my love; even as I have kept my Father's commandments, and abide in his love.

11 These things have I spoken unto you, that my joy might remain in you, and that your joy might be full.

12 This is my commandment, That ye love one another, as I have loved you.

13 Greater love hath no man than this, that a man lay down his life for his friends.

14 Ye are my friends, if ye do whatsoever I command you.

15 Henceforth I call you not servants; for the servant knoweth not what his lord doeth: but I have called you friends; for all things that I have heard of my Father I have made known unto you.

16 Ye have not chosen me, but I have chosen you, and ordained you, that ye should go and bring forth fruit, and that your fruit should remain; that whatsoever ye shall ask of the Father in my name, he may give it you.

17 These things I command you, that ye love one another.

THE WORLD'S HATRED

:18 If the world hate you, ye know that it hated me before it hated you.

19 If ye were of the world, the world would love his own; but because ye are not of the world, but I have chosen you out of the world, therefore the world hateth you.

20 Remember the word that I said unto you, The servant is not greater than his lord. If they have persecuted me, they will also persecute you; if they have kept my saying, they will keep yours also.

21 But all these things will they do unto you for my name's sake, because they know not him that sent me.

22 If I had not come and spoken unto them, they had not had sin; but now they have no cloak for their sin.

JOHN 15

23 He that hateth me hateth my Father also.

24 If I had not done among them the works which none other man did, they had not had sin: but now have they both seen and hated both me and my Father.

25 But this cometh to pass, that the word might be fulfilled that is written in their law, They hated me without a cause.

26 But when the Comforter is come, whom I will send unto you from the Father, even the Spirit of truth, which proceedeth from the Father, he shall testify of me:

27 And ye also shall bear witness, because ye have been with me from the beginning.

JOHN 16

:1 These things have I spoken unto you, that ye should not be offended.

2 They shall put you out of the synagogues: yea, the time cometh, that whosoever killeth you will think that he doeth God service.

3 And these things will they do unto you, because they have not known the Father, nor me.

4 But these things have I told you, that when the time shall come, ye may remember that I told you of them. And these things I said not unto you at the beginning, because I was with you.

5 But now I go my way to him that sent me; and none of you asketh me, Whither goest thou?

6 But because I have said these things unto you, sorrow hath filled your heart.

WHEN THE HOLY SPIRIT IS COME

JOHN 16

:7 Nevertheless I tell you the truth; It is expedient for you that I go away: for if I go not away, the Comforter will not come unto you; but if I depart, I will send him unto you.

8 And when he is come, he will reprove the world of sin, and of righteousness, and of judgment:

9 Of sin, because they believe not on me;

10 Of righteousness, because I go to my Father, and ye see me no more;

11 Of judgment, because the prince of this world is judged.

JOHN 16

12 I have yet many things to say unto you, but ye cannot bear them now.

13 Howbeit when he, the Spirit of truth, is come, he will guide you into all truth: for he shall not speak of himself; but whatsoever he shall hear, that shall he speak: and he will show you things to come.

14 He shall glorify me: for he shall receive of mine, and shall show it unto you.

15 All things that the Father hath are mine; therefore said I, that he shall take of mine, and shall show it unto you.

JESUS WILL GO TO THE FATHER

JOHN 16

:16 A little while, and ye shall not see me: and again, a little while, and ye shall see me, because I go to the Father.

17 Then said some of his disciples among themselves, What is this that he saith unto us, A little while, and ye shall not see me: and again, a little while, and ye shall see me: and, Because I go to the Father?

18 They said therefore, What is this that he saith, A little while? We cannot tell what he saith.

19 Now Jesus knew that they were desirous to ask him, and said unto them, Do ye inquire among yourselves of that I said, a little while, and ye shall not see me: and again, a little while, and ye shall see me?

20 Verily, verily, I say unto you, That ye shall weep and lament, but the world shall rejoice; and ye shall be sorrowful, but your sorrow shall be turned into joy.

21 A woman when she is in travail hath sorrow, because her hour is come: but as soon as she is delivered of the child, she remembereth no more the anguish, for joy that a man is born into the world.

22 And ye now therefore have sorrow: but I will see you again, and your heart shall rejoice, and your joy no man taketh from you.

23 And in that day ye shall ask me nothing. Verily, verily, I say unto you, Whatsoever ye shall ask the Father in my name, he will give it you.

JOHN 16   24 Hitherto have ye asked nothing in my name: ask, and ye shall receive, that your joy may be full.

CHRIST WILL PRAY FOR HIS FOLLOWERS

JOHN 16   :25 These things have I spoken unto you in proverbs: but the time cometh, when I shall no more speak unto you in proverbs, but I shall show you plainly of the Father.

26 At that day ye shall ask in my name: and I say not unto you, that I will pray the Father for you:

27 For the Father himself loveth you, because ye have loved me, and have believed that I came out from God.

28 I came forth from the Father, and am come into the world: again, I leave the world, and go to the Father.

29 His disciples said unto him, Lo, now speakest thou plainly, and speakest no proverb.

30 Now are we sure that thou knowest all things, and needest not that any man should ask thee: by this we believe that thou camest forth from God.

31 Jesus answered them, Do ye now believe?

32 Behold, the hour cometh, yea, is now come, that ye shall be scattered, every man to his own, and shall leave me alone: and yet I am not alone, because the Father is with me.

33 These things I have spoken unto you, that in me ye might have peace. In the world ye shall have tribulation: but be of good cheer; I have overcome the world.

THE HIGH PRIESTLY PRAYER OF CHRIST

JOHN 17   :1 These words spake Jesus, and lifted up his eyes to heaven, and said, Father, the hour is come; glorify thy Son, that thy son also may glorify thee:

2 As thou hast given him power over all flesh, that he should give eternal life to as many as thou hast given him.

3 And this is life eternal, that they might know thee the only true God, and Jesus Christ, whom thou hast sent.

4 I have glorified thee on the earth: I have finished the work which thou gavest me to do.

5 And now, O Father, glorify thou me with thine own self with the glory which I had with thee before the world was.

6 I have manifested thy name unto the men which thou gavest me out of the world: thine they were and thou gavest them me; and they have kept thy word.

7 Now they have known that all things whatsoever thou hast given me are of thee.

8 For I have given unto them the words which thou gavest me; and they have received them, and have known surely that I came out from thee, and they have believed that thou didst send me.

9 I pray for them: I pray not for the world, but for them which thou hast given me; for they are thine.

10 And all mine are thine, and thine are mine; and I am glorified in them.

11 And now I am no more in the world, but these are in the world, and I come to thee. Holy Father, keep through thine own name those whom thou hast given me, that they may be one, as we are.

12 While I was with them in the world, I kept them in thy name: those that thou gavest me I have kept, and none of them is lost, but the son of perdition; that the Scripture might be fulfilled.

13 And now come I to thee; and these things I speak in the world, that they might have my joy fulfilled in themselves.

14 I have given them thy word; and the world hath hated them, because they are not of the world, even as I am not of the world,

15 I pray not that thou shouldest take them out of the world, but that thou shouldest keep them from the evil.

16 They are not of the world, even as I am not of the world.

17 Sanctify them through thy truth: thy word is truth.

18 As thou hast sent me into the world, even so have I also sent them into the world.

JOHN 17

19 And for their sakes I sanctify myself, that they also might be sanctified through the truth.

20 Neither pray I for these alone, but for them also which shall believe on me through their word:

21 That they all may be one; as thou, Father, art in me, and I in thee, that they also may be one in us: that the world may believe that thou hast sent me.

22 And the glory which thou gavest me I have given them; that they may be one, even as we are one;

23 I in them, and thou in me, that they may be made perfect in one; and that the world may know that thou hast sent me, and hast loved them, as thou hast loved me.

24 Father, I will that they also, whom thou hast given me, be with me where I am; that they may behold my glory, which thou hast given me: for thou lovedst me before the foundation of the world.

25 O righteous Father, the world hath not known thee: but I have known thee, and these have known that thou hast sent me.

26 And I have declared unto them thy name, and will declare it; that the love wherewith thou hast loved me may be in them, and I in them.

THEY LEAVE THE UPPER ROOM

LUKE 22

:35 And he said unto them, When I sent you without purse, and scrip, and shoes, lacked ye any thing? And they said, Nothing.

36 Then said he unto them, But now, he that hath a purse, let him take it, and likewise his scrip: and he that hath no sword, let him sell his garment, and buy one.

37 For I say unto you, that this that is written must yet be accomplished in me, and he was reckoned among the transgressors: for the things concerning me have an end.

38 And they said, Lord, behold, here are two swords. And he said unto them, It is enough. [1]*When Jesus had spoken these words, [2]and when they had sung a hymn, [1]he went forth with his disciples over the brook Cedron, [2]into the Mount of Olives [1]where*

[1]John 18:1
[2]Mark 14:26

was a garden, into the which he entered, and his disciples.

PETER'S DENIAL FORETOLD A SECOND TIME

MATT. 26

:31 Then saith Jesus unto them, All ye shall be offended, because of me this night: for it is written, I will smite the shepherd, and the sheep of the flock shall be scattered abroad,

32 But after I am risen again, I will go before you into Galilee.

33 Peter answered and said unto him, Though all men should be offended because of thee, yet will I never be offended.

[1]Mark 14:30

34 Jesus said unto him, Verily I say unto [1]*thee, That this night, before the cock crow twice,* thou shalt deny me thrice.

[2]Mark 14:31

35 Peter said unto him, [2]*the more vehemently,* Though I should die with thee, yet will I not deny thee. Likewise also said all the disciples.

JESUS PRAYS IN GETHSEMANE

MATT. 26

:36 Then cometh Jesus with them unto a place called Gethsem'ane, and saith unto the disciples, Sit

[1]Luke 22:40

ye here, while I go and pray yonder, and [1]*Pray that ye enter not into temptation.*

[2]Mark 14:33

37 And he took with him Peter and [2]*James and John,* the two sons of Zeb'edee, and began to be sorrowful and very heavy.

38 Then saith he unto them, My soul is exceeding sorrowful, even unto death: tarry ye here, and watch with me.

[3]Luke 22:41
[4]Mark 14:35
on the ground

39 And he went a little further, [3]*and he was withdrawn from them about a stone's cast,* and fell [4]on his face, and prayed, saying, O my Father, if it be possible, let this cup pass from me: nevertheless, not as I will, but as thou wilt.

LUKE 22

:43 And there appeared an angel unto him from heaven, strengthening him.

44 And being in an agony he prayed more earnestly: and his sweat was as it were great drops of blood falling down to the ground.

ARRANGED AS A SINGLE NARRATIVE 203

LUKE 22　　45 And when he rose up from prayer, [5]*he cometh*
[5]Matt. 26:40　*unto the disciples, and findeth them asleep, and*
[6]Mark 14:37　*saith unto Peter,* [6]*Simon, sleepest thou?* [5]*What, could ye not watch with me one hour?*

MATT. 26　　:41 Watch and pray, that ye enter not into
[7]Mark 14:38　temptation: the spirit indeed is [7]willing, but the flesh
ready　　is weak.

42 He went away again the second time, and prayed, saying, O my Father, if this cup may not pass away from me, except I drink it, thy will be done,

43 And he came and found them asleep again: for
[8]Mark 14:40　their eyes were heavy, [8]*neither wist they what to answer him.*

44 And he left them, and went away again, and prayed the third time, saying the same words.

[9]Mark 14:41　45 Then cometh he to his disciples, [9]*the third time,* and saith unto them, Sleep on now, and take your rest: [9]*it is enough,* behold, the hour is at hand, and the Son of man is betrayed into the hands of sinners.

46 Rise, let us be going: behold, he is at hand that doth betray me.

THE BETRAYAL AND ARREST OF JESUS

MARK 14　　:43 And immediately, while he yet spake, cometh
[1]John 18:2　Judas, one of the twelve, [1]*which betrayed him,*
[2]John 18:3　[2]*having received a* [3]*band of men and officers from the*
[3]Mark 14:43　*chief priests* and [4]*scribes* [2]*and Pharisees, with*
multitude　　*lanterns and torches and weapons,* [for he] [1]*knew the*
[4]Mark 14:43　*place: for Jesus ofttimes resorted thither with his disciples.*

JOHN 18　　:4 Jesus therefore, knowing all things that should come upon him, went forth,

MARK 14　　:44 And he that betrayed him had given them a
[5]Matt. 26:48　[5]token, saying, Whomsoever I shall kiss, that same
sign　　is he; take him, [6]*hold him fast,* and lead him away
[6]Matt. 26:48　safely.

45 And as soon as he was come, he goeth
[7]Matt. 26:49　straightway to him, and saith, [7]*Hail,* Master,
[8]Matt. 26:40　Master; and kissed him, and [8]*Jesus said unto him,*

[9]Luke 22:48	*Friend, wherefore art thou come:* [9]*betrayest thou the Son of man with a kiss?*
JOHN 18	:4 ... and said unto them, Whom seek ye?

5 They answered him, Jesus of Nazareth, Jesus saith unto them, I am he. And Judas also, which betrayed him, stood with them.

6 As soon then as he had said unto them, I am he, they went backward, and fell to the ground.

7 Then asked he them again, Whom seek ye? And they said, Jesus of Nazareth.

8 Jesus answered, I have told you that I am he: if therefore ye seek me, let these go their way:

9 That the saying might be fulfilled, which he spake, Of them which thou gavest me have I lost none. |
| MARK 14 | :45 And they laid their hands on him, and took him. |
| LUKE 22 | :49 When they which were about him saw what would follow, they said unto him, Lord, shall we smite with the sword? |

PETER USES HIS SWORD

JOHN 18	:10 Then Simon Peter having a sword drew it, and smote the high priest's servant, and cut off his right
[1]Luke 22:51	ear. The servant's name was Malchus. [1]*And Jesus answered and said, Suffer ye thus far. And he touched his ear, and healed him.*

11 Then said Jesus unto Peter, Put up thy sword |
| [2]Matt. 26:52 | into the sheath, [2]*for all they that take the sword shall perish with the sword, the cup which my Father* hath given me, shall I not drink it? |
| MATT. 26 | :53 Thinkest thou that I cannot now pray to my Father, and he shall presently give more than twelve legions of angels?

54 But how then shall the Scriptures be fulfilled, that thus it must be? |
| MARK 14 | :48 [3]*In that same hour* Jesus answered and said |
| [3]Matt. 26:55 | [4]*unto the chief priests, and captains of the temple,* |
| [4]Luke 22:52 | *and the elders, which were come to him,* Are ye come out, as against a thief, with swords and with staves to take me?

49 I was daily with you in the temple teaching, |

ARRANGED AS A SINGLE NARRATIVE

⁵Luke 22:53 — and ye took me not: *⁵but this is your hour, and the power of darkness.*

MATT. 26 — :56 But all this was done, that the Scriptures of the prophets might be fulfilled. Then all the disciples forsook him, and fled.

THEY LAY HOLD ON A YOUNG MAN

MARK 14 — :51 And there followed him a certain young man, having a linen cloth cast about his naked body; and the young men laid hold on him:

52 And he left the linen cloth, and fled from them naked.

JESUS BROUGHT BEFORE THE HIGH PRIEST

JOHN 18 — :12 Then the band and the captain and officers of the Jews took Jesus, and bound him,

13 And led him away to Annas first; for he was father-in-law to Cai'aphas, which was the high priest that same year.

14 Now Cai'aphas was he, which gave counsel to the Jews, that it was expedient that one man should die for the people. *¹And with him were assembled all the chief priests and the elders and the scribes. ²And when they had kindled a fire in the midst of the hall,*

¹Mark 14:53

²Luke 22:55 — they sat *²down together.*

PETER IN THE HIGH PRIEST'S COURT

JOHN 18
¹Luke 22:54 — :15 And Simon Peter followed Jesus *¹afar off* and so did another disciple: that disciple was known unto the high priest, and went in with Jesus into the palace of the high priest.

16 But Peter stood at the door without. Then went out that other disciple, which was known unto the high priest, and spake unto her that kept the door, and brought in Peter, *²and he sat with the servants, to see the end.*

²Matt. 26:58

³Luke 22:56 — 17 Then ... the damsel that kept the door *³beheld*
⁴Mark 14:67 — *⁴Peter ³as he sat* by the fire, *⁴warming himself ³and earnestly looked upon him, and said, This man was also with ⁴Jesus of Nazareth.*

JOHN 18 — :18 And the servants and officers stood there, who had made a fire of coals, for it was cold; and they warmed themselves: and Peter stood with them, and warmed himself.

LUKE 22
⁵Mark 14:68

:57 And he denied him, saying, Woman, I know him not, *⁵neither understand I what thou sayest. And he went out into the porch; and the cock crew.*

⁶Mark 14:69

58 And after a little while another *⁶maid* saw him on *⁷the porch* and *⁶began to say unto them that stood by,* Thou art also one of them, *⁷with Jesus of Nazareth.* And Peter said, Man, I am not.

⁷Matt. 26:71

THE TRIAL BEFORE ANNAS

JOHN 18 — :19 The high priest then asked Jesus of his disciples and of his doctrine.

20 Jesus answered him, I spake openly to the world; I ever taught in the synagogue, and in the temple, whither the Jews always resort; and in secret have I said nothing.

21 Why askest thou me? ask them which heard me, what I have said unto them: behold, they know what I said.

22 And when he had thus spoken one of the officers which stood by struck Jesus with the palm of his hand, saying Answerest thou the high priest so?

23 Jesus answered him, If I have spoken evil, bear witness of the evil: but if well, why smitest thou me?

24 Now Annas had sent him bound unto Cai'aphas the high priest.

PETER DENIES CHRIST THE THIRD TIME

LUKE 22
¹John 18:25
²Mark 14:70
³Matt. 26:73

:59 And about the space of an hour after, *¹Simon Peter stood and warmed himself. They therefore* confidently affirmed, saying, of a truth, this fellow was also with him; *²for thou art a Galilean, ³for thy speech betrayeth thee.*

JOHN 18 — :26 One of the servants of the high priest, being his near kinsman whose ear Peter cut off, saith, Did I not see thee in the garden with him?

ARRANGED AS A SINGLE NARRATIVE

⁴Matt. 26:74
⁵Mark 14:71
⁶Luke 22:60
Man, I know not what thou sayest.
⁷Mark 14:72
LUKE 22

⁸Mark 14:72

27 And Peter denied again [and] ⁴*began* ⁶*to curse and to swear, saying, I know not the man* ⁵*of whom ye speak,* and immediately while he yet spake, the cock crew ⁷*the second time.*

:61 And the Lord turned, and looked upon Peter, and Peter remembered the word of the Lord, how he had said unto him, Before the cock crow ⁸*twice,* thou shalt deny me thrice.

62 And Peter went out and wept bitterly.

COUNCIL SEEKS FOR FALSE WITNESSES

MARK 14
¹Matt. 26:59

:55 And the chief priests and all the council sought for ¹*false* witness against Jesus to put him to death; and found none.

56 For many bare false witness against him, but their witness agreed not together.

57 ¹*At last* there arose ¹*two* and they bare false witness against him, saying,

²Matt. 26:61

58 We heard him say, I will destroy this temple ²*of God* that is made with hands, and within three days I will build another made without hands.

59 But neither so did their witness agree together.

60 And the high priest stood up in the midst, and asked Jesus, saying, Answerest thou nothing? What is it which these witness against thee?

61 But he held his peace, and answered nothing. Again the high priest asked him, and said unto him,

³Matt. 26:63

³*I adjure thee by the living God that thou tell us whether thou art the Christ,* the Son of the Blessed?

⁴Matt. 26:64

62 And Jesus said ⁴*Thou hast said* I am: and ye shall see the Son of man sitting on the right hand of power, and coming in the clouds of heaven.

⁵Matt. 26:65
⁶Matt. 26:67
MARK 14

63 Then the high priest rent his clothes, and saith, ⁵*He hath spoken blasphemy.* What need we any further witnesses? ⁶*Behold now.*

64 Ye have heard the blasphemy: what think ye? And they all condemned him to be guilty of death.

JESUS MOCKED AND BEATEN

LUKE 22
¹Mark 14:65

:63 And the men that held Jesus mocked him, and smote him, ¹*and began to spit on him.*

64 And when they had blindfolded him, they struck him on the face, and asked him, saying,

²Matt. 26:68

Prophesy, ²*unto us, thou Christ,* who smote thee?

65 And many other things blasphemously spake they against him.

JESUS BEFORE THE COUNCIL*

LUKE 22
¹Matt. 27:1
²Mark 15:1

:66 ¹*When morning was come,* and as soon as it was day, the elders of the people and the chief priests and the scribes came together, and ²*held a consultation against Jesus to put him to death,* and led him into their council saying,

67 Art thou the Christ? tell us. And he said unto them, If I tell you, ye will not believe:

68 And if I also ask you, ye will not answer me, nor let me go.

69 Hereafter shall the Son of man sit on the right hand of the power of God.

70 Then said they all, Art thou then the Son of God? And he said unto them, Ye say that I am.

71 And they said, what need we any further witness? for we ourselves have heard of his own mouth.

MATT. 27
³Luke 23:1

:2 And when they had bound him, ³*The whole multitude of them arose.* ⁴*Then led they Jesus from Caiaphas, unto the hall of judgment, and it was early,* and delivered him to Pontius Pilate the governor, ⁴*and they themselves went not into the judgment hall, lest they should be defiled: but that they might eat the passover.*

⁴John 18:28

---

*This is another council meeting held at break of day. The preceding account all seems to have taken place before day while Peter was yet present and before the cock had crowed the third time. Mark 15:1 says, "And straightway in the morning the chief priests held a consultation with the elders and scribes and the whole council, and bound Jesus and carried him away, and delivered him to Pilate." Also Matt. 27:1, "When the morning was come, all the chief priests and elders of the people took counsel against Jesus to put him to death." Luke is the only writer who gives an account of this council meeting.

JUDAS HANGS HIMSELF*

MATT. 27 :3 Then Judas, which had betrayed him, when he saw that he was condemned, repented himself, and brought again the thirty pieces of silver to the chief priests and elders. .

4 Saying, I have sinned in that I have betrayed the innocent blood. And they said, What is that to us? see thou to that.

5 And he cast down the pieces of silver in the temple, and departed, and went and hanged himself.

6 And the chief priests took the silver pieces, and said, It is not lawful for to put them into the treasury, because it is the price of blood.

7 And they took counsel, and bought with them the potter's field, to bury strangers in.

8 Wherefore that field was called, The field of blood, unto this day.

9 Then was fulfilled that which was spoken by Jeremiah the prophet, saying, And they took the thirty pieces of silver, the price of him that was valued, whom they of the children of Israel did value;

10 And gave them for the potter's field, as the Lord appointed me.

JESUS BEFORE PILATE

JOHN 18 :29 Pilate then went out unto them, and said, What accusation bring ye against this man?

30 They answered and said unto him, If he were not a malefactor, we would not have delivered him up unto thee.

---

*Matthew is the only one to mention the death of Judas in the Gospels. Peter speaks of him in Acts 1:15-19 as follows: "And in those days Peter stood up in the midst of the disciples, and said, (the number of names together were about an hundred and twenty,) Men and brethren, this scripture must needs have been fulfilled, which the Holy Ghost by the mouth of David spake before concerning Judas, which was guide to them that took Jesus. For he was numbered with us, and obtained part of this ministry. Now this man purchased a field with the reward of iniquity; and falling headlong; he burst asunder in the midst, and all his bowels gushed out. And it was known unto all the dwellers at Jerusalem, insomuch as that field is called in their proper tongue, A-cel'-da'ma, that is to say, the field of blood."

LUKE 23　:2 And they began to accuse him, saying, We found this fellow perverting the nation, and forbidding to give tribute to Caesar, saying that he himself is Christ a king.

JOHN 18　:31 Then said Pilate unto them, Take ye him, and judge him according to your law. The Jews therefore said unto him, It is not lawful for us to put any man to death:

32 That the saying of Jesus might be fulfilled, which he spake, *signifying what death he should die.

33 Then Pilate entered into the judgment hall again, and called Jesus, and said unto him, Art thou the King of the Jews?

34 Jesus answered him, Sayest thou this thing of thyself, or did others tell it thee of me?

35 Pilate answered, Am I a Jew? Thine own nation and the chief priests have delivered thee unto me: what hast thou done?

36 Jesus answered, My kingdom is not of this world: if my kingdom were of this world, then would my servants fight, that I should not be delivered to the Jews: but now is my kingdom not from hence.

37 Pilate therefore said unto him, Art thou a king then? Jesus answered, Thou sayest that I am a king. To this end was I born, and for this cause came I into the world, that I should bear witness unto the truth. Every one that is of the truth heareth my voice.

38 Pilate saith unto him, What is truth? And when he had said this, he went out again unto the Jews, and saith unto them, I find in him no fault at all.

39 But ye have a custom, that I should release unto you one at the passover: will ye therefore that I release unto you the King of the Jews?

LUKE 23　:5 And they were the more fierce, saying, He stirreth up the people, teaching throughout all Jewry, beginning from Galilee to this place.

MARK 15　:3 And the chief priests accused him of many things;

---

*'The Romans only used the method of crucifixon; the Jews, stoning.

MATT. 27 :13 Then said Pilate unto him, Hearest thou not how many things they witness against thee?

14 And he answered him to never a word; insomuch that the governor marveled greatly.

JESUS BEFORE HEROD

LUKE 23 :6 When Pilate heard of Galilee, he asked whether the man were a Galilean.

7 And as soon as he knew that he belonged unto Herod's jurisdiction, he sent him to Herod, who himself also was at Jerusalem at that time.

8 And when Herod saw Jesus, he was exceeding glad: for he was desirous to see him of a long season, because he had heard many things of him; and he hoped to have seen some miracle done by him.

9 Then he questioned with him in many words; but he answered him nothing.

10 And the chief priests and scribes stood and vehemently accused him.

11 And Herod with his men of war set him at nought, and mocked him, and arrayed him in a gorgeous robe, and sent him again to Pilate.

12 And the same day Pilate and Herod were made friends together; for before they were at enmity between themselves.

BARABBAS OR CHRIST

LUKE 23 :13 And Pilate, when he had called together the chief priests and the rulers and the people,

14 Said unto them, Ye have brought this man unto me as one that perverteth the people; and, behold, I, having examined him before you, have found no fault in this man touching those things whereof ye accuse him:

15 No, nor yet Herod: for I sent you to him; and, lo, nothing worthy of death is done unto him.

16 I will therefore chastise him, and release him.

MATT. 27 :15 Now at that feast the governor was wont to release unto the people a prisoner, whom they would.

LUKE 23 :17 (For of necessity he must release one unto them at the feast.)

MATT. 27 ¹Mark 15:7	:16 And they had then a notable prisoner, called Barab'bas, ¹*which lay bound with them that had made insurrection with him, who had committed murder in the insurrection.*
MARK 15	:8 And the multitude crying aloud began to desire him to do as he had ever done unto them.
MATT. 27	:17 Therefore when they were gathered together, Pilate said unto them, Whom will ye that I release unto you? Barab'bas, or Jesus which is called Christ? 18 For he knew that for envy they had delivered him.
LUKE 23	:18 And they cried out all at once, saying, Away with this man, and release unto us Barab'bas:
MATT. 27	:19 When he was set down on the judgment seat, his wife sent unto him, saying, Have thou nothing to do with that just man: for I have suffered many things this day in a dream because of him. 20 But the chief priests and elders persuaded the multitude that they should ask Barab'bas, and destroy Jesus. 21 The governor answered and said unto them, Whether of the twain will ye that I release unto you? They said Barab'bas. 22 Pilate saith unto them, What shall I do then with Jesus which is called Christ? They all say unto him, Let him be crucified.
LUKE 23	:20 Pilate therefore, willing to release Jesus, spake again to them. 21 But they cried, saying, Crucify him, Crucify him.
JOHN 18	:40 Then cried they all again, saying, Not this man, but Barab'bas. Now Barab'bas was a robber.
LUKE 23	:22 And he said unto them, the third time, Why, what evil hath he done? I have found no cause of death in him: I will therefore chastise him, and let him go. 23 And they were instant with loud voices, requiring that he might be crucified: and the voices of them and of the chief priests prevailed.

PILATE WASHES HIS HANDS

MATT. 27 :24 When Pilate saw that he could prevail nothing, but that rather a tumult was made, he took water, and washed his hands before the multitude, saying, I am innocent of the blood of this just person: see ye to it.

25 Then answered all the people, and said, His blood be on us, and on our children.

JESUS SENTENCED

MATT. 27
¹John 19:1

:26 Then released he Barab'bas unto them: ¹*Then Pilate therefore took Jesus, and scourged him* and when he had scourged Jesus, he delivered him to be crucified.

²Mark 15:16

27 Then the soldiers of the governor took Jesus into the common hall, ²*called Pretorium*, and gathered unto him the whole band of soldiers.

³Mark 15:17
purple

28 And they stripped him, and put on him a ³scarlet robe.

⁴Mark 15:19
⁵John 19:3

29 And when they had platted a crown of thorns, they put it upon his head, and a reed in his right hand: and they bowed the knee before him, ⁴*worshipped him* and mocked him, ⁵*and they smote him with their hands,* saying, Hail, King of the Jews!

30 And they spit upon him, and took the reed, and smote him on the head,

31 And after that they had mocked him, they took the robe off from him, and put his own raiment on him.

PILATE PLEADS AGAIN
WITH THE JEWS

JOHN 19 :4 Pilate therefore went forth again, and saith unto them, Behold, I bring him forth to you, that ye may know that I find no fault in him.

5 Then came Jesus forth, wearing the crown of thorns, and the purple robe. And Pilate saith unto them, Behold the man!

6 When the chief priests therefore and officers saw him, they cried out, saying, Crucify him, crucify him. Pilate saith unto them, Take ye him, and crucify him: for I find no fault in him.

JOHN 19

7 The Jews answered him, We have a law, and by our law he ought to die, because he made himself the Son of God.

8 When Pilate therefore heard that saying, he was the more afraid;

9 And went again into the judgment hall, and saith unto Jesus, Whence art thou? But Jesus gave him no answer.

10 Then saith Pilate unto him, Speakest thou not unto me? knowest thou not that I have power to crucify thee, and have power to release thee?

11 Jesus answered, Thou couldest have no power at all against me, except it were given thee from above: therefore he that delivereth me unto thee hath the greater sin.

12 And from henceforth Pilate sought to release him: but the Jews cried out, saying, If thou let this man go, thou art not Caesar's friend: whosoever maketh himself a king speaketh against Caesar.

PILATE'S FINAL PLEA

JOHN 19

:13 When Pilate therefore heard that saying, he brought Jesus forth, and sat down in the judgment seat in a place that is called the Pavement, but in the Hebrew, Bat'batha.

14 And it was the preparation of the passover, and about the sixth *hour: and he saith unto the Jews, Behold your King!

15 But they cried out, Away with him, away with him, crucify him. Pilate saith unto them, Shall I crucify your King? The chief priests answered, We have no king but Caesar.

[1]Mark 15:15
[2]Luke 19:25

16 Then Pilate [1]*willing to content the people* [2]*delivered Jesus to their will*, and gave sentence that

---

*"About the sixth hour" was about noon, Matt. 27:45 says there was darkness over all the land from the sixth to the ninth hour. This would be according to our time from 12:00-3:00 p.m. Luke gives the same time. However, Mark 15:25 says "it was the third", the time of the crucifixion. The Romans had a system whereby they divided the day into four parts and also the night. It could be that Mark was referring to this third part of the daylight hours as the third hour which would have been from noon unto three o'clock. It is generally accepted that Mark was writing to the Romans. This would be a natural way to describe the time of the crucifixion.

JOHN 19
³John 19:16
⁴Matt. 27:31

it should be as they required, ³*And they took Jesus and led him away* ⁴*to crucify him.*

THE CRUCIFIXION

LUKE 23
¹John 19:17
²Matt. 27:32
³Mark 15:21

:26 And as they led him away, ¹*and he bearing his cross went forth,* ²*and as they came out, they found a man,* ³*Simon a Cyre'nian, who passed by, coming out of the country, the father of Alexander and Rufus,* and they laid hold upon Simon . . . and on him they laid the cross.

27 And there followed him a great company of people, and of women, which also bewailed and lamented him.

28 But Jesus turning unto them said, Daughters of Jerusalem, weep not for me, but weep for yourselves, and for your children.

29 For, behold, the days are coming, in the which they shall say, Blessed are the barren, and the wombs that never bare, and the paps which never gave suck.

30 Then shall they begin to say to the mountains, Fall on us; and to the hills, Cover us.

31 For if they do these things in a green tree, what shall be done in the dry?

32 And there were also two others, malefactors, led with him to be put to death.

⁴John 19:17
⁵Matt. 27:37
⁶Luke 23:33
Mark 15:23
Golgotha
⁷Mark 15:23
wine
⁸myrrh

33 And when they were come unto a place, ⁴*in the Hebrew called* ⁶Calvary, ⁵*that is to say a place of a skull.*

34 They gave him ⁷vinegar to drink mingled with ⁸gall: and when he had tasted thereof, he would not drink.

MARK 15

:25 And it was the *third hour, and they crucified him,

MARK 15

:27 And with him they crucify two thieves; the one on his right hand, and the other on his left.

28 And the Scripture was fulfilled, which saith, And he was numbered with the transgressors.

---
*See footnote on John 19:14 on page 214.

LUKE 23 :34 Then said Jesus, **Father, forgive them; for they know not what they do.

JOHN 19 :19 And Pilate wrote a title, and put it on the cross [9]*over his head.* And the writing was, [10]Jesus of Nazareth the King of the Jews.
[9]Matt. 27:37
[10]Luke 23:38
This is the King of the Jews.

20 This title then read many of the Jews; for the place where Jesus was crucified was nigh to the city: and it was written in Hebrew, and Greek, and Latin.

21 Then said the chief priests of the Jews to Pilate, Write not, The King of the Jews; but that he said, I am King of the Jews.

22 Pilate answered, What I have written I have written.

23 Then the soldiers, when they had crucified Jesus, took his garments, and [12]made four parts, to every soldier a part; and also his coat: now the [13]coat was without seam, woven from the top throughout.
[12]Matt. 27:37 parted his garments
[13]vesture

24 They said therefore among themselves, Let us not rend it, but cast lots for it, whose it shall be: that the Scripture might be fulfilled, which saith, They parted my raiment among them, and for my vesture they did cast lots. These things therefore the soldiers did.

MATT. 26 :36 And sitting down they watched him there;

LUKE 23 :35 And the people stood beholding, and the rulers also with them derided him,

MARK 15 :29 And they that passed by railed on him, wagging their heads, and saying, Ah, thou that destroyest the temple, and buildest it in three days,

[14]Matt. 27:40 30 Save thyself [14]*if thou be the Son of God,* and come down from the cross.

31 Likewise also the chief priests mocking said among themselves with the scribes [15]*and elders,* He saved others; himself he cannot save.
[15]Matt. 27:41

32 Let Christ the King of Israel descend now from the cross, that we may see and believe.

MATT. 27 :43 He trusted in God; let him deliver him now, if he will have him: for he said, I am the Son of God.

44 The thieves also, which were crucified with him, cast the same in his teeth.

**First of Jesus' seven sayings from the cross.

LUKE 23	:36 And the soldiers also mocked him, coming to him, and offering him vinegar,
	37 And saying, If thou be the King of the Jews, save thyself.
LUKE 23	:39 And one of the malefactors which were hanged railed on him, saying, If thou be Christ, save thyself and us.
	40 But the other answering rebuked him, saying, Dost not thou fear God, seeing thou art in the same condemnation?
	41 And we indeed justly; for we receive the due reward of our deeds: but this man hath done nothing amiss.
	42 And he said unto Jesus, Lord, remember me when thou comest into thy kingdom.
	43 And Jesus said unto him, Verily I say unto thee, *Today shalt thou be with me in paradise.
MATT. 27 [16]Luke 23:44 earth [17]Luke 23:45	:45 Now from the sixth hour there was darkness over all the [16]land unto the ninth hour, [17]*and the sun was darkened.*
	46 And about the ninth hour Jesus cried with a loud voice, saying, *Eli, Eli, lama sabach'thani? that is to say, My God, my God, why hast thou forsaken me?
	47 Some of them that stood there, when they heard that, said, This man calleth for Elijah.
JOHN 19	:25 Now there stood by the cross of Jesus his mother and his mother's sister, Mary the wife of Cle'ophas, and Mary Mag'dalene.
	26 When Jesus therefore saw his mother, and the disciple standing by, whom he loved, he saith unto his mother,**Woman, behold thy son!
	27 Then saith he to the disciple, Behold thy mother! And from that hour that disciple took her unto his own home.
	28 After this, Jesus knowing that all things were now accomplished, that the Scripture might be fulfilled, saith,**I thirst.

---

*Second and third sayings from the cross.
**Fourth through fifth sayings from the cross.

MATT. 27 [18]Matt. 27:48	29 Now there was set a vessel full of vinegar: [18]*and straightway one of them ran, and took a sponge, and filled it with vinegar, and put it on a*
[19]John 19:29 hyssop	[19]*reed* and put it up to his mouth [18]*and gave him to drink.*
MATT. 27 [20]Mark 15:36 to take him down	:49 The rest said, Let be, let us see whether Eli'jah will come to [20]save him.
JOHN 19 [21]Luke 23:46 [22]Matt. 27:50	:30 When Jesus therefore had received the vinegar, he [21]*cried* [22]*again* [21]*with a loud voice*, and [21]*said, Father, *into thy hands I commend my spirit: and having said thus, he* said, *It is **finished: and bowed his head, and gave up the ghost.
MATT. 27	:51 And, behold, the veil of the temple was rent in twain from the top to the bottom; and the earth did quake, and the rocks rent;

MANY RAISED FROM THE DEAD AFTER HIS RESURRECTION

MATT. 27 [1]Mark 15:39 [2]Luke 23:47 Centurion saw what was done, he glorified God saying certainly this was a righteoeus man.	:52 And the graves were opened; and many bodies of the saints which slept arose, 53 And came out of the graves after his resurrection, and went into the holy city, and appeared unto many. 54 Now when the centurion, [1]*which stood over against him, saw that he so cried out and gave up the ghost*, [and] they that were with him watching Jesus, [2]saw the earthquake, and those things that were done, they feared greatly, saying, Truly this was the Son of God.
LUKE 23	:48 And all the people that came together to that sight, beholding the things which were done, smote their breasts, and returned. 49 And all his acquaintance, and the women that followed him from Galilee, stood afar off, beholding
[3]Mark 15:40	these things, [3]*among whom was Mary Magdalene, and Mary the mother of James the less and of Joses, and Salome;*
[4]Matt. 27:56	[4]*and the mother of Zebedee's children.*

---

*Sixth and seventh sayings from the cross.
**The Old Testament ceremonial law is fulfilled in Christ. New Testament begins.

ARRANGED AS A SINGLE NARRATIVE

MARK 15 :41 Who also, when he was in Galilee, followed him, and ministered unto him; and many other women which came up with him unto Jerusalem.

THE SIDE OF JESUS PIERCED*

JOHN 19 :31 The Jews therefore, because it was the preparation, that the bodies should not remain upon the cross on the sabbath, (for that sabbath day was a high day,) besought Pilate that their legs might be broken, and that they might be taken away.

32 Then came the soldiers, and brake the legs of the first, and of the other which was crucified with him.

33 But when they came to Jesus, and saw that he was dead already, they brake not his legs;

34 But one of the soldiers with a spear pierced his side, and forthwith came there out blood and water.

35 And he that saw it bare record, and his record is true; and he knoweth that he saith true, that ye might believe.

36 For these things were done, that the Scripture should be fulfilled, A bone of him shall not be broken.

37 And again another Scripture saith, They shall look on him whom they pierced.

THE BURIAL OF JESUS

MARK 15 :42 And now when the even was come, because it was the preparation, that is, the day before the
[1]Luke 23:50 sabbath, [1]*behold, there was a* [2]*rich* [1]*man named*
[2]Matt. 27:47 43 Joseph of Arimathe′a, [3]*a disciple of Jesus, but*
[3]John 19:38 *secretly for fear of the Jews,* an honorable counselor,
[4]Luke 23:51 [1]*and he was a good man and a just:* which also waited for the kingdom of God, [4]*(The same had not consented to the counsel and deed of them:)* came, and went in boldly unto Pilate, and craved the body of Jesus.

44 And Pilate marveled if he were already dead: and calling unto him the centurion, he asked him whether he had been any while dead.

---

*John is the only one of the four Gospels that mentions the piercing of Jesus' side.

MARK 15	45 And when he knew it of the centurion, he gave the body to Joseph.
	46 And he bought fine linen, and took . . . ⁵*down*
⁵John 19:40	*the body of Jesus.*
JOHN 19	:39 And there came also Nicodemus, which at the first came to Jesus by night, and brought a mixture of myrrh and aloes, about a hundred pound weight.
	40 Then took they the body of Jesus, and wound
⁶Matt. 27:59	it in ⁶*clean* linen clothes with the spices, as the manner of the Jews is to bury.
	41 Now in the place where he was crucified there was a garden; and in the garden a new sepulchre
⁷Matt. 27:60	⁷*which* Joseph ⁸*had hewn out in the rock:* wherein
⁸Luke 23:53 hewn in stone	was never man yet laid.
	42 There ⁹*in his own new tomb* laid they Jesus therefore because of the Jews' preparation day; for
⁹Matt. 27:60	the sepulchre was nigh at hand. ⁹*And he rolled a great stone to the door of the sepulchure, and departed.*
LUKE 23	:54 And that day was the preparation, and the sabbath drew on.
¹⁰Mark 15:47	55 And the women also, ¹⁰*Mary Magdalene and Mary the mother of Joses* which came with him from Galilee, followed after, and beheld the sepulchre, and how his body laid.
	56 And they returned, and prepared spices and ointments; and rested the sabbath day according to the commandment.

THE GUARD AT THE TOMB*

MATT. 27	:62 Now the next day, that followed the day of the preparation, the chief priests and Pharisees came together unto Pilate,
	63 Saying, Sir, we remember that that deceiver said, while he was yet alive, After three days I will arise again.
	64 Command therefore that the sepulchre be made sure until the third day, lest his disciples come by night, and steal him away, and say unto the people, He is risen from the dead: so the last error shall be worse than the first.

---

*Matthew is the only one to make any mention of the guard.

MATT. 27   65 Pilate said unto them, Ye have a watch: go your way, make it as sure as ye can.

46 So they went, and made the sepulchre sure, sealing the stone, and setting a watch.

THE RESURRECTION*

JOHN 20   :1 The first day of the week cometh Mary Mag'dalene early, when it was yet dark, unto the sepulchre, and seeth the stone taken away from the sepulchre.

2 Then she runneth, and cometh to Simon Peter, and to the other disciple, whom Jesus loved, and saith unto them, They have taken away the Lord out of the sepulchre, and we know not where they have laid him.

3 Peter therefore went forth, and that other disciple, and came to the sepulchre.

---

*The following appears to me to be a logical and consistent explanation for what seems to be conflicting reports among the Gospel writers. It appears that Mary Magdalene went into the sepulchre alone some while before day and found the stone rolled away, but she did not see the angel nor understand what had taken place. In her anxiety she hastens to tell Peter and John who also rush to the sepulchre and find it as she had said. In their perplexity, they leave and go to their own home.

With all the perplexity and confusion, and still hope that they would find the body or that it might be returned, Mary possibly did not tell Mary the mother of James and Salome of her earlier experience, but went ahead and joined them as had been planned, hoping for the best. When the three women arrive at the sepulchre, just as the sun was rising, they witnessed the angel sitting on the stone which had been rolled away. He tells them of the resurrection. Mary and Salome enter and see two angels who give the same report. Mary and Salome evidently leave to go tell the news. Mary had been awaiting outside having been earlier inside, still waits in wonder and amazement. She looks inside, after the others leave. Then the angel questions her and she repeats the words which she told to Peter and John earlier, "They have taken away my Lord and I know not where they have laid him". Then Jesus, her risen Lord, spoke to her, and she questions him, not knowing it was Jesus. Then he reveals himself unto her and tells her to go tell the brethren. She hastens to catch up with Mary and Salome and in the meantime he appears to them. Then they, the three of them, go and tell the eleven disciples who believe not. Then Peter goes (Luke 24:9-12) to the sepulchre the second time to view the situation and to consider the matter. When he arrived, the angels were gone. The same day, Jesus walks and talks with two disciples on the way to Emmaus (Luke 24:13-18). Later in the day (John 20:19), Jesus appears unto the disciples, Thomas being absent.

JOHN 20

:4 So they ran both together: and the other disciple did outrun Peter, and came first to the sepulchre.

5 And he stooping down, and looking in, saw the linen clothes lying; yet went he not in.

6 Then cometh Simon Peter following him, and went into the sepulchre, and seeth the linen clothes lie,

7 And the napkin, that was about his head, not lying with the linen clothes, but wrapped together in a place by itself.

8 Then went in also that other disciple, which came first to the sepulchre, and he saw, and believed.

9 For as yet they knew not the Scripture, that he must rise again from the dead.

10 Then the disciples went away again unto their own home.

MARK 16

:1 And when the sabbath was past, Mary Mag'dalene, and Mary the mother of James, and Salome, had brought sweet spices, that they might come and anoint him.

2 And very early in the morning, they came unto the sepulchre at the ¹rising of the sun ²*bringing the spices which they had prepared and certain others with them.*

¹Matt. 28:1 as it began to dawn toward the first day of the week
²Luke 24:1

3 And they said among themselves, Who shall roll us away the stone from the door of the sepulchre?

4 And when they looked, they saw that the stone was rolled away: for it was very great.

MATT. 28

:2 And, behold, there was a great earthquake: for the *angel of the Lord descended from heaven, and came and rolled back the stone from the door, and sat upon it.

3 His countenance was like lightning, and his raiment white as snow:

4 And for fear of him the keepers did shake, and became as dead men.

5 And the angel answered and said unto the

---

*This had taken place before Mary Magdalene had gone earlier. Evidently the angel was not present or had concealed himself at that time.

women, Fear not ye: for I know that ye seek Jesus, which was crucified.

MATT. 28

6 He is not here: for he is risen, as he said. Come, see the place where the Lord lay.

LUKE 24

:3 And they entered in, and found not the body of the Lord Jesus.

4 And it came to pass, as they were much perplexed thereabout, behold, *two men stood by them in shining garments: and ³ *a young man sitting on the right side clothed in a long white garment.*

³Mark 16:5

5 And as they were afraid, and bowed down their faces to the earth, they said unto them, Why seek ye the living among the dead?

6 He is not here, but is risen: remember how he spake unto you when he was yet in Galilee,

7 Saying, The Son of man must be delivered into the hands of sinful men, and be crucified, and the third day rise again.

8 And they remembered his words,

MARK 16

:6 And the young man said unto them, Be not affrighted: ye seek Jesus of Nazareth, which was crucified: he is risen; he is not here: behold the place where they laid him.

⁴Matt. 28:7 quickly

7 But go your ⁴ way, tell his disciples and Peter ⁵ *that he is risen from the dead and behold he goeth* before you into Galilee: there shall ye see him, as he said unto you. ⁵ *Lo, I have told you.*

⁵Matt. 28:7

8 And they departed quickly from the sepulchre with fear and great joy; and did run to bring his disciples word.

THE REPORT OF THE GUARD

MATT. 28

:11 Now when they were going, behold some of the watch came into the city, and showed unto the chief priests all the things that were done.

12 And when they were assembled with the

---

*It seems that four angels announce the resurrection. One rolls back the stone and sits on it and invites them to see where the Lord had lain (Matt. 28:2-6). Two angels inside proclaim the resurrection (Luke 24:34). Then an angel appearing as a young man sitting on the right side repeats the same story (Mark 16:7). The two angels that were standing are sitting as Mary Magdalene looks in after the others had left.

MATT. 28

elders, and had taken counsel, they gave large money unto the soldiers,

13 Saying, Say ye, His disciples came by night, and stole him away while we slept.

14 And if this come to the governor's ears, we will persuade him, and secure you.

15 So they took the money, and did as they were taught: and this saying is commonly reported among the Jews until this day.

JESUS APPEARS TO MARY MAGDALENE

JOHN 20

:11 But Mary stood without at the sepulchre weeping: and as she wept, she stooped down, and looked into the sepulchre,

12 And seeth two angels in white *sitting, the one at the head, and the other at the feet, where the body of Jesus had lain.

13 And they say unto her, Woman, why weepest thou? She saith unto them, Because they have taken away my Lord, and I know not where they have laid him.

MARK 16

:9 Now when Jesus was risen early the first day of the week, he appeared first to Mary Mag'dalene, out of whom he had cast seven devils.

JOHN 20

:14 And when she had thus said, she turned herself back, and saw Jesus standing, and knew not that it was Jesus.

:15 Jesus saith unto her, Woman, why weepest thou? whom seekest thou? She, supposing him to be the gardener, saith unto him, Sir, if thou have borne him hence, tell me where thou hast laid him, and I will take him away.

16 Jesus saith unto her, Mary. She turned herself, and saith unto him, Rabbo'ni; which is to say, Master.

17 Jesus saith unto her, Touch me not; for I am not yet ascended to my Father; but go to my brethren, and say unto them, I ascend unto my Father, and your Father; and to my God, and your God.

---

*Luke 24:4 says the angels were standing. When Mary and Salome left, they must have sat down.

MATT. 28	:9 And as they went to tell his disciples, behold, Jesus met them, saying, All hail. And they came and held him by the feet, and worshipped him.
	10 Then said Jesus unto them, Be not afraid: go tell my brethren that they go into Galilee, and there shall they see me.
LUKE 24	:9 And they returned from the sepulchre, and told all these things unto the eleven, and to all the rest.
	10 It was Mary Mag'dalene, and Joanna, and Mary the mother of James, and other women that were with them, which told these things unto the apostles.
	11 And their words seemed to them as idle tales, and they believed them not.
JOHN 20	:18 Mary Mag'dalene came and told the disciples
¹Mark 16:10	¹ *as they mourned and wept* that she had seen the Lord, and that he had spoken these things unto her.
MARK 16	:11 And they, when they had heard that he was alive, and had been seen of her, believed not.
LUKE 24	:12 Then arose Peter, and ran unto the sepulchre; and *stooping down, he beheld the linen clothes laid by themselves, and departed, wondering in himself at that which was come to pass.

JESUS APPEARS TO TWO DISCIPLES
ON THE WAY TO EMMAUS

MARK 16	:12 After that he appeared in another form,
LUKE 24	:13 And, behold, two of them went that same day to a village called Emma'us, which was from Jerusalem about threescore furlongs.
¹Mark 16:12	14 ¹ *As they walked and went into the country* and they talked together of all these things which had happened.
	15 And it came to pass, that, while they communed together and reasoned, Jesus himself drew near, and went with them.
	16 But their eyes were holden that they should not know him.
	17 And he said unto them, What manner of communications are these that ye have one to another, as ye walk, and are sad?

---
*When he was earlier at the sepulchre he went in (John 20:6-7).

LUKE 24

18 And the one of them, whose name was Cle'opas, answering said unto him, Art thou only a stranger in Jerusalem, and hast not known the things which are come to pass there in these days?

19 And he said unto them, What things? And they said unto him, Concerning Jesus of Nazareth, which was a prophet mighty in deed and word before God and all the people:

20 And how the chief priests and our rulers delivered him to be condemned to death, and have crucified him.

21 But we trusted that it had been he which should have redeemed Israel: and beside all this, today is the third day since these things were done.

22 Yea, and certain women also of our company made us astonished, which were early at the sepulchre;

23 And when they found not his body, they came, saying, that they had also seen a vision of angels, which said that he was alive.

24 And certain of them which were with us went to the sepulchre, and found it even so as the women had said: but him they saw not.

25 Then he said unto them, O fools, and slow of heart to believe all that the prophets have spoken:

26 Ought not Christ to have suffered these things and to enter into his glory?

27 And beginning at Moses and all the prophets, he expounded unto them in all the Scriptures the things concerning himself.

28 And they drew nigh unto the village, whither they went: and he made as though he would have gone further.

29 But they constrained him, saying, Abide with us; for it is toward evening, and the day is far spent. And he went in to tarry with them.

30 And it came to pass, as he sat at meat with them, he took bread, and blessed it, and brake, and gave to them.

31 And their eyes were opened, and they knew him; and he vanished out of their sight.

32 And they said one to another, Did not our

ARRANGED AS A SINGLE NARRATIVE

LUKE 24

heart burn within us, while he talked with us by the way, and while he opened to us the Scriptures?

33 And they rose up the same hour, and returned to Jerusalem, and found the eleven gathered together, and them that were with them,

34 Saying, The Lord is risen indeed, and hath appeared to Simon.

35 And they told what things were done in the way, and how he was known of them in breaking of bread.

JESUS APPEARS TO HIS DISCIPLES*

JOHN 20
[1]Luke 24:36

:19 Then the same day at evening [1] *as they thus spake*, being the first day of the week, when the doors were shut where the disciples were assembled for fear of the Jews, came Jesus and stood in the midst, and saith unto them, Peace be unto you.

LUKE 24

:37 But they were terrified and affrighted, and supposed that they had seen a spirit.

38 And he said unto them, Why are ye troubled? and why do thoughts arise in your hearts?

39 Behold my hands and my feet, that it is I myself: handle me, and see; for a spirit hath not flesh and bones, as ye see me have.

40 And when he had thus spoken, he showed them

[2]John 20:20

his hands and his feet, [2]*and his side. Then were the disciples glad, when they saw the Lord.*

41 And while they yet believed not for joy, and wondered, he said unto them, Have ye here any meat?

42 And they gave him a piece of broiled fish, and of a honeycomb.

43 And he took it, and did eat before them.

44 And he said unto them, These are the words which I spake unto you, while I was yet with you, that all things must be fulfilled, which were written in the law of Moses, and in the prophets, and in the psalms, concerning me.

---

*Thomas was not present on this occasion. Thomas asked for no more evidence than had already been given to the other disciples who also had doubts. Thomas is often condemned for not being present, but if Jesus had appeared earlier, Peter and John would have been absent (John 20:4-10, Luke 24:12).

LUKE 24

45 Then opened he their understanding, that they might understand the Scriptures,

46 And said unto them, Thus it is written, and thus it behooved Christ to suffer, and to rise from the dead the third day:

47 And that repentance and remission of sins should be preached in his name among all nations, beginning at Jerusalem.

48 And ye are witnesses of these things.

49 And, behold, I send the promise of my Father upon you: but tarry ye in the city of Jerusalem, until ye be endued with power from on high.

JOHN 20

:21 Then said Jesus to them again, Peace be unto you: as my Father hath sent me, even so send I you.

22 And when he had said this, he breathed on them, and saith unto them, Receive ye the Holy Ghost:

23 Whosesoever sins ye remit, they are remitted unto them; and whosesoever sins ye retain, they are retained.

THOMAS DOES BELIEVE

JOHN 20

:24 But Thomas, one of the twelve, called Did'ymus, was not with them when Jesus came.

25 The other disciples therefore said unto him, We have seen the Lord. But he said unto them, Except I shall see in his hands the print of the nails, and put my finger into the print of the nails, and thrust my hand into his side, I will not believe.

26 And after eight days again his disciples were within, and Thomas with them: then came Jesus, the doors being shut, and stood in the midst, and said, Peace be unto you.

27 Then saith he to Thomas, Reach hither thy finger, and behold my hands; and reach hither thy hand, and thrust it into my side; and be not faithless, but believing.

28 And Thomas answered and said unto him, My Lord and my God.

29 Jesus saith unto him, Thomas, because thou hast seen me, thou hast believed: blessed are they that have not seen, and yet have believed.

JESUS APPEARS TO DISCIPLES
AT SEA OF GALILEE

JOHN 21 :1 After these things Jesus showed himself again to the disciples at the sea of Tibe'ri-as; and on this wise showed he himself.

2 There were together Simon Peter, and Thomas called Did'ymus, and Nathan'a-el of Cana in Galilee, and the sons of Zeb'edee, and two other of his disciples.

UNPROFITABLE LABOR WITHOUT
CHRIST

JOHN 21 :3 Simon Peter saith unto them, I go a fishing. They say unto him, We also go with thee. They went forth, and entered into a ship immediately; and that night they caught nothing.

4 But when the morning was now come, Jesus stood on the shore; but the disciples knew not that it was Jesus.

5 Then Jesus saith unto them, Children, have ye any meat? They answered him, No.

6 And he said unto them, Cast the net on the right side of the ship, and ye shall find. They cast therefore, and now they were not able to draw it for the multitude of fishes.

JOHN 21 :7 Therefore that disciple whom Jesus loved saith unto Peter, It is the Lord. Now when Simon Peter heard that it was the Lord, he girt his fisher's coat unto him, (for he was naked), and did cast himself into the sea.

8 And the other disciples came in a little ship, (for they were not far from land, but as it were two hundred cubits,) dragging the net with fishes.

9 As soon then as they were come to land, they saw a fire of coals there, and fish laid thereon, and bread.

10 Jesus saith unto them, Bring of the fish which ye have now caught.

11 Simon Peter went up, and drew the net to land full of great fishes, a hundred and fifty and three: and for all there were so many, yet was not the net broken.

JOHN 21

12 Jesus saith unto them, Come and dine. And none of the disciples durst ask him, Who art thou: knowing that it was the Lord.

13 Jesus then cometh, and taketh bread, and giveth them, and fish likewise.

14 This is now the *third time that Jesus showed himself to his disciples, after that he was risen from the dead.

THE CALL OF GOD IS WITHOUT REPENTANCE.

JOHN 21

:15 So when they had dined, Jesus saith to Simon Peter, Simon, son of Jonas, lovest thou me more than these? He saith unto him, Yea, Lord; thou knowest that I love thee. He saith unto him, Feed my lambs.

16 He saith to him again the second time, Simon, son of Jonas, lovest thou me? He saith unto him, Yea, Lord; thou knowest that I love thee. He saith unto him, Feed my sheep.

17 He saith unto him the third time, Simon, son of Jonas, lovest thou me? Peter was grieved because he said unto him the third time, Lovest thou me? And he said unto him, Lord thou knowest all things; thou knowest that I love thee. Jesus saith unto him, Feed my sheep.

18 Verily, verily, I say unto thee, When thou wast young, thou girdedst thyself, and walkedst whither thou wouldest: but when thou shalt be old, thou shalt stretch forth thy hands, and another shall gird thee, and carry thee whither thou wouldest not.

19 This spake he, signifying by what death he should glorify God. And when he had spoken this, he saith unto him, Follow me.

20 Then Peter, turning about, seeth the disciple whom Jesus loved following; which also leaned on his breast at supper, and said, Lord, which is he that betrayeth thee?

---

*This could only refer to his meeting with the Apostles. He had been seen of the apostles of the First Resurrection Sabbath and again eight days later when Thomas was present. He had made three appearances before this: to Mary Magdalene, and again to Mary Magdalene with the other women, and again to the two disciples on the way to Emmaus.

JOHN 21	21 Peter seeing him saith to Jesus, Lord, and what shall this man do?

22 Jesus saith unto him, If I will that he tarry till I come, what is that to thee? follow thou me.

23 Then went this saying abroad among the brethren that that disciple should not die: yet Jesus said not unto him, He shall not die; but, If I will that he tarry till I come, what is that to thee?

24 This is the disciple which testifieth of these things, and wrote these things: and we know that his testimony is true. |

JESUS COMMISSIONS THE ELEVEN

MATT. 28	:16 Then the eleven disciples went away into Galilee, into a mountain where Jesus had appointed them.

17 And when they saw him, they worshipped him: but some doubted. |
| MARK 16 | :14 Afterward he appeared unto the eleven as they sat at meat, and upbraided them with their unbelief and hardness of heart, because they believed not them which had seen him after he was risen.

15 And he said unto them, Go ye into all the world, and preach the gospel to every creature.

16 He that believeth and is baptized shall be saved; but he that believeth not shall be damned.

17 And these signs shall follow them that believe; In my name shall they cast out devils; they shall speak with new tongues;

18 They shall take up serpents; and if they drink any deadly thing, it shall not hurt them; they shall lay hands on the sick, and they shall recover. |
| MATT. 28 | :18 And Jesus . . . spake unto them, saying, All power is given unto me in heaven and in earth.

19 Go ye therefore, and teach all nations, baptizing them in the name of the Father, and of the Son, and of the Holy Ghost.

20 Teaching them to observe all things whatsoever I have commanded you: and, lo, I am with you alway, even unto the end of the world. Amen. |

THE ASCENSION

LUKE 24 :50 And he led them out as far as to Bethany, and he lifted up his hands, and blessed them.

51 And it came to pass, while he blessed them, he was parted from them, and carried up into heaven [1]Mark 16:19 *[1] and sat on the right hand of God.*

52 And they worshipped him, and returned to Jerusalem with great joy:

53 And were continually in the temple, praising and blessing God.

MARK 16 :20 And they went forth, and preached every where, the Lord working with them, and confirming the word with signs following.

THE PURPOSE OF THE BOOK

JOHN 20 :30 And many other signs truly did Jesus in the presence of his disciples, which are not written in [1]John 21:25 this book: [1] *the which, if they should be written every one, I suppose that even the world itself could not contain the books that should be written.*

31 But these are written, that ye might believe that Jesus is the Christ, the Son of God; and that believing ye might have life through his name. Amen.

INDEX

THE INCARNATION OF THE WORD, JOHN 1:1-5, 9:14	1
THE GENEALOGY OF JESUS CHRIST BEGINNING WITH ABRAHAM, MATT. 1:1-17	1-2
THE BIRTH OF JOHN THE BAPTIST, THE FORERUNNER OF JESUS CHRIST, FORETOLD, LUKE 1:5-25	2-4
GABRIEL APPEARS UNTO MARY AND FORETELLS OF JESUS' BIRTH, LUKE 1:26-38	4-5
MARY GOES TO JUDAH TO VISIT ELISABETH, LUKE 1:39-56	5-6
THE BIRTH OF JOHN THE BAPTIST, LUKE 1:57-66	6-7
ZECHARIAH IS FILLED WITH THE HOLY SPIRIT AND PROPHESIES, LUKE 1:67-80	7-8
THE WORD BECOMES FLESH IN THE BIRTH OF JESUS THE CHRIST, MATT. 1:18-25, LUKE 2:1-7	8-9
THE SHEPHERD VISITED BY THE ANGELS, LUKE 2:8-20	9-10
MARY AND JOSEPH TAKE JESUS TO THE TEMPLE TO PRESENT HIM TO THE LORD, LUKE 2:21-38	10-12
THEY RETURN TO NAZARETH, LUKE 2:39-40	12
THE VISIT OF THE WISE MEN, MATT. 2:1-12	12-13
HEROD HAS ALL THE INFANTS SLAIN UP TO TWO YEARS OLD, MATT. 2:13-23	13-14
JESUS IN THE TEMPLE—AGE TWELVE, LUKE 2:41-52	14-15
JOHN THE BAPTIST BEGINS HIS MINISTRY, LUKE 3:1-2, 5-6; MARK 1:2; JOHN 1:7-8	15-16
THE PREACHING OF REPENTANCE FOR THE REMISSION OF SINS, MATT. 3:1, 2-6; LUKE 3:3	16
JOHN REPROVES THE PHARISEES AND SADDUCEES, MATT. 3:7, LUKE 3:8-9	16
CONVERSION LEADS TO ETHICAL CONDUCT AND DEMANDS, LUKE 3:10-15	17
CHRIST SHALL BAPTIZE WITH THE HOLY GHOST AND FIRE, LUKE 3:16-18, 21	17
THE BAPTISM OF JESUS, MATT. 3:13-16	17-18
THE GENEALOGY OF JESUS GOING BACK TO ADAM, LUKE 3:23-38	18-19
THE TEMPTATION OF JESUS, LUKE 4:1, 2-3, 5-6, 8-13 MARK 1:12-13, MATT. 4:4, 9, 11	19-20

THE TESTIMONY OF JOHN THE BAPTIST, JOHN 1:15-28	20-22
JESUS IS THE LAMB OF GOD, JOHN 1:29-34	22
THE DISCIPLES OF JOHN SEEK JESUS, JOHN 1:35-42	22-23
THE CALL OF PHILIP AND NATHANAEL, JOHN 1:43-51	23-24
BEGINNING OF MIRACLES AT THE WEDDING IN CANA OF GALILEE, JOHN 2:1-12	24
THE FIRST CLEANSING OF THE TEMPLE, JOHN 2:13-22	25
JESUS BEING DIVINE, KNOWS THE CHARACTER OF ALL MEN, JOHN 2:23-25	25
NICODEMUS VISITS JESUS, JOHN 3:1-15	26
GOD'S LOVE FOR THE WORLD, JOHN 3:16-21	27
DISCIPLES OF JOHN AND JESUS BAPTIZE BELIEVERS, JOHN 3:22-27	27
JOHN AGAIN BEARS WITNESS OF CHRIST, JOHN 3:28-36	27-28
JOHN THE BAPTIST IMPRISONED, LUKE 3:19-20	28
JESUS' MINISTRY IN SAMARIA, JOHN 4:1-43	28-31
JESUS MINISTERS AT NAZARETH AND IS REJECTED, LUKE 4:16-30, JOHN 4:44-54, MATT. 4:13-17	31-32
NOBLEMAN'S SON HEALED, JOHN 4:46	33-34
JESUS CALLS FOUR FISHERMEN, MATT. 4:18-22	34
JESUS' FAME REACHES INTO SYRIA, MATT. 4:23-25	34
JESUS' SECOND TRIP TO JERUSALEM DURING HIS MINISTRY THE HEALING AT THE POOL, JOHN 5:1-16	35-36
THE WORK OF THE FATHER AND SON ARE ONE, JOHN 5:17-35	36-37
JESUS HAS A GREATER WITNESS THAN JOHN, JOHN 5:36-6:3	37-38
THE SERMON ON THE MOUNT, MATT. 5:2-7:29	38-47
THE BEATITUDES, MATT. 5:2-13	38-39
THE LIGHT OF THE WORLD, MATT. 5:14-16	39
JESUS DECLARES THAT THE MORAL LAW IS STILL IN FORCE, MATT. 5:17-20	39-40
JESUS REPROVES THEM FOR THEIR DISTORTION OF THE LAW, MATT. 5:21-26	40
LOOKING AND LUSTING, MATT. 5:27-32	40-41

Arranged As a Single Narrative

OATHS, MATT. 5:33-42	41
LOVE YOUR ENEMIES, MATT. 5:43-48	42
GIVING, MATT. 6:1-4	42
PRAYER, MATT. 6:5-15	42-43
FASTING, MATT. 6:16-18	43
TREASURES CAN BE SECURE, MATT. 6:19-21	43
THE EYE: THE LIGHT OF THE BODY, MATT. 6:22-23	44
GOD AND MAMMON, MATT. 6:24	44
GOD ACCEPTS RESPONSIBILITY TO CARE FOR US, MATT. 6:25-34	44-45
JUDGING OTHERS, MATT. 7:1-6	45
THE PRAYER OF FAITH, MATT. 7:7-12	45
TWO WAYS, MATT. 7:13-14	46
FRUIT IDENTIFIES THE TREE, MATT. 7:15-23	46
BUILDING ON ROCK OR SAND, MATT. 7:24-29	46-47
JESUS CLEANSES A LEPER, MATT. 8:1-4	47
A CENTURION'S SERVANT HEALED, MATT. 8:5-13	47-48
A MAN WITH AN UNCLEAN SPIRIT, LUKE 4:33-37	48
JESUS HEALS SIMON'S MOTHER-IN-LAW, MARK 1:29, LUKE 4:39	48-49
JESUS HEALS MANY AT EVENING, LUKE 4:40, 41; MATT. 8:17	49
JESUS DEPARTS ON A PREACHING TOUR, MARK 1:35-39	49
THE GREAT CATCH OF FISH, LUKE 5:1-11	49-50
JESUS CLEANSES A LEPER, MARK 1:40-45	51
JESUS HEALS A PALSIED MAN, MARK 2:1-12	51-52
THE CALL OF LEVI, MARK 2:13-17	52-53
THE QUESTION ABOUT FASTING, MATT. 9:14, 16-17, LUKE 5:34-39	53-54
THE DISCIPLES PLUCK GRAIN ON THE SABBATH, MATT. 12:1-8	54
THE MAN WITH THE WITHERED HAND, LUKE 6:6-1	55
JESUS LEAVES THE SYNAGOGUE, MATT. 12:15-21	55-56
JESUS PREACHES TO A MULTITUDE BY THE SEASIDE, MARK 3:7-12	56
JESUS CHOOSES THE TWELVE APOSTLES, LUKE 6:12-13, MATT. 10:2-4	56-57
THE ORDINATION ADDRESS GIVEN TO THE TWELVE, MATT. 10:5-33	57-59
CHRIST VS. SIN EQUALS DIVISION, MATT. 10:34-11:1	59

JESUS MINISTERS TO A GREAT MULTITUDE,
  LUKE 6:17-42................................59-62
THE FRUIT IDENTIFIES THE TREE, LUKE 6:43-45,
  MATT. 12:34-37..............................61-62
THE ROCK IS THE RIGHT FOUNDATION,
  LUKE 6:46-49....................................62
A CENTURION'S SERVANT HEALED,
  LUKE 7:1-10.................................62-63
JESUS RAISES THE WIDOW'S SON AT NAIN,
  LUKE 7:11-17................................63-64
THE MESSENGERS FROM JOHN THE BAPTIST,
  MATT. 11:2, 12-15, LUKE 7:20-28, 29-35........64-65
WOES TO UNREPENTANT CITIES, MATT. 11:20-24......65-66
REST IS FOUND IN CHRIST, MATT. 11:25-30............66
JESUS AT THE HOME OF SIMON THE PHARISEE,
  LUKE 7:36-50................................66-67
SOME WOMEN ACCOMPANY JESUS,
  LUKE 8:1-3.......................................68
BLASPHEMY AGAINST THE HOLY GHOST,
  MARK 3:19-21, 30; MATT. 12:22-32.............68-69
THE RETURN OF THE UNCLEAN SPIRIT,
  MATT. 12:43-45...................................69
JESUS' MOTHER AND BRETHREN,
  MATT. 12:46-50...................................70
THE PARABLE OF THE SOWER,
  MATT. 13:1, 3-9; LUKE 8:4...................70-71
THE PURPOSE OF THE PARABLES,
  MATT. 13:10-17, MARK 4:13........................71
JESUS EXPLAINS THE PARABLE OF THE SOWER,
  MATT. 13:18-23...................................72
A CANDLE UNDER A BUSHEL, MARK 4:21-25..........72-73
THE MYSTERY OF GROWTH, MARK 4:26-29...............73
THE PARABLE OF THE MUSTARD SEED,
  MARK 4:30-32.....................................73
THE PARABLE OF THE WHEAT AND THE TARES,
  MATT. 13:24-30...............................73-74
THE PARABLE OF THE LEAVEN,
  MATT. 13:33......................................74
JESUS' USE OF PARABLES, MATT. 13:34-35;
  MARK 4:33..74
JESUS EXPLAINS THE PARABLE OF THE WHEAT
  AND THE TARES, MATT. 13:36-43................74-75

ARRANGED AS A SINGLE NARRATIVE

THE HIDDEN TREASURE, MATT. 13:44	75
THE PEARL OF GREAT PRICE, MATT. 13:45-46	75
THE NET, MATT. 13:47-50	75
TREASURES NEW AND OLD, MATT. 13:51-53	76
CONDITIONS FOR FOLLOWING CHRIST, MATT. 8:18-22	76
JESUS CALMS A STORM, MARK 4:25-41	76-77
THE GADARENE DEMONIAC HEALED, MARK 5:1-20; LUKE 8:35-37	77-78
JAIRUS' DAUGHTER AND THE WOMAN WHO TOUCHED JESUS' GARMENT, MARK 5:21-32, 35-43; LUKE 8:47-48	79-81
TWO BLIND MEN RECEIVE THEIR SIGHT, MATT. 9:27-31	81
A DUMB MAN SPEAKS, MATT. 9:32-34	81
THE HARVEST IS PLENTEOUS, MATT. 9:35-38	81
JESUS REJECTED AT NAZARETH, MARK 6:1-6	82
THE MISSION OF THE TWELVE, LUKE 9:1-6; MARK 6:11-13	82-83
THE DEATH OF JOHN THE BAPTIST, MARK 6:14-29	83-84
APOSTLES RETURN FROM THEIR MISSION, MARK 6:30-34	84-85
THE FEEDING OF THE FIVE THOUSAND, MARK 6:35-42; JOHN 6:4-15; MATT. 14:21-23	85-86
JESUS WALKS ON THE SEA, MATT. 14:24-33	86-87
JESUS HEALS THE SICK IN GENNESARET, MARK 6:53-56	87
THE PEOPLE SEEK JESUS, JOHN 6:22-29	87-88
JESUS THE BREAD OF LIFE, JOHN 6:30-59	88-90
THE WORDS OF ETERNAL LIFE, JOHN 6:60-71	90
THE UNBELIEF OF JESUS' BRETHREN, JOHN 7:1-9	91
THE THINGS THAT DEFILE, MARK 7:1-23; MATT. 15:13-15	91-93
THE SYROPHOENICIAN WOMAN'S FAITH, MARK 7:24-30, MATT. 15:23-25	93-94
JESUS HEALS A DEAF AND DUMB MAN, MARK 7:31-37	94

THE FEEDING OF THE FOUR THOUSAND,
   MARK 8:1-10 95
THE DEMAND FOR A SIGN, MATT. 16:1-4 95-96
THE LEAVEN OF THE PHARISEES,
   MARK 8:14-21 96
A BLIND MAN HEALED AT BETHSAIDA,
   MARK 8:22-26 97
PETER'S CONFESSION, MATT. 16:13-20 97-98
JESUS FORETELLS HIS DEATH,
   MARK 8:31-9:1 98
THE TRANSFIGURATION, MARK 9:2-13;
   LUKE 9:32-33; MATT. 17:5-13 99-100
JESUS HEALS A BOY WITH AN UNCLEAN SPIRIT,
   MARK 9:14-29 100-102
JESUS AGAIN FORETELLS HIS DEATH,
   MARK 9:30-31; LUKE 9:44-55 102
WHO IS THE GREATEST? LUKE 9:46 102
PAYMENT OF THE TRIBUTE MONEY,
   MATT. 17:24-27 102
WHICH OF THE APOSTLES SHOULD BE THE
   GREATEST, MARK 9:33-37 103
WHO IS THE GREATEST IN THE KINGDOM OF
   HEAVEN? MATT. 18:1-3, 5 103
HE THAT IS NOT AGAINST US IS FOR US,
   MARK 9:38-41 104
OFFENCES, MARK 9:42-50; MATT. 18:7-11 104-105
THE LOST SHEEP, MATT. 18:12-14 105
IF A BROTHER SINS AGAINST THEE,
   MATT. 18:15-20 105
THE UNFORGIVING SERVANT, MATT. 18:21-35 106-107
JESUS REBUKES JAMES AND JOHN,
   LUKE 9:51-56 107
THE COST OF DISCIPLESHIP, LUKE 9:57-62 107
JESUS' TEACHING ON DIVORCE,
   MATT. 19:1-12; MARK 10:3-12 108-109
THE SEVENTY SENT FORTH, LUKE 10:1-16 109-110
THE SUCCESS OF THE SEVENTY, LUKE 10:17-20 110
JESUS REJOICES IN SPIRIT, LUKE 10:21-24 111
THE GOOD SAMARITAN, LUKE 10:25-37 111-112
JESUS VISITS MARTHA AND MARY,
   LUKE 10:38-42 112
JESUS AT THE FEAST OF TABERNACLES,
   JOHN 7:10-24 112-113

Arranged As a Single Narrative

IS THIS THE CHRIST? JOHN 7:25-31	114
OFFICERS SENT TO ARREST JESUS, JOHN 7:32-36	114
RIVERS OF LIVING WATER, JOHN 7:37-39	114-115
DIVISION AMONG THE PEOPLE, JOHN 7:40-44	115
THE UNBELIEF OF THOSE IN AUTHORITY, JOHN 7:45-53	115
THE WOMAN CAUGHT IN ADULTERY, JOHN 8:1-11	116
JESUS THE LIGHT OF THE WORLD, JOHN 8:12-20	116-117
WHITHER I GO YE CANNOT COME, JOHN 8:21-30	117-118
THE TRUTH SHALL MAKE YOU FREE, JOHN 8:31-38	118
YOUR FATHER THE DEVIL, JOHN 8:39-47	118-119
BEFORE ABRAHAM WAS, I AM, JOHN 8:48-59	119-120
JESUS HEALS THE MAN BORN BLIND, JOHN 9:1-12	120
THE PHARISEES INVESTIGATE THE HEALING, JOHN 9:13-34	121-122
SPIRITUAL BLINDNESS, JOHN 9:35-41	122
THE PARABLE OF THE SHEEPFOLD, JOHN 10:1-6	123
JESUS THE GOOD SHEPHERD, JOHN 10:7-42	123-125
THE MODEL PRAYER, LUKE 11:1-4	125
EARNEST PRAYING, LUKE 11:5-13	125-126
CHRIST VS. BEELZEBUB, LUKE 11:14-23	126-127
THE RETURN OF THE UNCLEAN SPIRIT, LUKE 11:24-28	127
JONAH, A SIGN TO NINEVITES, LUKE 11:29-32	127-128
THE EYE SHOULD BE SINGLE, LUKE 11:33-36	128
JESUS DINES WITH A PHARISEE, LUKE 11:37-12:3	128-130
BEWARE OF HYPOCRISY, LUKE 12:1-3	130
WHOM TO FEAR, LUKE 12:4-12	130
CONFESSING CHRIST AND TRUSTING THE LEADERSHIP OF THE HOLY SPIRIT, LUKE 12:8-12	130-131
THE RICH FOOL, LUKE 12:13-21	131
SEEK FIRST THE KINGDOM OF GOD, LUKE 12:22-31	131-132
WHERE IS YOUR TREASURE? LUKE 12:32-34	132

The FOUR GOSPELS

BE READY FOR CHRIST'S RETURN,
  LUKE 12:35-40 132-133
PERSONAL RESPONSIBILITY, LUKE 12:41-48 133
CHRISTIAN CONVICTIONS CAUSE DIVISIONS,
  LUKE 12:49-53 134
DISCERNING THE TIMES, LUKE 12:54-59 134
REPENT OR PERISH, LUKE 13:1-5 134-135
THE FRUITLESS FIG TREE, LUKE 13:6-9 135
CHRIST'S ADVERSARIES ASHAMED,
  LUKE 13:10-17 135-136
THE PARABLE OF THE MUSTARD SEED,
  LUKE 13:18-19 136
THE PARABLE OF THE LEAVEN, LUKE 13:20-21 136
TWO WAYS, LUKE 13:22-30 136-137
O JERUSALEM, JERUSALEM, LUKE 13:31-35 137
THE DEATH OF LAZARUS, JOHN 11:1-16 138
JESUS THE RESURRECTION AND THE LIFE,
  JOHN 11:17-27 139
JESUS WEEPS, JOHN 11:28-37 139-140
LAZARUS BROUGHT TO LIFE,
  JOHN 11:38-46 140
CAIAPHAS PROPHESIES THAT ONE SHOULD DIE
  FOR THE NATION, JOHN 11:47-57 141
THE MAN WHO HAD DROPSY HEALED,
  LUKE 14:1-6 141-142
A LESSON ON HUMILITY, LUKE 14:7-14 142
THE PARABLE OF THE GREAT SUPPER,
  LUKE 14:15-24 142-143
COUNTING THE COST, LUKE 14:25-33 143-144
SALT CAN LOSE ITS SAVOR, LUKE 14:34-35 144
THE LOST SHEEP, LUKE 15:1-7 144
THE LOST COIN, LUKE 15:8-10 145
THE PRODIGAL SON, LUKE 15:11-32 145-146
THE PARABLE OF THE DISHONEST STEWARD,
  LUKE 16:1-15 146-147
THE LAW AND THE KINGDOM OF GOD,
  LUKE 16:16-17 148
DIVORCE AND REMARRIAGE, LUKE 16:18 148
THE RICH MAN AND LAZARUS, LUKE 16:19-31 148-149
OFFENSE WILL COME, LUKE 17:1-4 149
MUSTARD SEED, LUKE 17:5-6 149
WE ARE UNPROFITABLE SERVANTS,
  LUKE 17:7-10 149-150

ARRANGED AS A SINGLE NARRATIVE 241

JESUS CLEANSES TEN LEPERS,
   LUKE 17:11-19 ... 150
THE KINGDOM OF GOD IS WITHIN YOU,
   LUKE 17:20-25 ... 150-151
AS IN THE DAYS OF NOAH, LUKE 17:26-37 ... 151
THE WIDOW AND THE UNJUST JUDGE,
   LUKE 18:1-8 ... 151-152
THE PHARISEE AND THE PUBLICAN,
   LUKE 18:9-14 ... 152
JESUS BLESSES LITTLE CHILDREN,
   MARK 10:13-16 ... 153
THE RICH YOUNG RULER,
   MATT. 19:16-30 ... 153-154
LABORERS IN THE VINEYARD,
   MATT. 20:1-16 ... 154-155
JESUS FORETELLS HIS DEATH A THIRD TIME,
   MARK 10:32-34 ... 155-156
THE REQUEST OF JAMES AND JOHN,
   MATT. 20:20-28 ... 156-157
A BLIND BEGGAR HEALED NEAR JERICHO,
   LUKE 18:35-43 ... 157-158
TWO BLIND MEN RECEIVE SIGHT,
   MATT. 20:29-34 ... 158
BLIND BARTIMEUS RECEIVES SIGHT,
   MARK 10:46-52 ... 158-159
JESUS AND ZACCHEUS, LUKE 19:1-10 ... 159
THE PARABLE OF THE NOBLEMAN AND THE
   TEN SERVANTS, LUKE 19:11-28 ... 159-161
JESUS ANOINTED AT BETHANY,
   JOHN 12:1-8 ... 161
THE PLOT AGAINST LAZARUS,
   JOHN 12:9-11 ... 162
THE TRIUMPHAL ENTRY INTO JERUSALEM,
   LUKE 19:29-44; JOHN 12:12-19; MATT. 21:4-11;
   MARK 11:11 ... 162-164
THE CURSING OF THE FIG TREE,
   MATT. 21:18-22 ... 164
THE CLEANSING OF THE TEMPLE,
   MATT. 21:12-17 ... 165
THE LESSON FROM THE WITHERED FIG TREE,
   MARK 11:20-26 ... 165-166
JESUS' AUTHORITY QUESTIONED,
   LUKE 20:1-8 ... 166

THE PARABLE OF THE TWO SONS,
  MATT. 21:28-32 166-167
THE PARABLE OF THE WICKED HUSBANDMEN,
  MATT. 21:33-46 167-168
THE PARABLE OF THE MARRIAGE FEAST,
  MATT. 22:1-14 168-169
PAYING TAXES TO CAESAR,
  MATT. 22:15-22 169-170
THE QUESTION ABOUT THE RESURRECTION,
  LUKE 20:27-40 170-171
THE GREAT COMMANDMENT,
  MARK 12:28-34 171-172
THE QUESTION ABOUT DAVID'S SON,
  MATT. 22:41-46 172
JESUS DENOUNCES THE SCRIBES AND
  PHARISEES, MATT. 23:1-36 172-175
JESUS LAMENTS OVER JERUSALEM,
  MATT. 23:37-39 175
THE WIDOW'S OFFERING, MARK 12:41-44 175
SOME GREEKS WOULD SEE JESUS,
  JOHN 12:20-26 175-176
THE SON OF MAN MUST BE LIFTED UP,
  JOHN 12:27-36 176
BELIEVING PHARISEES AFRAID TO CONFESS
  HIM, JOHN 12:36-43 177
TO BELIEVE CHRIST IS TO BELIEVE IN GOD
  THE FATHER, JOHN 12:44-50 177-178
THE DESTRUCTION OF THE TEMPLE AND SIGNS BE-
  FORE THE END, MATT. 24:1-28; LUKE 21:13-24 ... 178-180
THE SIGN OF THE COMING OF THE SON OF MAN,
  MATT. 24:29-35 181
IN SUCH AN HOUR AS YE THINK NOT,
  LUKE 21:34-44 181-182
THE FAITHFUL SERVANT WATCHES,
  MATT. 24:45-51 182-183
THE VIRGINS—WISE AND FOOLISH,
  MATT. 25:1-13 183-184
THE PARABLE OF THE TALENTS,
  MATT. 25:14-30 184-185
THE JUDGMENT OF NATIONS,
  MATT. 25:31-38 185-186

ARRANGED AS A SINGLE NARRATIVE 243

THE LEADERS PLOT AGAINST JESUS,
   MATT. 26:1-5 186
JESUS ANOINTED AT BETHANY THE THIRD
   TIME, MATT. 26:6-13 187
SATAN ENTERS INTO JUDAS, LUKE 22:3-6 187-188
JESUS EATS THE PASSOVER WITH HIS DISCIPLES,
   JOHN 13:1; MATT. 26:17-25; LUKE 22:10-23;
   MARK 14:16-25 188-189
JESUS WASHES HIS DISCIPLES' FEET,
   JOHN 13:2-20 190-191
JESUS FORETELLS HIS BETRAYAL,
   JOHN 13:21-30 191
THE NEW COMMANDMENT, JOHN 13:31-35 191-192
THE THIRD DISPUTE ABOUT GREATNESS,
   LUKE 22:24-30 192
PETER'S DENIAL FORETOLD, JOHN 13:36-38;
   LUKE 22:31-34 192-193
JESUS THE WAY, THE TRUTH AND THE LIFE,
   JOHN 14:1-14 193-194
THE PROMISE OF THE HOLY SPIRIT,
   JOHN 14:15-31 194-195
JESUS THE TRUE VINE, JOHN 15:1-17 195-196
THE WORLD'S HATRED, JOHN 15:18-16:6 196-197
WHEN THE HOLY SPIRIT IS COME,
   JOHN 16:7-15 197-198
JESUS WILL GO TO THE FATHER,
   JOHN 16:16-24 198-199
CHRIST WILL PRAY FOR HIS FOLLOWERS,
   JOHN 16:25-33 199
THE HIGH PRIESTLY PRAYER OF CHRIST,
   JOHN 17:1-26 199-201
THEY LEAVE THE UPPER ROOM, LUKE 22:35 201-202
PETER'S DENIAL FORETOLD A SECOND TIME,
   MATT. 26:31-35 202
JESUS PRAYS IN GETHSEMANE,
   MATT. 26:36-46; LUKE 22:43-45 202-203
THE BETRAYAL AND ARREST OF JESUS,
   MARK 14:43-45; JOHN 18:4-9, LUKE 22:49 203-204
PETER USES HIS SWORD, JOHN 18:10-11;
   MATT. 26:53-56; MARK 14:48-49 204-205
THEY LAY HOLD ON A YOUNG MAN,
   MARK 14:51-52 205

JESUS BROUGHT BEFORE THE HIGH PRIEST,
    JOHN 18:12-14 205
PETER IN THE HIGH PRIEST'S COURT,
    JOHN 18:15-18; LUKE 22:57-58 205-206
THE TRIAL BEFORE ANNAS, JOHN 18:19-24 206
PETER DENIES CHRIST THE THIRD TIME,
    LUKE 22:59-62; JOHN 18:26-27 206-207
COUNCIL SEEKS FOR FALSE WITNESSES,
    MARK 14:55-64 207
JESUS MOCKED AND BEATEN,
    LUKE 22:63-65 218
JESUS BEFORE THE COUNCIL, LUKE 22:66-71;
    MATT. 27:2 208
JUDAS HANGS HIMSELF, MATT. 27:3-10 209
JESUS BEFORE PILATE, JOHN 18:29-39;
    LUKE 23:2, 5; MARK 15:3; MATT. 27:13-14 209-211
JESUS BEFORE HEROD, LUKE 23:6-12 211
BARABBAS OR CHRIST, LUKE 23:13-23; MATT. 27:15-22;
    MARK 15:8; JOHN 18:40 211-212
PILATE WASHES HIS HANDS,
    MATT. 27:24-25 213
JESUS SENTENCED, MATT. 27:26-31 213
PILATE PLEADS AGAIN WITH THE JEWS,
    JOHN 19:4-12 213-214
PILATE'S FINAL PLEA, JOHN 19:13-16 214-215
THE CRUCIFIXION, LUKE 23:26-43; MARK 15:25-32;
    JOHN 19:19-29; MATT. 26:36; 27:43-51 215-218
MANY RAISED FROM THE DEAD AFTER HIS RESUR-
    RECTION, MATT. 27:52-54; LUKE 23:48-49;
    MARK 15:41 218-219
THE SIDE OF JESUS PIERCED,
    JOHN 19:31-37 219
THE BURIAL OF JESUS, MARK 15:42-46;
    JOHN 19:39-42; LUKE 23:54-56 219-220
THE GUARD AT THE TOMB, MATT. 27:62-66 220-221
THE RESURRECTION, JOHN 20:1-10;
    MARK 16:1-8; MATT. 28:2-6 221-223
THE REPORT OF THE GUARD,
    MATT. 28:11-15 223-224
JESUS APPEARS TO MARY MAGDALENE,
    JOHN 20:11-18; MARK 16:9-11; MATT. 28:9-10;
    LUKE 24:9-11 224-225

Arranged As a Single Narrative

JESUS APPEARS TO THE DISCIPLES ON THE WAY
   TO EMMAUS, MARK 16:12; LUKE 24:13-35 225-227
JESUS APPEARS TO HIS DISCIPLES,
   JOHN 20:19-23; LUKE 24:37-49 227-228
THOMAS DOES BELIEVE, JOHN 20:24-29 228
JESUS APPEARS TO DISCIPLES AT SEA OF
   GALILEE, JOHN 21:1-2 229
UNPROFITABLE LABOR WITHOUT CHRIST,
   JOHN 21:3-14 229-230
THE CALL OF GOD IS WITHOUT REPENTANCE,
   JOHN 21:15-24 230-231
JESUS COMMISSIONS THE ELEVEN,
   MATT. 28:16-20; MARK 16:14-18 231
THE ASCENSION, LUKE 24:50-53; MARK 16:20 232
THE PURPOSE OF THE BOOK,
   JOHN 20:30-31 232

REFERENCE INDEX

MATTHEW

MATT 1:1-17	1-2
MATT 1:18-25	8
MATT 2:1-23	12-14
MATT 3:1	16
MATT 3:2-7	16
MATT 3:13-17	17-18
MATT 4:4	20
MATT 4:9	20
MATT 4:11	20
MATT 4:13-25	33-34
MATT 5:2-48	38-42
MATT 6:1-34	42-45
MATT 7:1-29	45-47
MATT 8:1-13	47-48
MATT 8:17	49
MATT 9:14	53
MATT 9:16-17	53-54
MATT 12:1-8	54
MATT 12:15-21	55-56
MATT 10:2-42	56-59
MATT 11:1	59
MATT 12:34	62
MATT 12:36-37	62
MATT 11:2	64
MATT 11:12-15	65
MATT 11:20-30	65-66
MATT 12:22-32	68-69
MATT 12:43-50	69-70
MATT 13:1	70
MATT 13:3-17	70-71
MATT 13:18-23	72
MATT 13:24-30	73-74
MATT 13:33-35	74
MATT 13:36-53	74-76
MATT 8:18-22	76
MATT 8:33	78
MATT 9:26-38	81
MATT 14:5	83
MATT 14:21	86

MARK

MARK 1:1	1
MARK 1:2	15
MARK 1:12-13	19
MARK 1:29	48-49
MARK 1:35-39	49
MARK 1:40-45	51
MARK 2:1-17	51-53
MARK 3:7-12	56
MARK 3:19-21	68
MARK 3:30	69
MARK 4:13	71
MARK 4:21-32	72-73
MARK 4:33	74
MARK 4:35-41	76-77
MARK 5:1-13	77-78
MARK 5:16	78
MARK 5:18-32	78-80
MARK 5:35-43	80-81
MARK 6:1-6	82
MARK 6:11	82
MARK 6:13-18	83
MARK 6:19-36	83-85
MARK 6:38	85
MARK 6:39-42	85
MARK 6:53-56	87
MARK 7:1-17	91-92
MARK 7:18-26	93
MARK 7:27-31	94
MARK 7:32-37	94
MARK 8:1-10	95
MARK 8:12	95
MARK 8:14-21	96
MARK 8:22-26	97
MARK 8:31-38	98
MARK 9:1-4	98-99
MARK 9:5-6	99
MARK 9:8-13	100
MARK 9:14-27	100-101
MARK 9:28-31	101-102

Arranged As a Single Narrative

LUKE

LUKE 1:5-80	2-8
LUKE 2:1-40	9-12
LUKE 2:41-52	14-15
LUKE 3:1-2	15
LUKE 3:5-6	15
LUKE 3:3	16
LUKE 3:8-9	16
LUKE 3:10-18	17
LUKE 3:21	17
LUKE 3:23-38	18-19
LUKE 4:1	19
LUKE 4:2-3	20
LUKE 4:5-6	20
LUKE 4:8-13	20
LUKE 3:19-20	28
LUKE 4:15-30	31-32
LUKE 4:33-37	48
LUKE 4:39-40	49
LUKE 4:41	49
LUKE 5:1-11	49-50
LUKE 5:16	51
LUKE 5:34-35	53
LUKE 5:39	54
LUKE 6:6-11	55
LUKE 6:12-13	56
LUKE 6:17-44	59-61
LUKE 6:45	62
LUKE 6:46-49	62
LUKE 7:1-17	62-64
LUKE 7:20-28	64-65
LUKE 7:29-35	65
LUKE 7:36-50	66-67
LUKE 8:1-3	68
LUKE 8:4	70
LUKE 8:35	78
LUKE 8:37	78
LUKE 8:47-48	80
LUKE 9:1-5	82
LUKE 9:6	82
LUKE 9:32-33	99

JOHN

JOHN 1:1-5	1
JOHN 1:9-14	1
JOHN 1:7-8	15-16
JOHN 1:15-51	20-24
JOHN 2:1-25	24-25
JOHN 3:1-36	26-28
JOHN 4:1-43	28-31
JOHN 4:44-54	32-33
JOHN 5:1-47	35-38
JOHN 6:1-3	38
JOHN 6:4-7	85
JOHN 6:8-9	85
JOHN 6:13	86
JOHN 6:14-15	86
JOHN 6:22-71	87-90
JOHN 7:1-9	91
JOHN 7:10-53	112-115
JOHN 8:1-59	116-120
JOHN 9:1-41	120-122
JOHN 10:1-42	123-125
JOHN 11:1-57	138-141
JOHN 12:1-11	161-162
JOHN 12:12-13	162-163
JOHN 12:16-18	163
JOHN 12:19	164
JOHN 12:20-50	175-178
JOHN 13:1	188
JOHN 13:2-35	190-192
JOHN 13:36-38	192-193
JOHN 14:1-31	193-195
JOHN 15:1-27	195-197
JOHN 16:1-33	197-199
JOHN 17:1-26	199-201
JOHN 18:4	203
JOHN 18:4-9	204
JOHN 18:10-11	204
JOHN 18:12-18	205-206
JOHN 18:19-24	206
JOHN 18:26-27	206-207
JOHN 18:29-30	209

MATTHEW

MATT 14:22-33	86-87
MATT 15:13-15	92-93
MATT 15:23-25	93
MATT 15:30	94
MATT 16:1	95
MATT 16:2-4	95-96
MATT 16:12	96
MATT 16:13-20	97-98
MATT 17:5-7	99
MATT 17:13	100
MATT 17:24-27	102
MATT 18:1-3,5	103
MATT 18:7	104
MATT 18:10-35	105-106
MATT 19:1-6	108
MATT 19:7-9	108
MATT 19:10-12	109
MATT 12:40	128
MATT 19:16-30	153-154
MATT 20:1-16	154-155
MATT 20:20-28	156-157
MATT 20:29-34	158
MATT 21:4-5	163
MATT 21:10-11	164
MATT 21:18-22	164
MATT 21:12-17	165
MATT 21:28-35	166-167
MATT 21:38-46	168
MATT 22:1-22	168-170
MATT 22:41-46	172
MATT 23:1-39	172-175
MATT 24:1-9	178-179
MATT 24:10-14	179
MATT 24:15-35	179-181
MATT 24:36-41	182
MATT 24:42-51	182-183
MATT 25:1-46	183-186
MATT 26:1-13	186-187
MATT 26:17-18	188
MATT 26:20	188
MATT 26:21-25	188-189

MARK

MARK 9:33-37	103
MARK 9:38-42	104
MARK 9:43-50	104-105
MARK 10:3	108
MARK 10:10-12	108
MARK 10:13-16	153
MARK 10:32-34	155-156
MARK 10:46-52	158-159
MARK 11:11	164
MARK 11:20-26	165-166
MARK 12:28-34	171-172
MARK 12:41-44	175
MARK 13:34-36	182
MARK 14:16	188
MARK 14:43	203
MARK 14:44-45	203-204
MARK 14:45	204
MARK 14:48-49	204-205
MARK 14:51-52	205
MARK 14:55-64	207
MARK 15:3	210
MARK 15:8	212
MARK 15:25	215
MARK 15:27-28	215
MARK 15:29-32	216
MARK 15:41	219
MARK 15:42-46	219-220
MARK 16:1-4	222
MARK 16:6-8	223
MARK 16:9	224
MARK 16:11	225
MARK 16:12	225
MARK 16:14-18	231
MARK 16:20	232

ARRANGED AS A SINGLE NARRATIVE

LUKE

LUKE 9:43	101
LUKE 9:44-46	102
LUKE 9:51-62	107
LUKE 10:1-42	109-112
LUKE 11:1-30	125-128
LUKE 11:31-54	128-130
LUKE 12:1-59	130-134
LUKE 13:1-35	134-137
LUKE 14:1-35	141-144
LUKE 15:1-32	144-146
LUKE 16:1-31	146-149
LUKE 17:1-37	149-151
LUKE 18:1-14	151-152
LUKE 18:35-43	157-158
LUKE 19:1-28	159-161
LUKE 19:29-35	162
LUKE 19:36-44	163-164
LUKE 20:1-8	166
LUKE 20:13	167
LUKE 20:27-40	170-171
LUKE 21:13-15	179
LUKE 21:20	179
LUKE 21:34-36	181-182
LUKE 21:37-38	186
LUKE 22:3-6	187-188
LUKE 22:10-12	188
LUKE 22:15-16	188
LUKE 22:17-23	189
LUKE 22:24-30	192
LUKE 22:31-34	193
LUKE 22:35-38	201-202
LUKE 22:43-45	202-203
LUKE 22:49	204
LUKE 22:57-58	206
LUKE 22:59	206
LUKE 22:61-62	207
LUKE 22:64-71	208
LUKE 23:2	210
LUKE 23:5	210
LUKE 23:6-16	211

JOHN

JOHN 18:31-39	210
JOHN 18:40	212
JOHN 19:4-16	213-215
JOHN 19:19-24	216
JOHN 19:25-29	217-218
JOHN 19:30	218
JOHN 19:31-37	219
JOHN 19:39-42	220
JOHN 20:1-10	221-222
JOHN 20:11-13	224
JOHN 20:14-17	224
JOHN 20:18	225
JOHN 20:19	227
JOHN 20:21-29	228
JOHN 21:1-24	229-231
JOHN 20:30-31	232

MATTHEW

MATT 26:31-39	202
MATT 26:41-46	203
MATT 26:53-54	204
MATT 26:56	205
MATT 27:2-10	208-209
MATT 27:13-14	211
MATT 27:15	211
MATT 27:16	212
MATT 27:17-18	212
MATT 27:19-22	212
MATT 27:24-31	213
MATT 26:36	216
MATT 27:43-44	216
MATT 27:45-47	217
MATT 27:49	218
MATT 27:51-54	218
MATT 27:62-66	220-221
MATT 28:2-6	222-223
MATT 28:11-15	223-224
MATT 28:9-10	225
MATT 28:16-17	231
MATT 28:18-20	231

LUKE

LUKE 23:17	211
LUKE 23:18	212
LUKE 23:20-21	212
LUKE 23:22-23	212
LUKE 23:26-34	215
LUKE 23:34	216
LUKE 23:35	216
LUKE 23:36-43	217
LUKE 23:48-49	218
LUKE 23:54-56	220
LUKE 24:3-8	223
LUKE 24:9-11	225
LUKE 24:12	225
LUKE 24:13-35	225-227
LUKE 24:37-49	227-228
LUKE 24:50-53	232